Not Simply Divine

BENEATH THE MAKE-UP, ABOVE THE HEELS AND
BEHIND THE SCENES WITH A CULT SUPERSTAR

Bernard Jay

A FIRESIDE BOOK
Published by Simon & Schuster
NEW YORK   LONDON   TORONTO   SYDNEY   TOKYO   SINGAPORE

To Michael and Sammy of the Hotel Hovi and La Sardi

 FIRESIDE
Rockefeller Center
1230 Avenue of the Americas
New York, New York 10020

The author notes that filmmaker John Waters was not interviewed
for this book and that the quotes attributed to him in this book
come from previously published sources, including his book, *Shock
Value*.

FIRESIDE and colophon are registered trademarks
of Simon & Schuster Inc.

Manufactured in the United States of America

10 9 8 7 6 5 4 3 2 1

Library of Congress Cataloging-in-Publication Data

Jay, Bernard, 1946–
  Not simply Divine : beneath the make-up, above the heels and
behind the scenes with a cult superstar / Bernard Jay.
    p. cm.
  "A Fireside book."
  1. Divine, 1945–1988. 2. Motion picture actors and actresses–
United States–Biography. I. Title.
PN1998.3.D58J39 1994
791.43'028'092–dc20
  [B]   94-4991
                                              CIP

ISBN: 0-671-88467-0

Contents

Acknowledgements   vii
Introduction   ix

1   Tragic Timing   1
2   No One's Christened 'Divine'   13
3   A Question of Taste   23
4   Comic Timing   37
5   But Who Will Provide the Pay Cheque?   48
6   Divine Does Discos   62
7   Fuck You Very Much!   76
8   Briefly Not the Bitch   86
9   The First Lady of Filth   101
10   Divine the Disco Diva   114
11   Spend . . . Spend . . . Spend   126
12   Welcome Home, Baby Glenn   140
13   Controversial . . . and Banned!   154
14   Divi Goes Legit   170
15   Bored, Depressed and Lonely   186
16   Bi-talented and Bi-coastal   201
17   A Household Name   212

Postscript   224

Acknowledgements

For their assistance in the publication of *Not Simply Divine* the author wishes to thank Anne Evans, Pati Mayfield, Mark D. Sendroff, Sol Gordon and Mitch Horowitz.

Introduction

It was a matter of two people being in the same place at the same time and having a mutual need: surely the best reasons for getting together.

He was the only son of American Baptist parents; I the middle child of an English Jewish family. He had already achieved notoriety as an actor playing female roles in underground movies and now craved fame. I had gained respectability in the world of theatre through an adventurous career, but had not achieved security in success. He loved my English accent and thought that my career background could help bring him the respect from his peers for which he yearned. I saw in him an under-appreciated actor with a terrific natural sense of comic timing, urgently in need of career guidance.

When we first teamed up in 1978 we were both 32, single, unsure of the next step to be taken in our lives – and broke.

We both loved a challenge.

It just seemed to make sense to put the elements together and go for it. Could we, working as a team, turn the Actor Most Unlikely To Succeed into a Household Name? And both become rich by doing it? Anyway, what had we got to lose? He had no one else offering to help him; and I had no one else offering me the possibility of an income.

I became Divine's Personal Manager.

We worked together for the next ten years, taking every conceivable liberty in bringing the name Divine to a worldwide audience. Eventually, we believed, the public would recognise his talents and the machinery of stardom would fall into place and make things easier. By 1988, at the time of his death, we knew we had achieved our first goal; Divine was becoming a household name. I'm immensely proud of him and what we strived for. Our second goal – the money – was, after ten incredibly frustrating years, clearly on the horizon. But it never arrived.

Why should I write a book about my colleague and our ten years at each other's side?

First, because I think he deserves a memorial. A record for posterity of a most extraordinary career; a long, hard struggle to succeed – against all odds – in the toughest industry of all. No one else has all the facts. In those final ten years of his life, it was just the two of us doing it all. Many helped, some hindered. But no machinery of stardom had yet come his way; there are no agents, lawyers, producers, accountants, financial advisers, office staff, road managers or fan club secretaries close enough to him to tell their stories about him. Not even long-term lovers. It's unlikely that either his film performances or disco recordings will stand the test of time and be acknowledged as classics. So I want there to exist a detailed record of this career, because I think his achievements were classic in themselves.

Second, because I believe there are many – from work associates, to devoted fans, to those who just glimpsed him as he crossed their paths – who would like to know more about Divine, the *man*.

Over the years, much has been written of him in press interviews, in-depth magazine articles and by John Waters in his book *Shock Value*. But to John, Divine will always remain the *female* character, the most notorious and outrageous member of the Dreamlanders; his 'leading lady', whom he helped 'create'. The journalists saw what they took as the contradiction to his screen image: a gentle, quiet man who knew well how to charm them without giving away much of himself. Divine's was a black-and-white public persona. I hope this book will show the very many shades of grey that were mostly hidden between the 'female character' and 'the man'.

Because of the lack of suitable professionals willing to take the risk and join us – and the scarcity of funds to offer fees or salaries to the few that might have – our relationship was unusually intense for that of artiste and manager. At different times I would be his father, his mother, his confessor, his confidant, his best friend – and, in his mind, his worst enemy. We were never lovers. But we often joked to each other that it was like being married. There were certainly the highs and lows of most domestic partnerships: the jealousies that arose from other intimate relationships; the mutual but never acknowledged dependence; the insensitivities created by two people living out of each other's pockets, day-in, day-out; the shared joys of success, the depressions of rejection. Even the frequent bickering over spending. And, most important of all, the unquestioned trust we had in each other. I believe I knew Divine well enough to write about him. And Divine deserves 'a book on the shelf'.

Not Simply Divine is not the bitter revenge of an unappreciated manager, eager now to get his share of the praise. Divine always generously acknowledged the role I played in his success; indeed, our teamwork was respected by those with whom we worked and by members of the media. I have no bitterness, although, curiously, I have experienced problems 'by association' in my own career, caused by the ignorance, prejudice and hypocrisy from which he suffered all his life. But I wouldn't have missed it for the world. What a fantastic merry-go-round to have ridden.

Neither is my book a gushing homage, as were most of the international epitaphs and tributes he received following his death, painting him as someone both saintly and legendary. I trust that his unique flamboyancy comes across in these pages and that his fans will recognise the icon they so adored. I truly hope the warmth, generosity and sense of humour he possessed – but displayed only when he wanted to – can be found too. But, as hackneyed as the phrase may be, I can only portray the star of *Not Simply Divine!* 'with warts and all'.

If, in my account, I have often drawn Divine as a selfish and insensitive person, then I do not apologise. For, in recollecting these memoirs, I have found him to have been so. However, such an extended period of time as we shared so closely together has to have included a love for each other, of a sort. Without hesitation, I can say there were many times when I loved Divine. But I'm not sure I can truly say that I really *liked* him.

There were, of course, some great times and I hope the reader will enjoy sharing these. But life with Divine was no bed of roses.

It was not simply divine.

Bernard Jay
Spain, 1992

1 Tragic Timing

'He was the Drag Queen of the Century. He called himself Divine and he was proud of his creation: a unique and hilarious high-camp cartoon, a Miss Piggy for the blissfully depraved. But he dreamed of the day when at last he would be seen as a gifted actor who could animate any number of fascinating characters. That day came just two weeks ago. . . .'

People, 21 March 1988

'LL BEAT THE BASTARDS YET,' he had assured me at breakfast. 'I'm not going to slave away in a fucking dress and tights just to pay off the government. There's got to be another way.' I didn't answer. I'd learned it was best not to fuel his personal fires during valuable moments of discussion over a meal together. There was a long, embarrassing pause: he knew he was in the wrong. 'Whatever it takes, I'm determined not to give up all that money just to pay taxes,' he declared.

On the morning of 6 March 1988, at Hollywood World Restaurant on Sunset Boulevard, I informed Divine that he was currently in tax arrears to the United States Government, New York State and the City of New York of a total in excess of $100,000. And they were not leaving him alone. Or, rather, they were not leaving me alone, as his representative and contact number.

I was seriously frustrated with his devious ways of avoiding this issue. Over his third bowl of cereal and just as his mountain-high pile of hot syrup waffles arrived at the table, I explained to him that I was trying to negotiate a new film deal for a fee of $100,000, which I thought to be a reasonable demand following his current success with *Hairspray*. If we were able to complete the deal, he could pay off his tax debt in total. This simple idea was the kind of easy-to-accept logic Divine liked to hear and I thought it might just lead to this stubborn, selfish debtor facing up to facts. It didn't seem relevant at the time to question how he would also pay my twenty per cent commission due on his fee, or continue to meet his own ever-increasing personal expenditure.

He listened while eating feverishly. Then, suddenly: 'There just has to be another way to get round this, Bernard. If you can't work it out for me, I'll just have to do it myself.' For him, the conversation was over.

Within less than twenty-four hours of that breakfast together, Harris Glenn Milstead – known worldwide as the film star, pop singer and celebrity, Divine – died in his sleep.

'You selfish idiot,' I screamed out aloud, soon after discovering his huge bulk, frighteningly still and already red and black from rigor mortis, lying in his bed at the Regency Plaza Suites Hotel. I recalled the previous morning's declaration from him; that he would find his own way out of his financial mess. 'Not this way.' Now I was whispering, sobbing. 'That's just not fair. What about me? You've escaped the tax man, but you're gone now. What's left for *me* to do?'

It was twelve years earlier that we had first met – a most unlikely couple at first glance. On reflection, I believe a great deal of our success as a business partnership (as we both liked to think of it) was due to the way our personalities complemented each other. Whatever the reasons were that we managed to stay working together for twelve years, this was certainly not how we had thought it would end.

Show business rarely produces genuine happy endings. Too many celebrities die in their forties of excesses created by the lifestyles inflicted on them: too much publicity; no private life; easy access to drugs, alcohol and sex. Too much money. Elvis Presley, Marilyn Monroe, James Dean, Janis Joplin, John Belushi . . . the list is legendary . . . and tragic.

But for Divine it hadn't happened that way. 'Created' in the late sixties – by King of Sleaze John Waters and Ugly-Expert Van Smith – as the epitome of excess and vulgarity, Glenn (as he was called to avoid confusion with his father, who also had the first name of Harris) was destined to become yet another gay hairdresser, catering to the wealthy, bored housewives of Baltimore. But this only child of strict Baptist parents was suddenly plunged into a world of underground film-making and notoriety, brought about not the least by his questionable task of eating dog shit at the end of Waters's early screen epic *Pink Flamingos*.

Cinematic history? Perhaps. Gross excess at the beginning – not end – of a career? Most certainly. Divine had spent over twenty years since then shocking the public by taking the image of his alter ego into realms that some dreamed of, but few dared emulate.

By March 1988, Glenn was finally able to see his long-held dream come true – an escape from the paranoia of being Divine. Although he lived as Divine and encouraged those around him to accept him as Divine, the public had created their own image of the *star* Divine, to which he could not live up.

'Who am I talking to exactly?' he would be asked. 'How much of you is Glenn Milstead and how much of you is Divine?'

'They're both just names,' was his response. 'Glenn is the name I was brought up with, Divine is the name I've been using for the past twenty-three years. I guess it's *always* Glenn and it's *always* Divine. Do you mean the character Divine or the person Divine? You see, it gets very complicated. There's the Divine you're talking to now and there's the character Divine, which is just something I do to make my living. She doesn't really exist at all. I hope not . . . if she did I'd be in prison or a mental hospital.'

No wonder even he was confused at times. In reality, he was a complete contradiction to the crazy, larger-than-life, establishment-bashing icon his public had made of him. He needed to escape from this identity crisis.

For twelve years, I had fought to bring him nearer to the life he dreamed of. And it often seemed that only I realised how very much Divine needed the acceptance of his peers in the entertainment industry and to be able to live like 'an old-fashioned film star', loved by all. Divine's immediate goal in 1988 was the middle-class respectability from which he had so willingly escaped all those years before.

He was so near to it. Finally, after suffering what was possibly the most extreme example of typecasting ever practised in the film industry, his peers were beginning – just beginning – to take Divine the character actor seriously. Divine could picture the day when the heels, the false eyelashes, the wigs, the tights, the sponges sewn into his pain-fully tight-fitting body-suits could all be thrown into the garbage bin for good as the excesses with which he had begun his acting career and on which he had depended to achieve his far-from-overnight fame were finally being put behind him. At last he could look forward to living his true identity.

In September 1987, on the island of Malta where he was performing his disco act, Divine had been forced to give up his addiction to marijuana. Cold turkey. There was just none available and our hosts had warned me that we would both be 'thrown off the island' should he be discovered smoking pot whilst there. It would seem Divine's reputation travelled ahead of him.

We were on Malta for five days. They were five days of hell for those around him who had to suffer Divine's ill-temper and frustration while he withdrew. But for him, it must have been much worse than hell. 'I was addicted to marijuana. I thought the marijuana was helping me, because it's no fun getting home from a show at 3 a.m. and not being able to fall asleep until five,' Divine admitted. 'But soon I found I was stoned all day, until I passed out. I started staying at home all the time because I didn't want to end up out in a club somewhere snoring. I didn't care about my career, my looks. It certainly didn't help my weight. When I was stoned I only ate once a day, but the meal lasted twenty-four hours. I had agents and managers fighting to create a career for me, and my attitude was "Fuck it, let's smoke." I became difficult to work with, and I had always prided myself on being so professional. I wasn't happy.

'Finally I realised that I had to do something. But it had to be on my own. I didn't want to go to a clinic only to be released and smoke my brains out. So I went to Malta and spent time by myself. I did all the corny things: counted my blessings, recalled the bad times when I was on welfare, recalled the good times, admitted that I was throwing away a good life. I couldn't afford to waste time being negative. And I bucked it. I moved on.'

From Malta, he flew via Gatwick to Ibiza for his late-summer holiday. At Gatwick airport I was to leave him once he had met up with a group of British friends who would join him at the luxury villa he rented each year. I took them aside. 'Don't smoke pot in front of Divine during the holiday,' I pleaded. I explained the recent five days in Malta. I was certain that he had not touched the weed during that time. All his friends were well aware how Divine's addiction to marijuana was threatening his career, with the laziness, boredom, apathy and increased eating that it brought about.

On the plane from Malta, Divine had promised me he would not return to the habit. He had assured me how much he realised that he needed to give it up in order to concentrate on his film career and his future. I believed him, although Divine rarely kept his promises to me. They were often just made to terminate a business conversation which bored him – but this time I *wanted* to trust him and therefore was prepared to lecture his friends.

While Divine made purchases in the airport gift store – another addiction which brought him great pleasure – I talked further with his friends. They were in joyful mood, eager to please Divine in any way necessary so that their host would be the life-of-the-party rather than the impatient, dissatisfied bore. I received their astonishment, then their joy, then their disbelief at the news. I was assured that they would most certainly do their best to avoid his returning to marijuana. I still feared, however, that they would be the first to offer it to him should his mood demand. But to the best of my knowledge, Divine never smoked pot again after his Maltese revelation that he was able to discipline himself and did not need that particular crutch for the future.

Anyway, Divine no longer needed the high the drug would give him. The acclaim he was receiving across America for his dual performances – as housewife Edna Turnblad and bigot Arvin Hodgepile – in John Waters's *Hairspray* was giving him the kind of rush he had always longed for, but none of the boring side effects. For the first time, both Divine and I were optimistic that a screen performance he had recently given could lead to other, lucrative offers. Interest from the worldwide media was tremendous. Divine was busy giving interviews.

He declared himself to be 'bi-talented', referring to his success as both actor and recording star, and he was enjoying life. *Variety* was printing weekly figures that made *Hairspray* look like becoming a 'cross-over' hit and Divine a 'box office marquee name'. Following his own personal successes in other recent movies – *Polyester*, *Lust in the Dust* and *Trouble in Mind* – the sycophants surrounding him declared each time that he had 'broken through' and offers would come tumbling in. But they didn't. Moguls' doors didn't open for him. I was offered no cigars. Divine was still considered to be a freak, a cross-dresser, a transvestite – in short, an actor who had to wear dresses to get a job.

But now, Belle Zwerdling, Divine's newly acquired Hollywood talent agent, was having her calls returned for the first time since she had started to represent him a year before. Belle, coincidentally also from Baltimore, was a fan of Divine's. We were both optimistic of her attempts to achieve the breakthrough he sought. The agency, which also represented the rebellious young film actor Mickey Rourke, was small but respected, and Belle appeared to have many credible contacts.

Belle had been keeping us regularly informed of her negotiations with the producers of Fox TV's syndicated sitcom, *Married ... with Children*. There was a possibility that the producers would offer Divine a one-episode cameo role as Uncle Otto. However, if the character was well received in its début appearance, the producers could be persuaded, Belle assured us, to introduce Uncle Otto on a regular basis. There could certainly be little better way of breaking through the type-casting barrier than being given regular exposure in a male character role on TV screens throughout the country. *Married . . . with Children* was doing well in the ratings and building a cult audience of 'thirty-somethings'.

He could hardly sleep for anticipation, imploring me to call Belle four times a day for news. In February 1988, a few days after the national release of *Hairspray*, Belle called to give us the date for Divine's first day of rehearsals on the Hollywood sound stage as Uncle Otto: 7 March. Divine was ecstatic. A male character role. His dressmaker was not so thrilled.

I had arranged air tickets for us to fly to California on Saturday 5 March. He had wanted to arrive earlier, but, as usual, it was necessary to arrange a personal appearance at a disco to enable him to have some cash for a trip to the West Coast. Pati Mayfield, my personal assistant in New York, had become an expert in calling disco owners and booking Divine. He had been earning his living performing in discos even prior to his first hit record in 1982. Since then, he had become the most successful and in-demand disco performer in the world and had spent most of the past six years on tour with his act, promoting his dance-music singles. However, his popularity and fame as a recording star were clearly on the wane. He hadn't had a decent chart success anywhere in the world for over a year and, despite some rather feeble efforts to continue, we were very conscious of how we could no longer rely upon this side of his career to bring in the cash. It was even more important now to build his reputation and success as a character actor in both television and film.

The gig, arranged for midnight on Friday 4 March, was at a Brook-lyn club named Earthquake. As was often the case, we had played there before in one of its earlier incarnations under another name. It was a huge cavern, filled to capacity with young Latinos, fiercely hetero-sexual in their attitude. This in itself was no problem for Divine; he had graduated from playing only gay discos years before. But the Brooklyn kids had a tough reputation and were restless. Divine had not had a hit record for too long – it was unlikely they were still dancing to any of his songs – and they were *very* young. Would they even know who this monstrous guy was, in his skin-tight, sequined catsuit?

Rob Saduski, Divine's personal assistant, had flown ahead to California to discuss Divine's wardrobe for the TV show, so Divine decided to take Stephen, a close friend of his, as Rob's replacement for the night. The limo picked us up in Manhattan for the one-hour drive to Brooklyn. Divine knew that Stephen and I were not friendly. Stephen had often been critical of me, partly because I had fought with him over the years about his irritating habit of bringing cream cakes and other fattening goodies whenever he visited Divine.

Divine had not prepared himself at all for this show. His mind was solely on getting to the west coast and becoming a TV star with 'money to burn'. He fell asleep immediately he hit the limo seat and snored heavily. Stephen looked out of the window on one side of the long, white car; I, the other. On waking Divine as we arrived, we received the usual grunts, groans, farts and other noises indicating his disapproval of being made to suffer the indignity of work.

I dealt with the club owners as best I could, knowing that, as the joint was now full and people were buying vast quantities of liquor at the bar, they would be wishing they had not committed themselves to paying the $2,500 fee we were to receive in cash before Divine stepped on stage. I had to wait for the money and so the show was 30 minutes beyond the scheduled performance time, which made Divine even more unreasonable. His left high heel snapped just before the show and he cursed everyone, except Stephen – the person who was being paid for ensuring that a spare pair of shoes had been packed. There was no spare pair.

Divine climbed onto the stage in stockinged feet. It was a ridiculous sight. The club owners used this as an excuse to demand part of their fee back from me. The sound system was appalling and Divine hurtled through his 40-minute act in less than 25. The crowd of dancing Latinos didn't care at all about him and Divine was clearly hating every minute. I anticipated his foul temper when he came off stage. He didn't disappoint – his mood was loathsome.

The limo drove us back in almost total silence, broken only by Divine's snoring. Stephen and I glanced at each other, but no words were suitable at this time. I resolved to put my foot down once and for all about Divine using his ineffectual friends as personal assistants on tour.

I knew that Divine's career as a disco star was coming to an end. Not only were hit records a thing of the past and club bookings increasingly more difficult for Pati – or any of our European agents – to arrange, but the star's own lack of interest and enthusiasm for this money-earning part of his life was showing in his performances and venues were no longer so eager for him to return. I hoped that the forthcoming trip to Los Angeles would bring instant results.

Divine took the earliest flight possible to LA on 5 March. I had to work at home during the day and was delighted not to have to sit with him for seven hours on a crowded 747, listening to his unsocial snoring and pretending not to notice the irritated stares of disgust from those passengers unlucky enough to be seated near us. During the brief moments he might have stayed awake – usually only when food threatened to come his way – we were sure to have started arguing about the rights and wrongs of the last night's escapade. Instead, I took the late afternoon flight from JFK and spent most of it wondering what the future held in store. After all these years working discos together – and the odd movie role – we were still both broke, up to our eyes in credit debt, yet used to a very comfortable way of living. Where was the cash to come from next month to sustain these comforts?

On arrival at our Los Angeles home-from-home, I was allocated my usual suite, on the first floor, immediately below Divine's. There was a note from my star waiting for me at the front desk. 'Hi. Welcome back to Hollywood. Hope you had a good flight. Miss you. See you in the morning. Love, Divi.'

I interpreted the note immediately: he was feeling guilty about his behaviour the night before; he realised he needed my enthusiasm and total support during this most important week in Hollywood; he wanted to avoid seeing me until Sunday morning, by which time he hoped I would have decided not to bring up the subject of Stephen. I smiled to myself, went out on the town and got drunk on the ambitious, enticing air of Hollywood at night.

The next morning Divine called me earlier than usual. 'Hi. It's me. How are you? Isn't life wonderful? Did you get my note? Come on, man . . . let's go and eat!'

I knew he was very nervous about his first meeting with the cast of *Married . . . with Children* the next day at noon. It was my job on this quiet, beautiful spring Sunday to bring him to earth gently and help him find the confidence he would need. I knew how to do this. And his asking me to have breakfast with him was a sure sign that he acknowledged his need. He knew I liked to be invited to eat with him just to gossip, laugh and plan the future. He liked to talk business over meals; I think the joy of eating somewhat overcame the boredom of having to receive my lectures about over-spending. Breakfast that morning at Hollywood World was one of those increasingly rare shared moments of give and take.

Divine had decided to apologise to me about Friday night's moods and – without giving me a moment to comment before moving on to his next chosen topic – declared he would never again ask a personal friend to work as his assistant. I was experienced enough to know that this declaration made to please me (and one to which he would have no intention of adhering in the future) would be followed by a request, presumably for more cash. I handed him another $100 note, not even asking where the $500 cash had gone that I had given him two nights before. Surely not on drugs any more? More likely, he'd been forced finally to pay off part of an old debt to a friend in Los Angeles.

We talked for two hours about possible television and movie roles, about our plans for me to produce a new musical on Broadway in which he would star, of his friends in Los Angeles, and of the decline in his recording career. It was a good meeting. He seemed to understand many of the problems and want to be more co-operative in the future. All was fine until I started to complain about his urgent and worrying tax debt.

After breakfast Divine went his own way. We agreed to meet at the hotel at 4 p.m. for me to take him to a television studio in the Motown office building along Sunset Boulevard. *Hairspray*'s success had spread to Australia and I had been asked if Divine would do a live TV interview for *The Mike Walsh Show*, syndicated from Sydney.

When we had been in Australia in 1984 Divine was a controversial disco star, with a current hit record. He had toured the clubs successfully, but their image of him at the time was also of an X-rated film actor; they had even labelled him a porno star. It would be good now for him to have the opportunity to appear on Australian television as a respected and successful film star.

Because of the dateline difference between Sydney and Los Angeles it was necessary for Divine to appear live on satellite at 5 p.m. Sunday for the Monday lunchtime show. He was in a good humour, dressed smartly in his favourite Tommy Nutter three-piece silk suit, Turnbull and Asser shirt and Maud Frizon shoes. An elegant sight, however expensive it came.

The Motown building was deserted on a Sunday, save for the tiny studio used by Australian television. Divine was at his very best, amusing the LA-based staff with anecdotes and bawdy side remarks. He waited patiently for the satellite to commence, being able to hear the Monday show live, but with no vision. He smiled at me. 'Isn't it strange?' he whispered. 'Having to do Monday's show *live* on Sunday!

However, you might as well get done what you can today, as you never know what will come up by surprise tomorrow.' That passing comment on a calm, promising Sunday afternoon will probably remain the most curiously prophetic statement I shall ever hear.

We left the world of Motown, wondering how it might have been if Divine had been signed as a recording artist to the famous company and not to the tiny independent labels he had had to suffer for the past six years. But all that was behind us now. On to bigger and better things. In Hollywood.

I dropped Divine back at the hotel as he needed to get ready for dinner that night. His friend, celebrity photographer Greg Gorman, had invited him out to a chic bistro along with some of his other friends. Divine was excited as it was to be his first time out in public in Hollywood since his acclaim for *Hairspray*. He felt every inch – all of them – a star. I didn't join them; Greg knew not to invite me. Divine and I rarely socialised together. He always told me that I inhibited him, as I would constantly talk about what he was doing – as was my job and usually requested by others present.

I returned to the hotel at about midnight. As I climbed the steps from the underground car park, I heard the familiar chesty laugh of my star and much merry noise by the courtyard pool. Divine had only just returned and was bidding his friends goodnight. I could tell that they had all had a good time. He came over and hugged me, then kissed me on the cheek, whispering in my ear, 'Thank you for bringing all of this to me. I really don't know what I'd do without you.'

I wished him goodnight, turned and waved goodbye to the small gathering by the pool and was about to go into my room when I suddenly heard Divine start a deafening chorus from *Arrivederci Roma*. He was standing, Evita-like, on the balcony at the top of the steps to his suite, waving his arms majestically and singing in that all-too-familiar voice usually reserved for his disco singles. We all laughed, happy to see him in such good humour. Divine turned and made a suitably theatrical exit into his room. I went to bed and slept peacefully.

Divine had asked me to meet with him at 10 a.m. on Monday to run through his lines for the rehearsal. At this time, the actor weighed about 375 pounds and so it was easy to know he was awake if you lived underneath his room. The heavy footsteps dragging around his hotel suite signalled that the day's business was about to begin. Soon there would be the familiar first phone call of the day: 'Hi. It's me. How are you? Did any cheques come in the mail today?'

I thought I had heard him earlier that morning while I was still half asleep. It didn't surprise me that he was up and about earlier than usual. I knew he would be very nervous. I waited until 10.15 a.m., but there was no sign of Divine and no more sounds from up above. I called his room: no answer. I tried again: still no answer. The front desk checked his phone and told me there was no apparent problem. Growing impatient and beginning to feel a familiar anger brew inside me, I waited. At 11 a.m. I knocked loudly on his door. I paced the fake lawn by the pool, watched by sun-worshippers with telephones stretching on long cords from their poolside rooms – in case that long-awaited call from the agent or the casting company should suddenly materialise.

He had woken early and gone for breakfast with a friend, I decided. He had either not noticed the time, or was back in his selfish mood of not wanting to spend time working with me. Rob Saduski called me from the TV studio, reporting that all was well and everyone was very keen to meet Divine at noon, as arranged. It was now 11.30 a.m. and no sign of our star, but I didn't hint of the problem to Rob. During this time it never occurred to me that anything could be seriously wrong. I had grown so used to Divine's erratic timekeeping that I presumed all along that he was out having a good time. Even when I asked the maid to let me into his suite and told the front desk to say we had left for the studio if anyone called, it was in the expectation that I would find some scribbled note giving me a clue as to who he was with for breakfast.

It was now just after midday. The 'Do Not Disturb' sign was still hanging on his door handle. It was then, as the maid turned her pass key in the lock, that I knew instinctively what had happened. It was as if a sixth sense took over and everything was absolutely clear. I experienced a brief moment of calm – a break in the anger and frustration that had been building up for the past two hours – as if I knew it was no longer necessary to be angry. The living-room area was its usual mess – dirty socks strewn across the floor waiting for Rob to come back from the studio and clear up after him, the script of the TV episode lying on the coffee table, open at the first page. Asking the maid to wait, I walked alone through the narrow corridor of his suite, past the kitchen and bathroom, and in through the open bedroom doorway.

I shivered. There he was, lying on his bed, the blankets neatly covering him, his diamond earring glistening. But Divine's bulk usually simulated a minor earthquake when sleeping. And now it was totally still. Deathly still. I had never seen a dead body before.

Divine suffered badly from what has been recently termed 'sleep apnoea'. It has been discovered that people with chronic snoring problems often suffer from this illness, which can lead to failing memory, personality changes, heart attacks, strokes and death. Medical faculties now conduct research on this cause of death among grossly overweight people. All the symptoms described in the studies are identical to Divine's day-to-day problems: constant fatigue; falling asleep while talking on the phone or behind the wheel of a car; struggling to get air while sleeping – and excessively anti-social snoring. The final probability for extreme sleep apnics is cardiac arrest while asleep – Divine's cause of death.

These symptoms caused Divine to be a very restless sleeper. He spent much of his adult life fighting the physical difficulties created by his weight. He hated his size. He was aware that his fierce morning tempers were caused by the fearful nights of restlessness, afraid to go to sleep in case he should not manage to catch his breath. His weight problems made it easier for him – and much more comfortable – to sleep propped up in a sitting position with many pillows behind his back and head. Within moments of his falling asleep, all sheets and blankets would be on the floor as he tossed and turned. Yet here he was with his head neatly placed on one pillow as most of us would sleep, the blankets and sheets lying in place over the lower half of his stomach.

On Monday 7 March 1988, in the early hours of the morning, he was at his happiest. No more addiction to marijuana. Hope for his future as a character actor. Adulation from fans and approval from peers. And, best of all, that same morning would bring his long-awaited career breakthrough into family television.

My belief is that he left his friends feeling better than ever, glanced at his script, felt confident enough to try to get a good night's sleep, went to bed and – completely relaxing for a brief moment in his new-found contentment – placed his head on the pillow. It would have been about 12.30 a.m. The coroner advised me that Divine had been dead for about twelve hours when I found him.

I like to think that – at the age of 42 and at the turning point of his life – Divine died of happiness.

No excesses. Just his new-found optimism.

'People who used to make fun are now fans. I had the last laugh. It makes you feel good inside.' (*Chicago Sun-Times*, 28 February 1988)

2 No One's Christened 'Divine'

'I told him he should take the stage name "Divine". I don't even remember how it came to me – probably something from my Catholic upbringing. He looked the word up in the dictionary and seemed satisfied. Yes, he agreed, ever so modestly, he truly was Divine.'

John Waters in *Vanity Fair*, June 1988

BUT CERTAINLY HE WASN'T CHRISTENED DIVINE. And no one is born *that* fat.

Harris Glenn Milstead was born at the Women's Hospital in Baltimore, Maryland, at 7.28 a.m. on Friday 19 October 1945. He weighed only 5 pounds 14 ounces. A mother in the next bed, who had just given birth to a 10-pound daughter, laughed about Glenn being so tiny. Mrs Milstead said, 'Let's compare our children when they are a little older.'

Harris Bernard Milstead and Diana Frances, née Vukovich, had waited seven long years for a baby of their own, an even more frustrating fact than usual considering they ran a children's nursery for a living. Glenn was an only child.

In the first few years of my knowing and working with Divine, he talked very little of his childhood. He seemed reluctant to make the effort to think back to before his days as a rebellious actor and, in his mind at least, a star. In quieter times, I would try to bring him out on the subject of his family, but at first he said little beyond telling me that his parents had moved away some years ago from their home town of Baltimore to the gentle suburbs of southern Florida, in an attempt to escape from the notoriety of having become 'the parents of Divine'. Frances Milstead denies this, always insisting that their move south was solely due to a change of climate essential for her husband's health – Harris Milstead has suffered for many years from debilitating muscular dystrophy.

'He was our godsend, our little star,' Frances Milstead told me. 'We thought our son was beautiful. We brought him home from the hospital after five days. I really wanted to do what was right for our little baby. He had a lot of visitors the week we brought him home. They came with gifts for the little star and they all learned to love him and

13

watch him grow into a handsome person. He was my first doll to love, dress, cuddle and rock. I had never had a toy in my lifetime and I loved him dearly. I was a possessive mother and I really wanted to do the best for him.'

It doesn't need a psychologist to interpret these words. There is no doubt that Glenn was spoiled from the day he was born. Indeed, with the best intentions in the world, it would seem that he was suffocated with love. From a very early age Glenn was used to getting his own way. As Divine himself admitted, 'I was an only child in, I guess, your upper middle-class American family. I was probably your American spoilt brat.'

'We were inordinately proud when he spoke his first words at the age of six months,' Frances continued. 'He was dedicated in the local Baptist church and was given a silver teething-ring. We always said he was born with a silver spoon in his mouth.' According to her, he was a good and healthy baby and a lovable child to raise. He also had a very good appetite; he loved his food. He had his own bedroom with pretty blue animal curtains and a white crib with teddy bears on it. At fifteen months, he started to walk and his parents only bought him the best shoes. For his second Christmas, 'Harris and I just gave him everything we thought Glenn would like,' his mother said. 'I shall never forget the morning he saw the tree and all the gifts and toys and the train going round the track. His expression was worth a million dollars. His little face lit up like a fire-cracker. I was so happy to see this that it made me cry.'

Frances went back to work at the nursery when Glenn was only two and, instead of taking him with her, she left him during the day in the care of his paternal grandmother. They were a close family, God-fearing and conservative. Harris Milstead was an officer of his Baptist church and after Glenn had graduated from cradle roll at the church he attended Sunday school every week.

He was taken on frequent trips to see his other grandmother and his cousins in Pennsylvania. His grandmother believed that flowers were meant to look pretty in the garden and she had a rule that they were not to be picked and brought in doors. But this was a rule totally ignored by Glenn when he visited her. She never admonished him. 'He could do things and get away with it with her,' his mother told me. 'All he had to say was, "Grandma, these are for you."'

In fact, as a child, Glenn always got away with things by switching on the charm. No one had the heart to reproach him.

At the age of five, he had his tonsils removed. His grandmother prepared a special meal for him of easily digestible food, but all he wanted was potato chips. By now his favourite foods were fried chicken, spaghetti and meatballs. As he grew older, his mother was aware that he loved to eat, but they thought there was nothing very wrong with that. In fact, knowing that he was hungry, his grandmother sometimes fed him before the family sat down to dinner, when he would eat again. When he was taken to watch a baseball game, he could not have cared less about who was winning. The excitement for him was in eating hot-dogs and peanuts and drinking cokes. He was never interested in sports. His parents, both baseball and football fans, would have loved him to have played for the Colts or the Orioles, but they soon realised that he was more interested in art and photography.

'I guess I wasn't rough and tough,' Divine recollected. 'I always liked to ride, I loved horses. I loved painting and I always loved flowers and things. I've always been into the arts and water sports, such as boating and swimming.'

A teacher actually told Frances that perhaps Glenn did not want to hurt himself by physical exercise. In any case, Glenn could do no wrong — even if he did gradually put on a lot of weight. 'We loved him,' his mother said, 'and we accepted anything he chose to do.'

The Milsteads were excited to see their young son start at his new school. 'He was so sweet in his Eton suit and blue bow-tie,' Frances remarked. 'His legs were chubby and cute.'

At the same time as she felt that her little baby was growing up and away from her, a trait of selfishness began to show itself in young Glenn. His mother tells of how he always managed to get another child to carry his bag back home after school. It might have been the boy up the street or even the girl next door. 'Glenn,' she would tell him, 'you ought to carry Judy's bag instead of her carrying yours.' He would just laugh and take no notice. His mother's astute verdict was that 'he was either too smart or too lazy'.

Glenn Milstead was born in the Baltimore suburb of Towson and lived in a house that F. Scott Fitzgerald had lived in. 'We had a lovely place,' recalled Divine. 'It was a small estate with a very big house on it. We had twenty-eight rooms. At one time F. Scott Fitzgerald and his wife Zelda had lived there for a couple of years while she was in and out of a nearby mental hospital called Shephard-Pratt. So I guess she had a few problems. One time, she had set the top floor on fire, so that part of the house had a newer roof than the other part. We met their daughter, Scottie. My mother wrote her a letter and she came to the house.'

In 1958, when Glenn was twelve, the family moved to Lutherville, just six houses away from Mr and Mrs Waters and their son John, who was the same age as Glenn.

Mrs Milstead remembers that Glenn always took part in the school play and sometimes had a leading role. 'He loved acting and would say "You and Daddy and Grandma better be there to watch me."' He obviously also loved an audience. During a summer holiday in Quebec when Glenn was thirteen there was a floor show at their hotel, with singers, dancers and a comedian. Glenn enjoyed it enormously. 'Do you know what I would like to do?' he said to his parents. 'I would like to be an entertainer, to make people laugh.' The following year, the Milsteads took Glenn to New York City for the first time and did all the usual things that tourists do, seeing all the sights. A highlight for young Glenn was seeing Barbra Streisand at Radio City Music Hall.

At about this time there were incidents suggesting antipathy, for whatever reason, towards the young Glenn. Some of the boys at school called him a sissy. His mother taught him to fight, but he would not retaliate even when the kids made fun of him. 'At one point, when I was in school, I had a lot of trouble, because I was very much left out,' Divine recalled. 'I was very much to myself and very shy. The kids always used to wait for me and beat me up, and then threatened that if I ever told anyone, they would kill me. They were very bad to the point where I was completely black and blue. I had to go to the doctor for some kind of physical, and, when I disrobed, he saw my body and was horrified. He called my parents and they had the police come in and it just got very dramatic.

'A car picked me up,' he continued, 'and took me to school, which made it even worse then, because I was fourteen or fifteen years old. So that set me aside from the kids even more. I was fat. They said I was a fat fruit. I was fat, but that was as far as it went. Kids can be very cruel. A friend of mine in school wore glasses and had the shit kicked out of him almost every day too, but what could you do?'

In all probability, Mrs Milstead was more concerned about this bullying than was Glenn, who seemed to take it all in his stride. 'Then my parents went there with the police and had six or seven kids expelled from school, but then I had to walk down the hall and listen to "Ah, there's the squealer. There's the squealer." I had that for two years of school, to carry around with me.' In any case, nothing appears to have affected his schooling. He was a good student and got passable grades.

Divine also admitted to an inclination towards effeminacy while at school. In his book *Shock Value*, John Waters quotes him: 'I never went out of the house. I was with my parents always. Always. Until I was fifteen years old I was constantly with my mummy and daddy. I didn't have any brothers or sisters, so I used to play with this imaginary person, Jim. We just talked all the time; I would get dressed up and talk to him. I only had about an hour and a half alone when I got home from school before my parents came home. Once I got caught by my grandmother – I had on a slip and a big hat and she chased me across the lawn.'

When Glenn was fifteen, he decided to take a part-time job. He chose to work in a florist's shop. He liked his boss and was taught to make floral designs. He learned fast. That Christmas he used his new expertise to help him decorate his parents' house quite beautifully – 'Better than I ever could,' said Mrs Milstead. He was accepted at The Alfred Institute to study horticulture, but characteristically soon became bored with the idea, especially when a new activity suggested itself.

One day he went to collect his mother at the beauty shop where she was having her hair done. While waiting for her, he took a wig from a stand and combed it into a beehive style. The owner told him that he was exceptionally creative and could obviously do things with hair that even he and his staff could not manage. Horticulture was abandoned in favour of cosmetology.

He also made strenuous efforts to lose weight. By the time he entered his senior year, he had reduced from 180 pounds to 145 pounds. 'He looked terrific,' said his mother. 'His whole personality changed. He was a good-looking fellow.'

Divine too talked of this period. 'Finally I went on a diet,' he said. 'It did make a world of difference. People talked to me, but I didn't like them anyway. They were just talking to me because I lost eighty pounds or sixty pounds or whatever. But I did have more fun that year. I did go to the school dances and things like that which I had never really done before.'

His reward was to be given his mother's Visa card to buy new clothes. His taste was good. It was also expensive. 'He looked like he'd stepped out of a bandbox when he was dressed to go to church or when he went out to something special,' Frances enthused. 'The family were all proud of him and told him so.' She tells a story of her son buying a red sportscoat for a particular occasion when he was chosen to read the lesson in church, where he regularly sang in the choir. The minister, the Reverend Leland Higginbotham, exchanged jackets with him, declaring, 'Red is too loud to wear in the pulpit.'

Glenn learned to drive and his parents bought him a car, a second-hand Plymouth. This led to a number of arguments at home when he allowed his friends to drive it and collected endless parking tickets, which were always paid by his parents. Mr and Mrs Milstead were nothing if not indulgent. 'Go for it,' Divine admitted to having thought at the time. 'When you're young, what do you care? I didn't care about anything. You'd make as many people laugh as you'd want, and your parents would pay the bill. You could always ask Dad for twenty bucks, and he was always good for it and the car keys. If he wouldn't give them to you, you could go to your mother. But you got them some-how. And if nobody gave them to you, you stole them. You got pun-ished the next day, but that only lasted for one day. You took chances. Who cared? Every day was a party.'

His mother remembers that in 1963, at the time of her 25th wedding anniversary, Glenn was already crazy about movie stars, his favourites being Elizabeth Taylor and Marilyn Monroe. He also loved to go dancing. She claims to have taught him and they did a much admired cha-cha together at a supper club, as well as the twist. Indeed, those skills were never lost. Divine would always boast, 'I'm light on my feet.'

Mrs Milstead had high hopes that her son might one day marry Diane Evans, who accompanied him to his senior prom and with whom he exchanged class rings. Frances liked Diane, whose little sister Lisa attended the Milsteads' nursery, and would have welcomed her as a daughter-in-law. In the essentially respectable, close-knit circle in which they lived and worked, no reason stood out for Frances to put an unusual interpretation on any of her son's behaviour and she believes to this day that Glenn ceased dating Diane only because she went out with another boy. But Divine told me he quit going out with Diane because she wasn't the only one of this partnership who was dating another boy.

'When I was seventeen they sent me to a psychiatrist,' he recalled. 'That was when I first realised that I was attracted to boys as well as girls, which they thought was strange. They used to lay such heavy trips on me. I thought if you touched a girl with your finger she got pregnant!'

That summer Glenn attended the Marinella Beauty School. When he graduated, he was recognised as a really good hairstylist. He found immediate work at a hairdressing salon with an excellent reputation. He was quick to learn and soon built a personal following. He really enjoyed his job and it was not long before he moved to another establishment, the one his mother patronised, where he was very well liked. Mrs Milstead loved his style. 'He would experiment on my hair,' she said. 'I would cringe when he teased it. "Don't pull so hard," I told him, but I was a glutton for punishment and let him do it time and time again, because it always looked great when he'd finished. "You want it to stay put and to stay high, don't you?" he used to say.'

'After doing hair for five or six years,' Divine said, 'I had my own salon that my parents gave me, but I'd had enough. I just left one day. It was horrible. It was like being a psychiatrist. I mean, you stood there and while you were doing their hair you listened to their problems. I had problems of my own that I wanted someone to listen to . . .'

Glenn, however, was also becoming a problem for his mother. Frances put it down to the fact that 'he started to get big headed'. She probably meant that he had big ideas – and expensive ones, leading to frequent financial embarrassment for the family. Glenn was already extravagant and used money in a way that was not favoured by his conservative, respectable and cautious parents. They gave him money to enable him to attend a night course in interior decoration. Whether he ever intended to join the course, or whether he simply got bored with the idea, the fact is that he pocketed the money. Frances, curiously, was less annoyed about this than the fact that he borrowed her new car to visit his friends instead of attending the Maryland Art Institute. But 'He always knew how to get round me,' she admitted. 'He could really sweet talk me into anything.' In 1966 he finally wrecked the Plymouth and promptly put down a first instalment on a new black and white Buick Skylark Convertible, assuring his parents that he could afford to pay for it. His payments, however, were often late.

He had a current bank account, but seemed not to know or care how much money he had in it. If he wanted something, he merely signed a piece of paper as if that would magically provide the necessary funds. I suppose he knew that, in the last resort, his devoted parents would help him out. They received a telephone call one day from an attorney representing Glenn, asking them to attend court where their son was being charged over a bad cheque he had issued. Of all things, it was for an expensive antique baby crib. Glenn was ordered to pay the full amount and was put on probation for a year. This outcome in no way bothered him. What did infuriate him was that his own lawyer had informed his parents. When his mother finally faced him, asking why on earth he had bought such a useless object, all he could say was that 'it was for a friend'.

Glenn's extravagance sometimes *seemed* to be not entirely selfish, although lessons were to be learned. Frances had to get used to paying for her son's generosity to herself. On one occasion when he visited her in hospital, he brought her three dozen roses and a bottle of Joy perfume. She later discovered that he had charged these items to her account. 'I know he meant well,' she excused him. There were many similar instances when his parents bailed him out in slightly dubious financial matters. 'In our eyes he could do no wrong,' Mrs Milstead confessed, although she became tired of receiving bills for her son's many parties.

In what was a very much more serious matter than any of this, the young Glenn was entirely innocent. He was actually involved briefly in a murder investigation, being a prime suspect in the murder of a friend in a case publicised in the newspapers as 'The Hairdressing Party Mystery'.

Glenn used to bring his friends home from time to time when they would fix one another's hair. On a particular Friday night in December 1964, when Glenn was nineteen, there was such a hairdressing party which began at the Milsteads' house and went on to the home of a friend of Glenn's named Sally. The following day Glenn was picked up at work by the police, along with a number of his pals. Sally had been strangled with a necktie soon after midnight. It seems she had put up quite a fight.

His parents knew that Glenn had returned home by midnight. They gave him good advice: simply to tell the truth. The police invited everyone to attend the police station voluntarily to take lie-detector tests. Glenn and the others were promised that, in return for their cooperation, no names would be given to the press. Glenn being almost the central character in the affair, they all met up first at his home before going together to the station. Unfortunately for the Milsteads, the police were unable to keep the names out of the newspapers and, horribly conscious of what the neighbours might believe, Mrs Milstead's first concern was that people seemed to think it was not Harris Glenn Milstead, but his father Harris Bernard Milstead, who was involved. However, the news soon gained currency, quite unfairly, that

Glenn was the chief suspect. 'Did you know that your son was a murderer?' was a question actually put in one form or another to Mrs Milstead. She indignantly demanded that people should not judge until they knew the facts. Such ghoulish enquiries caused her, as she put it, 'to blow my stack and lose my religion'. Mr Milstead had to prevail on the minister to refer positively to Glenn in his sermon the following Sunday, after which there was some closing of ranks and the congregation at least supported the family.

This was undoubtedly a more difficult time for his parents than it was for Glenn, who, after all, knew that he was innocent. There might even have been an element of enjoyment on his part in his sudden notoriety. In any case, it was all soon forgotten when the real murderer was caught. Sally, it appears, was his eleventh victim and he was arrested when he tried to kill a twelfth.

If anyone, however, could take such dramatic events in his stride, Glenn was surely that person. By the following year he had already teamed up with John Waters and was making his first movie. He had started to become involved in a bizarre world of his own. His parents had no idea what he was up to, or, for that matter, what he was in to. The thought that he could be involved in something so outside their own experience would never have occurred to them. Some years later, when Mrs Milstead saw a movie featuring her son she recognised an old-fashioned beige gown he was wearing on the screen as one she had once found in his closet. At the time she had thought that it must have belonged to a girlfriend of his. Divine certainly did not inherit his mother's naivety.

She also recognised the blue station wagon that she had, at the time, called the police to tow away from their property. 'We never even guessed that he was making movies,' she told me, almost incredulous at her son's secrecy. At this time Glenn was still working as a hairdresser and it would have been impossible for him to have told his parents about his new additional activity. They actually believed he had 'straightened out' and put his financial problems behind him.

One can imagine the Milsteads' shock when, on another occasion, they saw his car. 'Glenn could never find a parking spot,' Mrs Milstead said, 'and one day he parked his car on the church lot. When the good minister called me to ask Glenn to move his car, I went down myself. Harris drove me so that I could park it where Glenn worked and tell him about it. Boy! When I saw the upholstery in his car, I was so embarrassed. There were dirty words written all over the leather seats!'

She told her son to hide them with a cover until he could clean them off. She also told him never to park in the church lot again.

Glenn was strangely cool about the whole incident. He merely told his mother that he did not know who had committed such sacrilege. Well, come to think of it, hadn't she already suffered enough with this only child without yet having to find out about the Dreamlanders?

'Glenn was born before civil rights, gay rights, or women's rights . . . God doesn't want people created out of a Xerox machine . . . The tragedy is that Glenn was cut off right at the point of becoming who he really was, and the world will never see how that flower could have unfolded.' (The Reverend Leland Higginbotham in his Eulogy at Divine's funeral; Baltimore, Maryland, March 1988)

3   A Question of Taste

'When he met Waters and his wild cronies, Divine said, "I thought
. . . God, what a sleazy crew they are. Everybody liked living in
poverty and filth. No one I knew lived like that. I was stuck in a
middle-class mentality."'

San Francisco Chronicle, March 1988

I T WASN'T A LEGENDARY director-actress partnership in comparison
with those of Josef Von Sternberg and Marlene Deitrich, or Victor
Sjeastrom and Greta Garbo. It wasn't even the intimate friendship
that they both loved the media to believe. They helped each other.
They used each other. They liked each other to a degree. But they were
both fiercely – and individually – ambitious, which would lead to problems that didn't exist among other members of the Dreamlanders, most
of whom were quite content to follow their one particular pied piper.
To be blunt, John Waters and Divine became each other's meal tickets.
And why not? Their public loved the creative combination.

Waters's stock-in-trade was deliberate bad taste. He set out, in his
own words, 'to make the trashiest motion pictures in cinema history'.
His Dreamland Productions was initially located in his bedroom at his
parents' home in Baltimore and the Dreamland Lot was their front
lawn. Working on shoestring budgets, he created the Dreamlanders.
He certainly didn't select actors for their beauty or respectability. It
would seem that it was a positive advantage to be ugly and outrageous.
For the most part, the Dreamlanders was an eccentric group of young
grotesques.

'I had noticed him . . . waiting on the corner for a school bus, shun-
ned by other students, but proud all the same,' said John Waters of his
first becoming aware of Glenn Milstead. 'I was formally introduced to
him by a rebel friend named Carol who lived across the street from
him. They used to play cards and gamble for pimple medicine. I had
already made one teenage underground movie that was sorely lacking
in star power, and when I saw Glenn dancing the Dirty Boogie at a local
swim club, I knew I had met my goddess.'

Divine, although recalling their meeting in less specific detail, knew
an opportunity – even then – when it presented itself. 'We met in high

school in suburban Baltimore, where we were refugees from the fraternity and sorority life. We were not very popular,' he commented. 'We grew up together. He said he always thought that this talent was in me.'

John Waters describes his parents as 'very straight'. 'From the first sign of my childhood obsessions,' he wrote in *Shock Value,* 'they realised I was not likely to turn out to be the all-American boy.' He graduated from a private grade school, followed by public school for two years before joining a Catholic high school. His conservative parents somewhat reluctantly gave John the financial support he needed for his early films. It's easy to see how young Glenn fitted neatly into John's plans and even easier to realise why Glenn hid this new extra-curricular activity from *his* parents. Glenn was the perfect actor for John, and John the perfect escape for Glenn. He threw himself with abandon into whatever was required of him and partly because of his size and personality, but also because of his natural acting ability, he quickly became the Dreamlanders' star player. The more outrageously he was required to behave, the more fun he seemed to have.

For Glenn, Baltimore was a drab, faceless place in which to grow up. Although it is no more than a two-hour train ride south of New York and only a few minutes north of Washington DC, it is also something of a Southern city in character: very class conscious and hypocritical in its attitude to minorities. At least, that was the case when John Waters and Divine were setting out on their unconventional road. 'You can look far and wide,' John would say, 'but you'll never discover a stranger city with such extreme style. It's as if every eccentric in the South decided to move north, ran out of gas in Baltimore, and decided to stay.'

John Waters usually denies that he was making any political statement in his early films. Certainly, by appearing in them, Divine was doing little more than having fun, although he was the first to admit that he quickly saw in this peculiar and unlikely group of thespians with their weird leader a possible way out of his seemingly drab future and—who knows?—an avenue to fame and fortune. After all, 'When you live in Baltimore,' Divine said, 'you don't think anything could ever happen.' He was already astute enough to have a method in his madness.

In 1964 John Waters made his first film, *Hag in a Black Leather Jacket.* However, it wasn't until 1966 that he used Glenn Milstead, in *Roman Candles,* which he described as 'all home movies of my friends shoplifting, modelling their shoplifted dresses, that kind of thing'. As it is actually three 8mm films shown simultaneously, it's rarely, if ever, that the 40-minute movie is seen publicly. It was at this time that Glenn's director renamed him. Divine's role was small, but it gave him a taste for glamour and the director began to see the star potential of his protégé. 'He had a little part and people liked it,' said Waters, 'So I responded to what people liked. I knew from *Eat Your Make-Up* that people started to recognise him. From then on, I just always sort of had him in the lead.'

In *Eat Your Make-Up* (1968), Divine was cast as Jackie Kennedy. The film is about a governess who kidnaps models and forces them to model themselves to death and eat their make-up. The 45-minute black-and-white film, which the director calls his first feature, is also virtually impossible to show because it is made up of sixteen frames per second and the sound is on separate tape.

The highlight of this movie is the Kennedy assassination with Divine in the Jackie Kennedy outfit. Divine could never quite understand why people didn't fall about with mirth when it was originally shown. Perhaps it had something to do with the fact it was then only a few years after the Kennedy assassination?

'I was at a party with Jackie a few years ago,' Divine told *People* magazine sixteen years later. 'We were wearing the same dress. We didn't talk, just glared at each other across the room.'

Waters was surely a master of poor taste way before he adopted this particular label with *Pink Flamingos*.

The next Waters/Divine partnership is rarely mentioned by John in his interviews, nor is it listed in his official filmography in *Shock Value*. However, it is a matter of history that John Waters shot *The Diane Linkletter Story,* staring David Lochary, Mary Vivian Pearce, and Divine as Diane, the day after the real-life suicide took place of Art Linkletter's daughter.

Divine's first official move away from his parents' home was at the age of 23. 'I went to Provincetown with some friends of mine – John Waters was one,' Divine recalled. 'I stayed there and loved it, worked there that summer in a gourmet shop, selling cooking utensils and pâté. I lived there that winter and, the following summer, I opened Divine Trash, which was a nostalgia shop when it very first started, when old clothes and thrift stores were real popular. Everybody – well, everybody I knew – shopped in them in the early seventies.

'It really hit me,' he continued. 'I got into it and I told my parents that that was what I wanted to do. They bought me a station wagon and rented the shop for me in Provincetown.' Frances Milstead recalled that, at about this time, her son's car was repossessed and, in a temporary change of heart, she and her husband refused to help him any further with repayments, although that didn't stop them lending their own van to him. Just three weeks later, he returned it badly damaged, saying that he had been run off the road by a bad driver. 'We decided maybe he had told the truth,' Frances said, 'so we bought him a brand-new Pontiac station wagon and told him we would make the payments until he could afford to take them over.'

His mother also recalls that it was on the doctor's advice that he gave up hairdressing for a living 'as it made him nervous'. The truth has to be that Divine had become more and more involved with John Waters and decided to make this his priority in life. Unfortunately there was no way in which John could, or did, make up his salary, so Divine moved back home for a time. 'He had so many expenses he couldn't meet,' his mother explained, 'so we paid them, and he came back home to live and to get himself together.'

Frances Milstead was clearly concerned about her son at this time although she believed, wrongly, that he had no occupation. In fact, he was now part of the Dreamlanders, making underground movies. She was right however in her belief that he was earning little or no money. 'It got to the point,' she said, 'that I didn't think Glenn knew what he wanted to do.'

The entire budget for *Mondo Trasho* (1969, B/W 16mm, 90 minutes, starring Divine, David Lochary, Mary Vivian Pearce and Mink Stole) was $2,000 so how much, if anything, could Divine or any of the actors have been paid? However, Divine did continue to receive modest twice-yearly royalty cheques from John for his participation in these early movies.

John Waters describes this as his gutter film. 'I wanted to make real trash this time,' he stated, 'and I knew Divine would make the perfect star.' Divine's role was that of a 'portly blonde bombshell' who was meant to be driving along a country road when she is startled by a male hitchhiker who she imagines to be nude, causing her to run over a young 'fashion-fanatic' (Mary Vivian Pearce). John Waters chose to shoot the scene one Sunday morning at Baltimore's Johns Hopkins University. Mark Isherwood, who played the hitchhiker, was acting totally nude and in freezing weather when he was confronted by a campus policeman, resulting in John Waters, Isherwood and three other actors being charged with conspiracy to commit indecent exposure.

The case was eventually dismissed by a judge with an apparent sense of humour. When offered tickets for the eventual opening of the film, he declined, saying, 'If it's as bad as some of the underground films I've seen in New York, I wouldn't be anxious to see it.'

Divine's name was not associated with the trial because the first thing John did when Mark was confronted by the policeman was to remove his star from the scene. Mr and Mrs Milstead told me that they were not at all aware of this minor scandal involving their son. Although the story made the front page of *Variety* – 'Balto Mondo Trasho in Campus Pincho of Its Figleaved Hero' – they would hardly have made the connection anyway.

It was Divine's appearance in *Mondo Trasho* that earned him the credit that was to follow him for the rest of his career: 'The Most Beautiful Woman In The World. Almost'. John Waters was already depending on stylist Van Smith, an essential member of the Dreamlanders, to create the particular visual images for his characters. John and Van gradually gave birth to the brightly painted female persona that Divine was to live with, though not always with gratitude. 'John always liked cartoons, especially the wicked stepmother in *Cinderella*, the evil queen of *Snow White* and the bad witch in *The Wizard of Oz*,' Divine explained. 'He combined all three for the character Divine and wanted the look to be something like Jayne Mansfield, but an original character. We did not want for me to look like a real woman, because I'm not. I can't be and don't want to be.'

It was also from this film that Divine received the wonderfully ambiguous comment from the *Los Angeles Free Press*, 'The three-hundred-pound sex symbol, Divine, is undoubtedly some sort of discovery.'

The budget for John's next film, *Multiple Maniacs* (1970, B/W 16mm, 90 minutes, starring Divine, David Lochary, Mary Vivian Pearce, Mink Stole and Edith Massey) – his first talking picture – was still only $5,000, but John was beginning to learn his art and his work was starting to receive some attention. He has described *Multiple Maniacs* as his favourite among his own movies. Yet again, Waters chose a subject matter of extreme questionable taste, as the movie was suggested by the sensational 'Manson Family' murder in 1969 of Sharon Tate. 'Since the real killers hadn't been apprehended yet,' he said, 'I decided that Divine would take credit for the murders in the film. I figured that if the murderers were never caught, there would always be the possibility that maybe Divine really did do it. We wanted to *scare the world*. As I was completing the film, the Manson Family was caught, so I quickly changed the ending, explaining that Divine really hadn't done it.'

The *Baltimore Evening Sun* noted that *Multiple Maniacs* was 'not only uglier and more repulsive than *Mondo Trasho*, it is even more repugnant than *The Conqueror Worm* and, as usual, the audience laughed most when Waters was at his sickest. Is this part of the *new world* they have in mind?' *KSFX* in San Francisco, however, remarked that 'Divine is incredible! Could start a whole new trend in films.'

In the complicated plot of *Multiple Maniacs*, Divine plays Lady Divine, who runs The Cavalcade of Perversion with her boyfriend, Mr David (David Lochary). The ordinary people lured to the travelling freak show of 'junkies, pornographers and homosexuals' are robbed and even murdered by Lady Divine and her associates. A barmaid (Edith Massey, making her film début) informs Lady Divine that her boyfriend is having an affair. Divine's character is then seduced by a religious pervert (Mink Stole) – who gives 'rosary jobs' – and they plot together to murder Mr David and his lover. Lady Divine eats the guts - of her victims and then performs one of the scenes for which he became most notorious and which firmly became one of his fans' favourites: she is attacked and raped by Lobstora, a fifteen-foot broiled lobster. Totally losing her mind, she creates panic on staggering into the street and is finally gunned down by the National Guard.

A small but vocal cult following for Waters's movies was beginning to sit up and take notice of Divine. The actor had, unintentionally, become the essential parody of a drag queen.

'The early movies were first shown in Baltimore, at the annual Flower Market Day,' Divine told me. 'They have all these booths where they sell lemons with peppermint sticks, potted plants and other precious, girly, homemade things to raise money for crippled kids. We wanted an audience so John rented a church hall and sold tickets for forty cents for a showing of one of them, and the showings kept selling out. So he said, "Well, maybe there's something to these things. Maybe people really like them."'

In May 1971 an incident occurred which led to a ten-year separation between the Milstead parents and their only child. Frances told me of how she learned her son had taken a trip in the Pontiac station wagon from Provincetown to Florida, going through Baltimore without even contacting them. She had gone to the local gas station, where the manager knew the family well, and was shocked to hear that Divine had, just a few days earlier, taken in the vehicle for extensive repairs.

'Boy! Your son sure did mess up his new wagon,' the manager innocently remarked. Divine had burned up the transmission, and ordered a new one to be put in, telling the manager to charge the bill to his parents. Once again, his mother seemed more upset about the fact that he had not called to see them, than the liberties he continued to take with their money. 'Harris and I decided that the more we did for him, the less he appreciated it, that he was taking advantage of us,' Frances concluded.

She had the manager bring the wagon to their home, paid the bill, and told her son, when he phoned asking for the car, that they were selling it and he could get back to Cape Cod the best way he could. He came home, collected his dog, Bo Bey, and left with his friends. 'When he left, I cried and felt guilty as hell,' Frances admitted. 'I prayed that he would straighten himself out and forgive us. I prayed that we would see him again.' They never dreamed at the time that it would be about ten years before they were all to be together again.

By now, Divine had made five films and had had an enticing taste of fame, however slight. But what to do with it? John Waters never had specific plans for his next production, and having managed to break away from his parents' claustrophobic grip and made new, if strange, friends, Divine yearned for more.

In an interview with England's *Ritz*, Divine retold the story – and his immediate solution to his problem.

D: So anyway, I decided to quit my store in Provincetown – money was tight at the time – and apparently the Cockettes had seen my movies and were screaming for me.
Ritz: Yes, they used to scream so well.
D: So I flew out to San Francisco wearing a dress – and Van Smith said, 'trust me – we've got to shave your head and eyebrows otherwise they're going to think you're just another drag queen.'
Ritz: Who's they?
D: Oh, yes. I forgot to mention – a press reception had been arranged for me at the airport, so there I was on the plane with my bra full of lentils.
Ritz: What are lentils?

D: The stuff you put in your soup.
Ritz: Why did you have stuff to put in your soup in your bra?
D: Well, it made the bra swirl round like a woman's . . .
Ritz: Oh, I see –
D: So there I was on the plane, full of lentils – and the stewardess couldn't get me off that plane fast enough.
Ritz: I bet –
D: So I got off the plane – and I couldn't believe it. People were screaming out for me. The newsreels were out. The bulbs were flashing. It was just as if all my dreams were coming true. . . . So, anyway, the airport area had to be cleared just for me to get through. It was the most wonderful experience of my life.

Along with John Waters and Van Smith, Divine travelled to San Francisco, to make what was probably his first *official* personal appearance, at a special screening at the Palace Theatre of *Multiple Maniacs*. Divine soon proved he was prepared to do anything to gain self-promotion. Most of the other Dreamlanders were content to wait in Baltimore for John to beckon once again, but Divine was impatient. After all, how many opportunities would he have in the future to achieve stardom? He was determined not to miss any possibilities. When John Waters returned to San Francisco to screen *Mondo Trasho*, Divine ran on stage in skintight Capri pants and seven-inch heels, threw dead fish at the audience and struck a series of 'exhibitionist poses'. 'It *was* glamour, but glamour gone berserk,' Divine decided.

He took part in the Miss Demeanour Pagent – a drag beauty contest held in a church – for which the ever-present ugly-expert, his friend Van Smith, designed latex burns and scars for his make-up and John Waters wrote a speech with which Divine could shock the audience: 'I smuggle rotten fruits into California and I eat pounds and pounds of white sugar! I had to come to California because I killed a couple of cops back East! Don't you realise? I killed Sharon Tate, and they've arrested the wrong people!'

'Divine and I did lots of interviews with the underground press,' John Waters remembered, 'and always got a confused reaction when he would grandly announce, "In my next film I plan to eat dogshit."'

Divine spent a crazy, wild, uninhibited time in The City By The Bay. The sexual revolution was in full swing – gays were flocking to their new-found homeland. Divine felt welcome; experimenting, seeking other pleasures than just waiting to become a film star. He visited the burgeoning gay pleasure palaces which offered all sorts of hitherto unfound possibilities; and quick and uncomplicated access to sexual encounters. He had neither the conventional face nor figure for young hunks to want to approach, however. While he fantasised about touching, undressing, making love to those extrovert, cute young guys so openly parading themselves each day in front of the kerbside cafés and bars, he had to satisfy his lust with visits to the infamous back rooms; dark, mysterious, instant contact – where his stretching, sagging flesh could press anonymously against a tight, smooth, firm body.

At these times, he was certainly no longer Glenn – as far as he was concerned, Glenn had been left, for ever, in Baltimore – but he wasn't Divine, the actor in women's clothes, the cult star, the public freak. What was his identity at these moments? Who was Divine the Man, with everyday, ordinary longings of his own?

It was a time to evolve. To 'come out' even further. It was 'all terribly exciting,' he told me. 'I remember when a policeman shot a faggot in the leg in The Stud Bar!'

He would have gladly stayed in San Francisco, savouring his local fame, growing adulation and freedom to discover who he was. But the pied piper called: time to make another film. 'All right,' John Waters told him. 'Now we're going to do the big one.' Without hesitation, Divine packed his bags and headed back to Baltimore.

'The Cult Film To End All Cult Films'. 'The Most Disgusting Movie Ever Made'. 'A Trip Through Decadence'. *Pink Flamingos* (1972, 16mm, Colour, 93 minutes) has probably received as many labels as it has screenings around the world. The producers' own choice of subtitle, *An Exercise In Poor Taste*, seems somewhat mild and unworthy of the debate and furore the film has created.

'John put up $12,000 for it,' Divine said, 'set up location at a trailer park near Baltimore, and suddenly all the old friends were back together once again.' Divine's co-stars were David Lochary, Mary Vivian Pearce, Mink Stole, Danny Mills and Edith Massey.

Divine starred as Babs Johnson, 'the filthiest person alive'. Babs resides in a neo-classic, silver-lined trailer with some loosely related characters: Crackers, a chicken-loving nymphomaniac; Cotton, an emotionally barren voyeur; and Edie, Bab's crabbed, egg-eating mother. Babs Johnson, while riding in her early-sixties white Cadillac 'Coupé-de-Vile' and defecating on manicured lawns, sets out to wage war against her pretenders, Raymond and Connie Marble. Fun-loving citizens, opting for the coveted title of the filthiest people alive,

Raymond and Connie run a baby-ring. The money from the ring, which supplies bastard children for lesbian couples, provides front money for elementary-school heroin pushers and porno shops. The contest reaches a climax when the Marbles are brought before a kangaroo-court presided over by Babs, Crackers and Cotton. Reporters from major tabloids are in attendance as Babs Johnson convicts Connie Marble of 'asshole-ism'. Raising her pistol to carry out the sentence she declares, 'Filth is my politics, filth is my life.'

Then comes the final scene. Divine scoops up a plopping poodle turd, puts it in his mouth and turns to the camera with – to coin a phrase – a great big, shit-eating grin.

John Waters is on record as saying about this legendary moment: 'We talked about that scene for a year before we shot it. I knew we were making a movie with no budget, so we had to do something that was so far out on a limb that people would never forget it. It wasn't easy for Divine to eat dog shit. I figured it probably would taste better than health food. It's a first, and probably a last, in film history. It's one scene that will always be remembered. Divine went through ten seconds of hell, but it was worth it.'

Divine comments: 'It was all a publicity stunt, a publicity stunt of the seventies. John Waters said, "Are you willing to take a chance? You won't have to swallow it, just put it in your mouth and spit it out. Let me get one take. If it works, you'll be a new star; if it doesn't, you'll be back doing hair or working in another junk store and never heard of again." In fact, the poodle belonged to a girlfriend of mine. She fed it steak for three days beforehand. I felt sorry for the dog having to put up with the cameras following him around all the time. God, I wanted to be famous so bad, I'd wanted to be a movie star since childhood. I wanted it so bad I used to say I could taste it. Yes, I tasted it, it was hideous, and I spat it out immediately. Then I rushed back to my best friend's house in Baltimore and used her toothbrush to get rid of the stain!'

And – for now – the last word on the subject: '*Pink Flamingos* certainly does not present any alternative to our society. The movie ends with Divine eating poodle shit on her way to Boise, Idaho, and eating poodle shit is not much of an alternative.' (The *Pennsylvania Voice*, 13 February 1974.)

One thing was for certain: if this movie ever got a public screening, if the critics ever got to review it, there could be no turning back for John Waters and his star. Whoever Divine the Man might be, John Waters had now immortalised the 'actress'; to many of their future supporters and followers, the director would never be able to live up to, and the star never live down, the infamy created by – and the extraordinary list of admirable atrocities contained in – *Pink Flamingos*.

'*Pink Flamingos* was one filthy word after the other because it was a $12,000 movie playing up against *Superman*, which cost $40 million, and something had to be done to get us noticed,' Divine explained. 'It was a gimmick. And whether people liked it or hated it, they talked about it and they wrote about it. It was designed to shock and make everyone aware of who we were. Except, talk about having a hard act to follow!'

In 1973, Divine and Mink Stole moved back to San Francisco, impatient for something to happen with the film they had just completed. While John Waters did the rounds trying to persuade people to sit through an entire screening of his *Poor Taste*, the two decided to cash in on the notoriety they had gained from the earlier movies and became involved in the stage productions at San Francisco's Palace Theatre.

The Cockettes, a ragtag, stoned-out, bearded band of gender-benders, quickly saw the potential in persuading the two cult stars to join them. They treated Divine like royalty and he returned the compliment with his enthusiasm and joy. He was soon starring in such productions as *Divine and Her Stimulating Studs*, *Divine Saves the World* and *Vice Palace*.

'I was starring in one with him,' Mink Stole recalled. 'Divine played a countess, entertaining while the bubonic plague was raging outside. It was an occasion for many dance numbers. I did another play with him around that same time in San Francisco that we renamed *Ladies in Retirement*. In that, we both played older women. Divine played an old frump with a grey wig. It was absolutely, totally unglamorous. And he was breathtakingly good. It really impressed me because there was no glamour to fall back on. It was a situation where he had to play a character. He couldn't be a larger-than-life, brassy, big woman. And he was absolutely convincing.'

Other titles of theatrical endeavours in which Divine participated – and remembered, not always fondly, by his San Francisco aficionados – include *Journey to the Center of Uranus* and a flop of gigantic proportions, *The Heartbreak of Psoriasis*.

'Divine bought lots of flashy new outfits and made personal appearances at the drop of a hat,' said Waters of this period. 'I loved it when he told the press, "I always wanted to be a movie star, and now I *am* and I'm quite happy about it." '

Pink Flamingos had virtually sat on the shelf for a year and its cast was becoming despondent. But not so its director. A small distribution company based in New York, New Line Cinema, told John Waters that, if he could get fifty people into Greenwich Village's Elgin Theatre (which seated 1200), he could show the movie for one night.

'So, John and five friends did a lot of phone work for a week and when the night came, the show was sold out, lines of people had to be turned away – and it was snowing,' Divine recalled. 'Then the theatre said we could do the show two nights a week – oh, I forgot to mention, these shows were on at midnight, something unheard of in those times – and finally the movie was showing seven nights a week. And this continued for three years. In fact, it's even been shown at the Museum of Modern Art as a Comedy Classic.'

Pink Flamingo's fast-growing success – albeit as a cult movie– spurred John Waters into preparing his next Dreamland Production. The idea behind *Female Trouble* 'began to spread like cancer' in his mind. In 1974, with a scraped-together budget of $25,000, a rented apartment for location and the inquisitive interest of New Line Cinema in the background, Divine and all the other Dreamland stars returned to Baltimore to start work again.

This is how the writer/director himself summarises *Female Trouble*'s plot:

The story of a headline-seeking criminal named Dawn Davenport (Divine). The film traces her life from teenage years as a suburban brat to her untimely death in the electric chair. After quitting school and running away from home, Dawn heads to the big city in search of 'the fast life', something not always easy to find in downtown Baltimore. She soon becomes involved with a fat lout named Earl (Divine also, playing a man's role) and has his illegitimate child, Taffy (Mink Stole). As the years pass, Dawn marries Gator (Michael Potter), a macho hairdresser, but soon divorces him because of problems with his fag-hag aunt, Ida (Edith Massey). Taffy grows into a severely maladjusted young lady, tracks down her father, and kills him, and in one final act of rebellion, turns Hare Krishna to get on her mother's nerves.

Sick of motherhood, bored with life in general, Dawn meets Donald and Donna Dasher (David Lochary, Mary Vivian Pearce), two fascist beauticians who run the Lipstick Beauty Salon. Flattered by their elitist attention, Dawn soon falls for the Dashers' brainwashing and mind-control technique. Egged on by bizarre beauty treatment and promises of stardom, Dawn becomes the Dashers' guinea pig and plunges headlong into their 'crime is beauty' program. Dawn's peak of criminal success occurs when she goes beserk during her trampoline act in a local nightclub and begins shooting members of the audience for 'art'. Finally apprehended by the authorities, she is sentenced to die in the electric chair, a death she welcomes because of her neurotic belief that the death penalty is the equivalent to the Academy Award in her chosen profession of crime.

This remained Divine's personal favourite of his films. To many, including myself, his final scene in the electric chair was proof beyond doubt that he possessed a natural acting talent that deserved to be channelled into a career. He was aware of this too and was, by now, thoroughly determined to make acting his full-time occupation and his road to fulfilling his ultimate ambition: to be a film star.

Divine was also thrilled that he was playing a male role in addition to the starring female. The scene in which Dawn (Divine) is raped by Earl (Divine) gave the star one of his most popular retorts to those heckling him at disco appearances in later years. 'Go fuck yourself!' some jealous, loud-mouthed lout would frequently scream at him in mid-song. 'I've done that already,' he would respond, quick as a flash over the continuing music. 'Now you go and try it.' Those in the audience who knew his film roles would roar in appreciation.

It's interesting to note that Divine was not only taking his own potential career seriously at this time, but also giving some considered thought to his screen image. In 1976, he told journalist Jacques le Sourd, 'The characters I play in the movies are very sad in a way. They do have lots of problems. The movies are billed as comedy, but *Female Trouble*, for instance, I found very sad. This character I played was just really bananas and easily influenced and convinced of things at the drop of a hat.'

Dreamland's own nine première screenings of *Female Trouble* in Baltimore were a sell-out, almost creating a riot for tickets. New Line Cinema quickly launched the film nationally – blowing it up to 35mm – and Divine was over the moon when he discovered that John Springer Associates had been hired as press agents to handle the movie. Springer represented Divine's all-time idol, Elizabeth Taylor.

'Of all the entertainers I haven't performed with, the one I hold in highest esteem is Elizabeth Taylor,' Divine said. 'To this day she's still the reigning queen of Hollywood. She has a little waist problem now and then, but I have that problem too. The fact that she's gotten her act together is unbelievable, and she's never looked more beautiful.'

Divine instantly reassured his new press agent that he would agree to share interviews with any other of his major clients whenever required.

Female Trouble was receiving a professional media launch. *Pink Flamingos* was being screened at midnight all over the United States. New Line Cinema had also picked up *Mondo Trasho* and *Multiple Maniacs* for distribution. Posters appeared all over New York promoting the new movie, carrying Divine's name and face in star billing – together with the warning 'While designated X, preview audiences have also indicated that *Female Trouble* includes scenes of extraordinary perversity and may be seen as morally and sexually offensive.'

Judith Christ, in *New York*, wrote, 'It can't be dismissed. As vulgar and gross as the porn genre can get . . . talent working its way up from the muck. Divine is marvelously funny!' Then Rex Reed's legendary comment appeared: 'Where do these people come from? Where do they go when the sun goes down? Isn't there a law or something?'

'No doubt about it,' Divine giggled to himself on reading the papers, 'I'm a film star.'

'I love action movies – Sylvester Stallone, Chuck Norris, Arnold Schwarzenegger. Gets me in the mood for my shows. I watch them while I'm doing my make-up. And Nazi movies. In the movies they always kill Hitler, so the bad guys always die.' (Divine, *New Musical Express*, 28 February 1987)

4 Comic Timing

'I've been chased down streets by people yelling "Why do you look
like that, you're so hideous, look at yourself, you're a freak". Never-
theless . . . I don't want to look like anyone else, I want to look like
an individual – I don't bother anybody and don't want to be
bothered.'

Divine, the *New York Post*, May 1975

T WAS 8 AUGUST 1976. I was 30 years old and living a good life,
working as a producer with a London-based theatre company. We
presented stage shows around the world and I regularly commuted
between my bachelor penthouse in London's Chelsea district and
the elegant sophistication of the Algonquin Hotel in New York. I
travelled first class, used limousines from airports and gave glamorous dinner parties for our stars, which at the time included Sir
Michael Redgrave and Douglas Fairbanks Jr. I had also discovered
the hedonistic joys of New York in the seventies, where every type of
instant gratification was available for the price of a subway ride to
Greenwich Village.

This particular Sunday afternoon in New York, I had bought a ticket
– I almost always went to the theatre on my own so that I could choose
to leave in the interval if I wished – to a new production of *Guys and
Dolls* on Broadway.

The theatre was full of blue-rinse ladies. I was bored and irritated. I
disagreed with the gimmick casting of an all-black company. I stood in
the sun on the pavement outside the Broadway theatre during the intermission, a glass of wine in my hand and with a sure feeling that I
wouldn't return for the second act.

'Are you enjoying the show, ladies?' I heard a voice enquire. I looked
round and there was a colourful young man asking the two matrons
beside me what they thought of their matinee outing.

'Why, yes, it's wonderful isn't it?' one gladly replied. 'All those gorgeous songs and such lovely voices.' Then he followed with the
strangest nonsequitur. 'You know, you should go to see another great
show down in the Village. It's called *Women Behind Bars*. Have you
heard of it? It's terribly funny.'

I had been reading about this off-Broadway show called *Women Behind Bars*. All I knew so far was that it appeared to attract a gay audience and starred *something* called Divine. It certainly didn't seem to be the kind of attraction one recommended to little old ladies. How strange that this man would have chosen to deliver his speech to the two by my side. But that's what I loved about New York: full of surprises and odd-ball conversations.

My curiosity got the better of me. I returned to the Algonquin without bothering to find out if this particular street-wise, jive-talking Sky Masterson got his girl, changed from my suit into regulation denim and headed for the East Village to find the Truck and Warehouse Theatre; off-Broadway at its most adventurous, hidden in a menacing street on the East Side and surrounded by its namesakes, deathly still on a Sunday evening. On the street outside the theatre was an assortment of beautiful, crazy, happy gay guys. Gay liberation was at its peak and these boys were out for a good time: publicly, proudly. London's gay life was still contained up narrow stairs, behind dark windows. I enjoyed this new sense of freedom; the flaunting of outrageousness.

The theatre foyer was covered in sawdust; popcorn and peanuts were served in one corner, and it seemed from the conversation before the show that everyone except myself had been there – seen it, done it – at least three times before.

Women Behind Bars was a spoof of old 'B' movies of women's prisons. Written by a Village resident, Tom Eyen, who had by this time achieved a cult following (and later was to find fame with the TV series *Mary Hartman, Mary Hartman* and the Broadway hit musical *Dreamgirls*), it was a two-hour comedy of one-liners and camp innuendoes, principally at the expense of the female sex. It frequently had its devoted audience rolling in the aisles, almost literally and sometimes very closely attached to each other.

Divine played Pauline, the unrelenting Matron of the Women's House of Detention, arriving on stage in mid-flight with her assault on the incarcerated – and, it seemed, the audience – 'The fuckin' party's over!' From then on, we were both offended and delighted by every stereotypic female wrong-doer imaginable: Cheri, a full-bosomed girl of questionable lineage and mores; Jo-Jo, a no-nonsense black dyke; Guadalupe, a cha-cha Puerto-Rican; and Mary-Eleanor, 'the innocent raped by the system'.

I was almost choking with laughter. Although the overall staging concept was fun, I was aware the play was unstructured and loosely directed. It had the appearance of being improvised, although my knowledge of theatre comedy told me it wasn't. In the centre of it all, taking charge as if his/her life depended upon it, was this oversized whale, this blown-up doll of Elizabeth Taylor at her worst, this caricature of Jayne Mansfield at her best. A person – was it a fat, extraordinary woman or a wild, freakish drag queen? – called Divine. As the show continued it became very clear to me why it worked so well. Divine held it together brilliantly, feeding lines to the others on stage in quick-fire succession and then stealing all the laughs by over-reacting to their scripted gags. *After Dark* best summed it up: 'At the bulldozing head of this oddly assorted troupe of actors is the "legendary" Divine. Magnetic, inventive, with a splendid sense of timing, Divine plays her unsympathetic role like Hitler, without the charm.'

I was having a ball. So was the rest of the audience. We all adored this elephantine presence on the stage and applauded loudly at its every entrance and exit. However, nothing in the flimsy theatre programme gave away the true identity of the star. The short bio was genderless. It seemed Divine had appeared in some cult movies, of which I knew nothing at the time, and was a popular celebrity in New York. I knew instinctively that he was a natural comedic actor, deserving success beyond trucks and warehouses. Perhaps I could bring this show to London? On the condition, of course, that Divine came with it.

After the final curtain, I waited in the foyer and asked an usher if I could speak with someone who represented this show. I took the time to explain to him that I was a London producer interested in doing it there. This news elicited great excitement.

'Please just wait a minute here, sir,' he asked. 'I'll go fetch the producer. He'd love to meet you.' I waited and waited. I was about to leave, impatient and embarrassed, when the producer of *Women Behind Bars* came bounding into the foyer, gushing with apologies and concern over my being kept waiting.

I felt an immediate respect for Otto Grun Jr; after all, any producer who walks around Broadway during intermission times, approaching the most unlikely of candidates in order to recommend his own East Village production, has guts. He was delighted to hear that his efforts outside the Broadway theatre that same afternoon had at least attracted me to the show, although, so far, not the two matrons.

'Oh yes, we'd love to come to London. How thrilling,' he shrieked, to my considerable embarrassment. 'Oh *my*, who can I tell first? This lovely young man is taking us all to London!' Then, 'Oh yes. You just *must* come right now and meet Divine. Divine will be out of her mind to have the chance to visit the Queen for tea!'

I was not ready for this. I was making no commitment. He was far too pushy for me. Perhaps I could just deal with his lawyers, or the playwright's agent, tomorrow? And I was certainly not ready to meet this gross, loud-mouthed woman (he had referred to Divine as 'her'). What would I say to her? Before I could think further, I was being dragged backstage.

'Come in,' a rather gentle, husky voice announced. Otto Grun Jr and I entered Divine's tiny, damp dressing room. Squatting in one corner on some huge old cushions was an almost bald, ageless, sweet-looking fat man. It was obviously too uncomfortable for him to get up from the floor to shake my hand as I offered it. I withdrew with some amount of shock. Here was Divine, so quiet, so gentle-mannered – and it appeared, from every point of view, unsuited to the pronoun 'she'.

'Thank you so much for waiting to see me until I changed,' he whispered. He was now dressed in a very baggy pair of dirty cotton trousers and an oversized T-shirt covered in make-up and displaying the legend 'Female Trouble' 'Is it true you want to take me to London? I'm a great fan of the Royal Family, you know.'

I was sold. But could he really be as naive and vulnerable as he now appeared?

'I have to get ready for our second show tonight. You must do this show Mr Producer. I'd love to work for you. I'll call you. My name's Divine.' He spelled it out, 'D-I-V-I-N-E'.

His bright blue eyes stared at me as I wrote my London office telephone number on a piece of paper. Not the usual thing to give a show's star before negotiations start, but this was no regular star. And certainly no regular meeting. He sat almost motionless, save for the folds of stomach moving up and down under the T-shirt with his every breath. I made my exit, while he gave me his 'until next time' speech: 'Goodbye, Mr Producer. Please promise me I'll have tea with the Queen.'

Circumstances didn't allow me to produce *Women Behind Bars* but about six months after my meeting Divine in the East Village, I received a call from him. 'Hi, it's Divine. D-I-V-I-N-E.' As if there was another.

He was in London rehearsing the play for producer Paul Raymond. And very unhappy. On arriving in the country, he had discovered that he was taking second billing in this production to Fiona Richmond, a protégée of Mr Raymond's and now his regular leading lady in British soft-core sex farces. The play was no longer Divine's 'vehicle'; but it was most certainly being promoted as hers. In London he feared he would not even become a cult star; he had been here three weeks and still not had tea with the Queen.

I took him to dinner and attempted to flatter his ego by making idle conversation about producing a play for him one day in the future. We talked of our mutual love for the city of San Francisco. Perhaps we would work together there one day? Pipe dreams. It was a polite meeting on my part with no expected outcome.

Women Behind Bars opened in London to critical pans and its run was brief. The *Evening Standard* did, however, note, 'But it is a bravura drag (I presume) performance from the massive Divine that gives the show its relentless fascination. As Matron, this mountainous parody of outsize womanhood strides the stage like some great white winsome blancmange, with a coy outrageous eye on the audience.' At least he didn't leave London completely unnoticed.

A year or so later, my life had changed considerably. Our producing company was suddenly forced into liquidation because it had overextended its activities. I packed my bags: off to Los Angeles, determined to grab this opportunity to break into TV production. I arrived on the West Coast almost penniless, with no work permit and indefinite permission to stay at a friend's home in Hollywood. After three days I was going crazy with the lack of anything to do. It appeared that my long list of credits in the theatre was virtually worthless in this land of television, film and recording companies. My confidence was at a very low ebb.

The phone rang. 'Hi, it's Divine. D-I-V-I-N-E.'

He informed me that he had just finished starring off-Broadway in *The Neon Woman*, a sequel to *Women Behind Bars*, written specially for him by Tom Eyen.

On leaving London, I had mailed out change-of-address cards to my business contacts, one of whom was Bridget Aschenberg, an agent with International Creative Management in New York. Bridget's clients included Tom Eyen. Divine was now pushing anyone and everyone for a continued run – anywhere – of *The Neon Woman*. I think Bridget had chanced upon my change-of-address card lying on her desk and given the number to Divine to get him off her phone.

'Isn't it wonderful that you're now living in California and I just *happen* to be available,' he exclaimed over the phone from New York. 'Now you can produce *The Neon Woman* in San Francisco, just like you promised me in London!' Promised? What promise?

'OK, Divine,' I said, to get rid of him. 'I'm not really thinking about doing more theatre work at the moment, but tell Bridget to put a copy of the play in the mail to me. She has my address in Los Angeles. Once I've read it, I'll think about the possibilities and get back to you. Give me your number in New York.'

Divine mumbled something about staying at a friend's apartment and not actually having a number where I could reach him. He assured me he would stay in touch with me. Somehow, I didn't doubt it.

The following morning Divine was on my doorstep in Los Angeles. Perhaps he just didn't trust the US mail system, but this was certainly an expensive way of delivering a script. I was having my first experience of this actor's sheer determination to get what he wanted. I was to have many more.

I had hardly been living in the United States for one week. With my last $1,000 I optioned the Californian stage rights to produce the play, *The Neon Woman*. In my beat-up, convertible white Buick and with a seriously overweight, kaftan-clad actor by my side, I started visiting Divine's 'friends' who he assured me would invest in the $85,000 capitalisation I estimated I would need to open the play in California.

Divine was extraordinary; I had never experienced anyone quite like him, although I admit I was enjoying his company and loved his over-the-top enthusiasm. But his ability to beg, borrow and steal (often, it seemed, all at the same time) was certainly new to me. My gentlemanly, business-like instincts were quickly thrown over the side of the convertible; I was getting a speedy lesson in street-wise, Hollywood deal-making from one of the best. Divine was funny, devious, determined and in a hurry. He made many appointments for me to discuss finance. At most, he would insist on being by my side as if he were my co-producer. Through Divine's personal contacts, I was offered cocaine, heroin, luxury trips to Las Vegas and the services of both male and female prostitutes in return for shares in the production. I often had to dissuade Divine from accepting these offers on my behalf.

He was used to living with no cash. He had no problem with staying at friends' homes and using them – and their facilities – in every way possible until they persuaded him to go. Suddenly he was camped-out on the living-room floor of my friend's home, eating his way through the refrigerator and running up huge telephone bills. He had no shame. His excuse was simply that a show needed to be produced so that he could live like a star again.

A few months later, we had raised the $85,000 and I had found a perfect theatre, the Alcazar, in the heart of San Francisco. Truthfully, my conversation with Divine all those months ago in London about our working together one day in this magical city had had no firm intention behind it. I certainly hadn't thought we would be on this side of the world doing exactly that only one year later.

Although I was determined not to let Divine believe he was a co-producer of this venture, he allowed me no choice but to hire several personnel from the New York production of The Neon Woman, including Ron Link, the director, and Divine's 'personal assistant', Jay Bennett (masquerading as the show's spotlight operator, a position which Divine considered to be absolutely essential and an operator he considered irreplaceable).

The Neon Woman was a combination burlesque-murder mystery. Divine played Flash Storm, the owner of Baltimore's Club Neon Woman, a strip joint threatened with closing by various forces, including the vice squad and a family relation. It was set in the early sixties and, just as the Women Behind Bars cast was made up of a retinue of inmates, this comedy's supporting players were the other strippers, including a totally deaf-and-dumb ecdysiast. Not to mention Divine's virginal daughter, who suffers 'a swift moral decline at the hands of her own mother'. Sound familiar?

Divine rented a spacious apartment in downtown San Francisco and immediately commenced decorating it in his inimitable style: huge cushions, giant plants and an assortment of esoteric teapots.

The show opened to great reviews and a healthy advance box office. Divine was a pleasure to work with, highly professional in his attitude and wonderfully co-operative in promoting the show and, of course, himself. I was, however, having many problems coping with Ron Link and some members of the cast as there seemed to be serious differences of opinion between my and their behaviour patterns when it came to basic work disciplines. I also worried a lot about Divine's constant voice problems. We were forever visiting local throat specialists in an effort to discover why he would suddenly lose his voice, unconnected with any other apparent ill-health symptom. Ron Link assured me that this was part of Divine's history as a stage actor and nothing could be done about it. My own training in the theatre found this explanation difficult to accept.

The play continued to do well until the sudden crisis of a severe petrol shortage hit us – and every other theatre in town – in 1979. We closed, and in an effort to keep the entire company together, I arranged a one-week visit of the show to Toronto, Canada, where Divine received one of his favourite press reviews, from the *Globe and Mail:* 'Divine is the decaying backbone of the venture. With the body of a restless dirigible, variously stuffed into taffeta, chiffon, or gold lamé, a sweep of hair like a bleached tumbleweed, she flicks her tongue like a cobra, clenches her false eyelashes, flexes her stomach rolls and, with flawless timing, growls thoughts and desires that would make a stevedore blush.'

After Toronto, we moved on to Provincetown, Massachusetts, a tiny seaside resort at the very tip of the Cape Cod Peninsula.

Betty and Phyllis owned the historic, but run-down Pilgrim House Hotel. 'P-Town' had become a popular holiday location for East Coast gays. Judy Garland-like cabaret divas were all the rage, competing with each other—and the transplanted New York drag queens—in the many tiny cabaret rooms and piano bars. Phyllis and Betty can best be described as two women always on the lookout for the last available dollar. They had heard of our show, had the good sense to realise that Divine could be a huge draw—with the town's proximity to New York—and had already found out that he was not available simply as a cabaret drag act.

To add to our potential in attracting an audience and competing with the various other camp attractions in town, Divine and I agreed to invite Holly Woodlawn, Andy Warhol's superstar, to take over a supporting role. So now I was the employer of the two most famous transvestite screen stars in the world.

Divine invited Holly to share a cute little beach house for the season. I lived at the other end of the one street. Teatime was traditionally spent at Divine's and soon became one of the very few pleasures to look forward to throughout the summer. Tea from Fortnum and Masons in London, sent to Divine by friends, would be brewed and ever available, served alongside the lethal afternoon cocktails prepared by Divine's neighbours, two hilariously funny local lesbians who mended fuses, repaired toilet seats and generally looked after Divine whenever necessary.

It was a hot summer—the weather as well as the temperaments—and Divine soon became quite a tourist attraction, all 300 pounds of him clad in the tiniest of bikini briefs and floating on a huge black rubber tyre in the Atlantic Ocean, slowly sinking into it as he dozed under the effects of marijuana and the heat.

The play was a huge success, breaking all records for an attraction in this resort town and overshadowing all other attempts at competing entertainments. However, I was having the most miserable time of my life, not being used to every one of my movements and conversations being inaccurately reported all over town as daily gossip. The acting company had become complacent with the sun and all-night partying. No amount of lectures from me would improve either their backstage or onstage discipline.

Somewhat to my amazement, but also to my great relief, Divine would stay aloof from the rest of the actors' shenanigans and would often lose his temper with an actor for being late or behaving improperly. Divine and I were gradually becoming aware of our mutual respect for the business we were in and, consequently, less and less patient with those we were contractually 'married' to for the summer.

I was also beginning to find out how cunningly self-protective Divine could be. To enable us to work for the minimal fee offered by The Ladies Of The House, I had to turn the production into a non-union one, paying lower than American Actors' Equity minimum salaries. Being a registered producer with the union myself – and Divine being a paid-up member – Equity's offices in New York had been pointing guns at us both since the beginning of this summer season, threatening to withdraw Divine's membership and my future permission to employ their members unless we either withdrew the current production or turned it into one with fully approved contracts.

We had spent the best part of the summer avoiding phone calls, telegrams and personal visits from union officers. Finally, an officer had managed to obtain the phone number of the apartment where Divine was living in Provincetown. One sultry afternoon, Divine innocently picked up the phone to find he was unwillingly talking to the head of his union in New York. 'Divine, why are you continuing to work with non-union actors after we have sent you warning telegrams and letters?' the officer barked down the instrument.

'Non-union actors?' my star purred inquisitively. 'I don't know what you mean.'

'Divine, you know full well that there are actors on stage with you each night that are not members of our union and have not signed *our* contracts with your producer. On joining our membership, you agreed not to work under such conditions. We must now insist that you cease performing with these actors as of today.'

'Oh!' Divine exclaimed as if he had suddenly discovered the meaning behind the existence of mankind. 'You must mean the *extras*. I don't talk to *extras*. I'm the star. I have nothing to do with *extras*. I know nothing about them!' On which he slammed down the phone and self-righteously announced to whoever was in his apartment that afternoon – playing his role to the hilt – that he could not understand why some-one in New York would have the audacity to believe that such a *star* as he would even care to know any meagre facts about supporting actors.

The ten-week run dragged to its eventual close. Phyllis and Betty made their money out of Divine, and my production. Neither of us, however, had managed to save a cent and the future, again, was bleak.

Determined to squeeze a little more from this venture, I made a few phone calls, resulting in a ten-day run of *The Neon Woman* in Chicago; a triumphant one, selling every ticket and allowing Divine to snatch another, albeit brief, moment of fame and adoration. Although the chosen venue was a rock club (and, by virtue of its tables-and-chairs layout and licence to serve drinks during the performances, ideal for the play), the promoters, Jam Productions, had invited the major Chicago theatre critics – second only in national importance to those in New York – to cover the opening. Divine and I waited up through the night for the *Tribune*'s first edition. He was excited; he knew the opening night had gone well. I have rarely seen him so devastated as when we read our notice: 'Divine is awful. Not awful for what he presents or represents, but awful because he pretty much fails to do *anything*. His voice is hollow, his movements are awkward, and most of the time he merely stands there like a huge, plastic statue, seemingly unembarrassed by his ineptitude.'

We called an emergency meeting with Jam Productions, who were not put off by this outright pan. 'Wait for the *Sun-Times* tomorrow,' they implored. 'Don't be downhearted. Advance bookings are good. We'll get through.'

We waited for the *Sun-Times*. Amazingly, it was one of those only too frequent times when one wonders if two critics reviewing a show on the same night actually saw the same production. The paper noted: '. . . more than anything else it is a vehicle for the talents of Divine, a 300-pound male actress (we are still talking about real life, now) who is surely the most unique character to ever grace America's stages.' Divine took that as a huge compliment. I was never certain the critic actually meant it as such.

On the closing night, the director Ron Link, who had never left our side during the entire run and continued to infuriate the cast by giving them notes after each and every performance, attempted to videotape the show without obtaining my permission. By this time, we had once again become a full union production and to do such taping was strictly against all the rules. It resulted in the fight between Link and myself that everyone else had been expecting, but I had avoided since the beginning of this entire episode. Ours was a totally intolerable and impossible working relationship from the start. We came from absolute opposite ends of work disciplines and we had a serious conflict of personalities. Much against my will, I was forced into a screaming match with Ron Link in front of Divine in his dressing room during the intermission of the last performance.

My final memory of our year with *The Neon Woman* is one of Ron Link and I fighting out our differences, while Divine tried in vain to repair his own make-up to commence Act Two. Ron Link's last words to me were '. . . and I'll make certain, you scum-bag, that you never work with a Tom Eyen play or Divine again.'

We went to New York. Divine chose, independently, never to work with Ron Link again. Coincidentally, he never again lost his voice during a stage run. I signed a personal management contract with Divine and spent the next ten years working by his side.

' "Would you like to be a serious actress like Meryl Streep?" I asked Divine. "I *am* a serious actor," he replied. "But I don't want to play the kind of roles she plays. They're for ugly people." ' (*Village Voice*, 29 April 1986)

5 But Who Will Provide the Pay Cheque?

'And then there's always the dream of an Oscar. I went to a person's house in Hollywood and he had a couple of them sitting on the shelf. So I stood there holding them – but they had the wrong name! And I thought, wouldn't it look good to see my name there? *Divine*.'

Heartbreak Hotel, February 1988

WHEN I STARTED TO WORK WITH DIVINE on *The Neon Woman*, he was represented by a talent agent in Los Angeles. In the time that Divine had been on his books, the agency had not managed to obtain any work for him, and my own dealings with the office on the contract for the play had been less than happy. I had to approach Divine directly to sign his contract before the opening as we were both frustrated by what we felt to be an unnecessary delay.

Following this action, I received a letter from his agent advising me that my direct dealings with Divine constituted 'no way to run a rail road'. Divine subsequently informed his agent that it might be a good idea if he realised his actor was now starring in a play in San Francisco and not working on a rail road.

The fact remained that, between the Dreamland films and the Eyen plays (for which the services of an agent or other representative had not been essential) he had no other offers of paid work. It was all very well being a celebrity, a cult star, recognised in the streets. But who was going to pay the bills?

Certainly, in the mid-seventies, Divine rarely seemed to be with nothing to do. He determinedly exploited his new fame and the access it brought to the media. He adored being in the gossip columns and, it would seem, the journalists welcomed this exotic diversion from the run-of-the-mill, out-of-work Hollywood stars eager to be written about just because they attended a cocktail party. With Divine, there was always an interesting – usually unique – angle.

The fame also brought him celebrity friends to mix with. Divine could hardly believe the succession of stars who would gladly visit him in his tiny, cramped dressing room after his plays in New York. They all seemed to be happy – and often keen – to be photographed with him – Jack Nicholson, Rudolph Nureyev, Lotte Lenya, David Hockney, Mick Jagger. . . . And Elton John became quite a fan. 'Elton came to see *The Neon Woman* and came backstage. He was wonderful to the cast and took about twenty of us to dinner,' Divine enthused. 'He came back to see the show about three times. I went to Chicago and Kentucky with them and attended the concerts. Then, I participated in the shows at Madison Square Garden at the end of the tour. I was brought up on to the stage on a lift and ran down steps throwing bananas. I sang backup with the backup people and did a "kick line" with Elton, the lead guitarist, and the bass player.'

It was clear that Divine was learning to maintain his unique celebrity status, without yet knowing how to sustain a career. He travelled, mainly at the expense of these newly acquired followers, and visited the West Coast frequently, cleverly developing this love affair with the media on both coasts.

'*After Dark* honored Mae West with their Ruby Award at the Beverly Wilshire Hotel, and all the party maniacs were on hand,' the Los Angeles press reported on the social activities of America's chic entertainment magazine.

As Mae was wheeled into a cheering audience the only guest with a long face was Divine. It seems that Divi had really been looking forward to meeting Mae, but the situation was slightly marred by the insistence of *After Dark* that Divine obey the dress code and come in black tie. Divine looked great in black cashmere, but what a rush it would have been if she had worn the emerald green taffeta fantasy dress they made her leave at home.

While achieving and promoting his new status in life, Divine kept in touch with his film producer. They were discovering their mutual usefulness and John Waters, understandably and to his star's delight, took full advantage of Divine's current popularity with a desperately trying-to-be-liberated public. 'He moved to Provincetown, San Francisco, Los Angeles and finally New York,' John reported. 'He'd do anything to be a star, walking the streets in full Divine regalia for promotion, and actually causing car accidents in the best Jayne Mansfield tradition. I remember dragging him in full costume with me to showings of the films at colleges. We'd have to eat at professors' homes beforehand and watch their children at the dinner table trying to be nonchalant but staring at Divine in disbelief and horror.'

'We travelled around like George and Gracie,' Divine would say of those days. Seemingly, he gave very little thought – if any – during this time of fun and frivolity to whether the constant media coverage might actually be extending further than New York and Los Angeles. Perhaps, even, to South Florida?

'We moved to Florida on July 1st 1972,' Frances Milstead told me, 'to make new friends and to have happiness. We didn't hear from Glenn and didn't know his whereabouts. My only concern was for my husband. In 1974 we did receive a card from Glenn asking us for money he needed for a new apartment, which we gave him, and then we didn't hear from him for another year. We continued to receive cards but no return address. He said he was doing a show, but we didn't know what he was talking about.

'Then one month,' she continued, 'I happened to pick up a *Time* magazine in a doctor's office. Would you believe me when I say I got the shock of my life? It was an article written by John Waters, saying "When Divine's mother found out that he was making underground movies they moved away and never told him." I never knew John, but remember Glenn saying his name. Then all of a sudden a thought came to me. While living up north, the maid asked me to help her turn the mattress over on Glenn's bed. There was a paper under the mattress and I began to read it. It was a script, with names like Divine and David Lochary and several of the girls that Glenn knew. I never asked him about it because I didn't want him to think I was snooping. I was hurt to think people would say did that to our son, when we didn't know where he was. We honestly did move to Florida due to his dad's health, nothing else.'

However, on being interviewed by *People* in 1984, Mrs Milstead then admitted: 'We always wanted Glenn to be perfect and were always afraid he would get involved with the wrong kids. The nursery schools were our bread and butter. We didn't want him to do anything that would disgrace our reputation.'

Studio 54, the most talked-about, written-about, beleaguered venue in the history of disco, was at the pinnacle of its fame in New York. It was impossible to gain instant entrance without being intimate friends of the owners or fucking one of the doormen. The alternative was to be willing to bear the indignity of standing in line – often for hours – waiting, hoping to be one of the chosen few. Or you had to be a celebrity. Celebrities – those who could truly attract media hype – were royalty in the VIP lounges of New York's fashionable dance clubs and all-night private bars.

Divine had never been so popular: friend after friend would call him constantly. His room-mate's phone became a hot line to 'invite Divi out'. It didn't take long for Divine to learn that, in exchange for a link with his arm in order to gain access to the latest place-to-be-seen in the early hours of the morning, he could obtain a first-class meal at Mr Chow's or L'Odéon earlier in the evening. And Divine was generous to his true friends, who, more often than not, were also wondering where the next meal would come from. He never had any hesitation in bringing along a friend or two, whether they were invited or not–probably as much as a safeguard against personal boredom as in generosity. Phillip Miller, his room-mate, was at least receiving something as 'payment in kind' for the huge phone bills.

In the disco Divine sat, gossiped and often danced (knowing that would attract the flashbulbs most of all) with Halston, Liza Minnelli, Andy Warhol, Bianca Jagger, Truman Capote, Grace Jones and all the other publicity-seeking demi-gods of the era. And these pre-dawn acquaintances were also more than happy to benefit from the additional publicity they could gain from knowing this bizarre, very-much-larger-than-life colleague.

People splashed the story:

'I thought it was disgusting and in very bad taste,' sniffed disco queen Grace Jones at her birthday party after Divine, a hefty transvestite, sat squarely in the 1,510-pound birthday cake and started lobbing gobs of it at fellow celebrants. Before Divine's arrival, the cake had been topped by 6,000 carnations and a Honda 400. 'Some people will do anything for a picture,' scolded Jones, who a few moments before had left $300 worth of heel marks on a rented Lincoln Continental she had been posing on for New York paparazzi. 'I wanted to get down on the dance floor,' she explained, 'but then I didn't want to step in all that cake and ruin my $90 shoes.'

But none of these occasions produced a pay cheque and Divine's daytime standard of living was not measuring up to the media image of his nocturnal outings.

He received an invitation from his friend Richard Bernstein–contemporary pop artist, celebrated for his front-cover illustrations of the famous in *Andy Warhol's Interview*–to attend a gala reception at the Lincoln Center. Divine was flattered; he had read that this was to be a particularly glamorous occasion. Richard was adamant that a uniquely extravagant gown should be created for Divine for this event. The following week, Arthur Bell, in his widely read and influential *Village Voice* gossip column wrote: 'When Divine arrived recently at a Lincoln Center benefit for young writers, wearing pink and blue finches on his head, many patrons turned around and looked at him in amusement.'

Divine told me it was this particular press item that made him finally take stock of his situation and look at the future. He did not want to become a joke, known only as a narcissist who would truly do *anything* to get publicity. He knew only too well that others of his male contemporaries who were earning limited fame by playing female roles — Candy Darling, Jackie Curtis and Holly Woodlawn among them — were not receiving this attention from the media. He wanted to believe — he *did* believe — that his fame and the public's interest in him were earned through his acting ability. He hated the labels 'drag queen' or 'transvestite' that seemed to accompany him everywhere.

In his own mind, Divine was never anything but a man. Contrary to press speculation and gossip, he never had the slightest reason to consider, for either psychological or career purposes, any changes to his natural looks, needs, feelings, behaviour. Male. Dressing as a woman was uncomfortable and time-consuming. 'But I *am* a man,' Divine would insist time and time again. 'It's a simple, inescapable fact. I mean, all the plumbing's intact. I think I can interpret male roles as well as I can female roles. You'd be surprised at how many people think I'm just as cute as a guy.'

He could identify with the need to put on a costume — female or otherwise — to play a role on the stage, or on screen. But it was making no sense to him to be joining the true transvestites and drag exhibitionists, on display each night for no other reason than the thrill they obtained from doing it. He got no thrill. And he got no money.

From now on, he decided, he would develop his public image as he would normally dress. As this, at the time, included flowing Zandra Rhodes designed kaftans and much adornment of the ears — he certainly was no longer Brooks Brothers — he didn't feel it would be too great a disappointment to the fans. He would only accept invitations from those who were happy — keen — to be seen with Divine the Man. But would he still receive invitations? Would the papers still want to write about him, the photographers notice him? He needed help, advice, guidance, he decided. What was it he had read recently? 'Professional Career Counselling', that's it.

**A glamour
shot from the
early seventies.**
(Roy Blakey)

Baby Glenn at
six months.

With proud mother,
Frances Milstead.

Glenn's first day at school.

A picture of innocence,
Glenn as a choirboy.

Growing up and gaining weight—Glenn at ten.

Glenn at fifteen years, and 220 pounds!

Glenn's graduation photograph.

Glenn with local prom date Diane Evans.

Divine in an early 1970s production of *The Heartbreak of Psoriasis*, San Francisco.

As Flash Storm in *The Neon Woman,* **San Francisco, 1979.**
(Daniel Nicoletta)

With the author
on the way to a
midnight personal
appearance,
Provincetown,
Massachusetts,
1979.

Taking a dip in Provincetown, Massachusetts, 1979.

As Pauline in *Women Behind Bars,* New York, 1976.

As Pauline in *Women Behind Bars,* London, 1977.

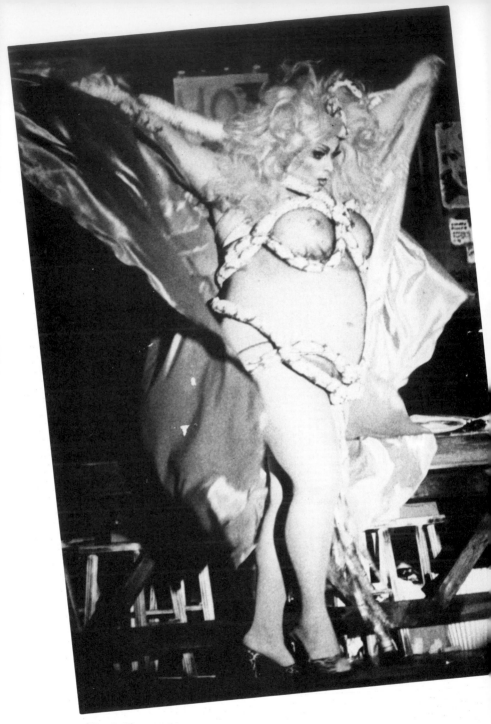

Flash Storm bares almost all in
The Neon Woman, San Francisco, 1979.

A 1978 portrait, taken
in New York by
Francesco Scavullo.

Divine sweats it out on stage at The Red Parrot, New York, 1983.
(Cathy Miller)

Divine on stage.

**A terrified Divine hides
from ravaging outlaws
in *Lust in the Dust*.**
(New World Pictures)

**Divine as Edna Turnblad
on location for *Hairspray*.**

A personal appearance
with John Waters.

Getting into character as Arvin Hodgepile, Divine's other
role in *Hairspray*.

A 1980s Baltimore group shot. Back row (*left to right*): Debbie
Harry, Pat Moran, Divine. Front row (*left to right*): Van Smith,
Zandra Rhodes, John Waters.

**With Jack Nicholson in
New York, mid-1970s.**
(Zarko Kalmic)

With Elton John in New York, mid-1970s.
(Zarko Kalmic)

With Rudolph Nureyev in New York, mid-1970s.
(Zarko Kalmic)

With Grace Jones in New York, mid-1970s.
(Zarko Kalmic)

With Lily Tomlin in the early 1970s.

The author at Divine's fortieth birthday party at the Hippodrome, London, in 1985.

With parents Harris and Frances Milstead in Margate, Florida, Christmas 1987,

Off duty and relaxing in 1986.

Simply Divine.

'I need a manager,' was his summary of his present predicament.

I don't recall an actual conversation ever taking place about my becoming his personal manager. It was just clear at the time that he badly needed representation and that I equally needed an income.

One morning in Provincetown he showed me a letter he had received, inviting him to lecture to students at Stoneybrook College in Long Island, New York. New Line Cinema, who held the distribution rights to the John Waters movies, had a division of their company that provided movie celebrities on a potentially lucrative lecture circuit. 'They've been after me for ages,' Divine told me, 'but there's never been anyone to negotiate with them on my behalf. Why don't you do it? Then I could go round the country talking about myself and earn lots of money.'

We packed our bags and returned to New York, he depositing himself on Phillip Miller's floor and I subletting an apartment on West 55th Street. All we possessed between us were prodigous amounts of optimism and determination.

'Hi. It's Divine. D-I-V-I-N-E,' the voice purred at 7.30 the morning after we had moved back to New York. 'Is the contract signed yet for the lecture?'

Full marks for pushiness, and I admit that was a quality which attracted me to him as I too liked to deal with matters quickly. But not quite that quickly. However, having little else to do, I called New Line Cinema, spoke with Kenny Rahtz of the New Line Presentations Division, introduced myself, somewhat hesitantly, as Divine's manager and negotiated the deal for Divine to be paid $1,500 to lecture to students the next month.

I suppose that was when I became Divine's personal manager. The contract arrived from New Line, made out to me to sign on his behalf. Divine came over to see me and, in my established method of doing business *correctly*, I told him I really couldn't sign it on his behalf without authorisation from him to do so. Without further thought, he asked me to type a letter of intent from him to me, pending a formal personal management contract. 'Put something on paper, man, and I'll sign it,' he said. As simple as that.

On 16 October 1979, after many meetings with my attorney, followed by a bill of over $3,000 for the attorney's services in drawing up a suitable document, Harris Glenn Milstead (professionally known as Divine) and Bernard Jay signed an eight-page contract binding themselves professionally for the next five years. I created

Bernard Jay Management and he wandered off in the direction of Rumplemeyer's Ice Cream Parlour on Central Park South to celebrate the fame and fortune he presumed I would instantly bring him by his adding his signature to this document.

On the very day that Divine was provided with a limo to go to Stoneybrook for the day I took advantage of some frequent-flyer airline mileage to go to Los Angeles and visit the film producer Allan Carr on the set of his current movie, *Can't Stop the Music*.

During the run of *The Neon Woman* in San Francisco, Carr had visited the production, invited himself backstage and enthused to Divine about his performance in the play. 'You *must* be in my next movie,' he insisted to the star. 'Tell your manager to get in touch with my office. We'll do lunch.' Divine was amused and excited. It was the first time he had been propositioned to 'do lunch' with a Hollywood producer! Unfortunately, neither he nor I realised that Allan Carr was known for this kind of magnanimous gesture everywhere he went.

Can't Stop the Music was a vehicle to introduce the phenomenally successful gay disco group the Village People to the movie-going public. They seemed to be the perfect stars to combine with the extrovert screen personality of Divine, without taking too many risks for anyone in doing so.

The week I went West to find fame and fortune for Divine, location for the film was in the car park of West Hollywood's Studio One, one of the most successful gay discos in the United States. I had visited it often when living in Los Angeles the previous year, and took this opportunity to renew my acquaintance with the owner, Scott Forbes. I recall Scott's surprise at hearing I had become Divine's personal manager and his telling me of the tremendous success his disco was now having by presenting late-night personal appearances, *live on stage*, of the current disco divas. 'What a shame Divine doesn't make disco records,' he remarked.

I spoke with Carr briefly. He agreed that Divine should play a cameo guest role in *Can't Stop the Music*. 'Call my office the day after tomorrow and we'll discuss everything,' he said. 'Would Divine be free to come out here immediately?'

It has always been my policy to advise my clients exactly what I am doing on their behalf. I try not to mislead, but also feel that I have no right to represent their lives without keeping them in touch. Divine was ecstatic with my news, heaping praise on me and grinning from ear to ear. He then told me of how successful he had been at Stoneybrook and how keen he was – now that he was secure he could be a lecturer – to follow up Kenny Rahtz's earlier suggestion of putting together a campus tour for Divine.

Things were looking good. A film role and a lecture tour would take care of the immediate future for both of us.

The next morning I called Allan Carr's office. I continued to call twice daily for seven days, each time being told that he had received my message and would get back to me. I wouldn't leave my apartment for fear of missing his call. It never came. I called Kenny Rahtz at New Line. The talked-of lecture tour never materialised. Our first lesson in West Coast bullshit and East Coast rhetoric: when possibly on to a good thing, never say no in case you may want to roll with the wagon at a later date . . . but not saying no doesn't mean yes.

I was also having my first experience of Divine's severe insecurity. Like most in his profession, he did not take rejection at all well. On our facing up to the fact that neither of these attractive projects was realistic – and that both of us were looking at instant 'poverty' – he became frighteningly moody. He turned on me. 'Why the fuck did you tell me I had the role?' he screamed. 'I've told everyone I'm going to LA to appear in *Can't Stop the Music*. What do I do now? It's all your fault. You've made a fool of me.' It was two days before he decided to speak with me again. Many months later, when the movie was crucified by the critics, he actually thanked me for getting him out of it. Divine liked to see things in his own way!

He had no idea at the time that I was as insecure as he, and his selfishness in presenting the entire problem as being my fault was an eyeopener as to how our relationship might well continue. Indeed, how it did.

Divine, I realised, had never had to compete for his work as an actor. John Waters had written the film roles specifically for him and he had been invited to join the cast of *Women Behind Bars*. *The Neon Woman* was also created for him and even my own production of the play was contingent on Divine being the star. This was the beginning of his having to control his own destiny and he had not given a thought to the possibility that something might go wrong. A pattern emerged that I was to live with for the next nine years: two days of sulking, blaming me for everything and not wishing to communicate at all, followed by the realisation that, as long as he refused to talk to me, he was not going to get news of any work, nor of any money he could spend.

Then the telephone would ring: 'Hi, it's Divine.' I think it was at about this time that he decided he no longer needed to spell his name to me. It was also time for me to get used to calling him Divi, as all his close friends did. The familiar follow-up to his phone introduction was now to become 'What's happening, man?'

As his mother had discovered earlier, Divine would show tremendous keenness for a new project, but quickly became bored, especially when things didn't develop his way instantly. It wasn't difficult to engage his total enthusiasm in a good idea at an early stage, but he soon lost interest if the dollars didn't roll into his pocket.

It was necessary for me to spend a good deal of spare time with him in order to give him confidence in my faith in his career. But this proved difficult as our personal lifestyles were so very different and we never, in all the time we spent together, successfully managed to socialise with each other. I would find excuses to visit him and Phillip over on East 58th Street. Although Divine spoke many times of the depth of this relationship, they appeared to be very good friends, but no more. Phillip slept on the banquette seating in the apartment's narrow hallway while Divine snored heavily on an old double mattress thrown onto the floor of the one bedroom. By day, this bedroom would become the communal living room. Phillip was hugely supportive and caring about Divine. He was also the one wage earner in the home through his freelance work as an interior designer.

Perhaps recalling some of the people who had, in the past, exploited Divine for their own ends, Phillip was at first overtly suspicious of my increasing closeness to his friend. There were other people too who felt they had some sort of proprietorial interest in the celebrity, fearing that I might change what they enjoyed taking credit for having helped him become. Divine appeared to be very fond of Pat Moran and her husband, Chuck. Indeed, Divine was proud of being godfather to their two children, Greer and Brook. Pat managed Baltimore's Charles Theatre, showing movies when not working full-time as John Waters's personal assistant. Divine often invited himself to stay with the family when he visited Baltimore. I was rarely included on these excursions and, if they coincided with his work and I had to be in Baltimore with him, I was given a polite but cold welcome by Pat. I knew that many of his friends were warning him that I would probably run off with his money some time in the future.

Divine would laugh at these lectures and freely turn them into comic anecdotes, entertaining other friends at dinner parties with stories of 'the evil Englishman in my life'. Of course, it all made my own personal dealings with his friends somewhat difficult, more than ever when they would unhesitatingly turn to me to ask my assistance in recovering from Divi the money he had recently borrowed from them.

'Laid back' was a popular phrase in the seventies and certainly one applicable to the atmosphere at East 58th Street. The aroma of marijuana was ever present and I soon realised quite how dependent Divi was on the drug. He would light a joint as soon as he woke, usually drifting through his morning thoroughly stoned. I've never smoked pot, so I found it difficult to understand the problems it caused, especially when I needed to talk business with Divine.

'Oh, come on, man,' he would say with a grin. 'Have a joint. Lighten up. Relax. You'll be more fun then.' When I would respond by reminding him that I was not there to be fun, but to try to make us both some money, he would seem quite offended. I would then relate whatever thoughts I had–and any suggestions for the future–to a stubborn silence, eventually taking my leave and continuing my day with no awareness whatsoever of any reactions my client may have had to my proposals. I suppose I felt I had done my duty, but, to say the least, it wasn't a very inspiring way of continuing what I looked upon as a partnership.

It didn't take me long to realise that Divi was beginning to use me in all the very same ways he had used his parents. An example of this concerned his relationship with his landlord, Sam, who would frequently demand cash for the monthly rent a few days before it was due, in order to meet his own gambling debts. Sam didn't hesitate to scream abuse and threaten eviction if the cash wasn't instantly handed over. In such circumstances, Divi would position himself in a corner of his apartment and not move out for fear of bumping into Sam in the hallway. One day Divine had the splendid idea that dealing with an enraged landlord should now be the responsibility of his personal manager and he proudly delivered a letter to Sam informing him that in future his "business manager' would settle the rent on his behalf.

Sam did not hesitate from this moment onwards to call me daily to request advances, turn up at my doorstep whenever he felt like it and harass the porters in my apartment building if they said I was not there. No amount of discussion with Divine could persuade him to take back this responsibility and it led to many heated arguments between us.

The jealousies our working relationship had created among some of his friends also led to gossip. The question of whether Divi was actually in love with me or not came up frequently in the first year or so of our working together. I knew he wasn't. True, Divi never liked to be rejected for a quick sexual liaison and this certainly did lead to a few embarrassing incidents. He was of course a big boy, weighing in at the time at almost 300 pounds. He was aware of how he could use his physical bulk to bully others.

It was not only at our late-night talks in hotel rooms, but even at daytime business meetings in my New York apartment, that Divine would suddenly, without warning, make his move. It always seemed rather comical to me. Regardless of my own sexual preferences, I certainly had no interest in becoming a 'chubby chaser' or in allowing him to mix business with pleasure. I was adamant: his groping hands were to be put down aggressively, along with his heavy breathing. It was difficult physically to push him off me, so I had to make it clear verbally that his apparent lust for me was not to be satisfied. Over a period of some months I managed to do this without compromise on my part. I actually think he just lost interest and moved to easier conquests. I was certainly to learn that he had no discretion whatsoever in his choice of quick tricks. Several business colleagues of ours would discreetly complain to me in the future of similar repeated attempts at seduction. Divi just thought everyone was fair game.

I busied myself daily making phone calls to anyone and everyone on Divine's behalf. Certain things I initiated, others came our way. I received a phone call from Richard Gayer in London. He introduced himself as the producer of the film *Andrew Logan's The Alternative Miss World,* which was due to open in London shortly. Would Divine like to attend the official première?

During the previous year, while I was busy preparing the production of *The Neon Woman* in San Francisco, Divine had vanished from my side for a week, telling me a friend had sent him an air ticket to London. As I didn't know Divine well at the time, I didn't question this act of generosity and was glad to be on my own for a few days. The facts now came to light about that particular week.

While in London in 1976 performing in *Women Behind Bars,* Divine had made some good friends, which helped to relieve him of the boredom of playing supporting actor. These friends included the eccentric young artist Andrew Logan; his assistant, Michael Davis; the Australian fashion photographer, Robyn Beeche, and the acclaimed, controversial fashion designer, Zandra Rhodes. Such friendships were in fact to prove surprisingly durable. I think what attracted him to them – and vice-versa – was an admiration of eccentricity combined with talent. In the seventies none of John Waters's movies had yet been shown publicly in England and these friends welcomed Divine as a legitimate stage actor. They were all people who had built, or were in the process of building, successful careers based on their talents, while not supressing their very individual personalities. It must have been immediately reassuring to Divine to meet others who had the courage to flaunt convention in similar ways to himself.

After Divine had returned to the States, he kept in touch with this group, making long phone calls and sending expensive gifts, charging them to credit accounts he had no intention of paying. Just as he had as a child, he adored creating this image and was determined to keep it up, no matter at whose expense.

Apparently, during that quick return visit to England to see his friends in 1978, he had appeared on stage as a guest compere for a bizarre evening of high camp presented in a circus tent on London's Clapham Common. 'Once a year, on the same night as the Miss World Pageant in London, my friend Andrew Logan – who is a poor Andy Warhol of London – gives a mock Miss World contest,' Divine explained. 'It is not a drag show. Men, women and children are in it. If a dog could dress up, he could be in it. The categories are Day Wear, Evening Wear, Bathing Suits, and Questions and Answers. The contestants put much time into their costumes, which included that year outer-space beasts and boxes of chocolates.'

Divine had been sent the air ticket to England so that the most outrageous drag star of all could take part in that year's *The Alternative Miss World*. What no one could have foreseen was that Divine would have a very bad bout of flu during his visit, so, being heavily sedated, his participation was far from outrageous. 'Andrew wasn't paying me anything to do it,' Divine told me later, 'so I didn't think it mattered if I was dreadful. Anyway, you should have seen the contestants. They made me look like Vivien Leigh.'

I told Divine of the invitation to the première and couldn't help but ask him whether he was aware or not that he was about to have another movie open in which he was the star. As the original stage event had happened prior to my signing a contract with my client, I had no right to be angry but I still felt somewhat surprised that he had never thought of advising me of this development in his career.

He responded with equal surprise. 'Well,' I told him, 'either I'm mad and I've totally misunderstood the situation, or you made a film without knowing it.' And that's exactly what it was. He had been so heavily under the influence of the drugs he was taking to fight the flu that he had no recollection of the event being filmed.

'Do you want to go to London?' I asked.

'Of course, but what will I wear?' he immediately replied. 'And I can't go now without my personal manager to escort me. Tell them we want two first-class air tickets and a hotel – what's that place called? – you know, the one on the River Thames with the famous suites.' And then, as the obvious afterthought: 'Will the Queen be there too?'

In reality, Andrew provided two economy-class tickets (for Divine and Van Smith) and Divi paid for mine on credit. We all stayed at friends' homes as no hotel rooms – let alone river suites – were part of the deal. Divine and I occupied the 'royal box' at the film's première, held at midnight in the vast Odeon Cinema in Leicester Square.

He was very much the 'guest of honour' (his screen credit for his participation) and was greeted by fans, both outside and inside the cinema, with roars of approval when they caught sight of the full-length, white sheath dress with fishnet tail that Van had specially designed for the occasion. At Divine's request, I hired white tie and tails from Moss Bros and escorted 'her' in grand fashion. It was a fun night.

The film turned out to be a straightforward video documentary of the actual event on Clapham Common, with an illogical prologue of a tour of Andrew Logan's flat facing the Tower of London. Divine, although billed on the posters as the star, did not appear on screen very often and, when he did, he was only too obviously sedated by drugs (to fight the flu). Andrew had given him a bare minimum of a script from which to improvise introductions to the contestants. The script itself was unfunny and, given Divine's lack of talent for improvisation, he came off very flat indeed. His appearance was outrageous, but his delivery deadpan. Fortunately, it didn't seem to matter very much since the film was not about him, but the odd assortment of participants.

The invitation-only audience greeted the première with rapture and the usual late-night celebrations followed. But Divine and I were, at this stage, more interested in the potential of the next day's breakfast we had arranged with Andrew and his business colleagues.

The following morning the sedate, upper-class patrons of Harrods' breakfast room witnessed a truly unusual group of would-be film-makers haggle over a deal. 'Is this what those famous Hollywood deal-making breakfasts at Chasens are going to be like for us?' Divine and I wondered, not totally, we hoped, in jest.

It was explained to us how they intended to release the film around the world and that Richard Gayer was about to travel to New York to set up an American deal. While Divine continued to eat his hot porridge, I spelt out to them that he had never been made aware that his contribution to that night of not-so-innocent fun on Clapham Common was to be recorded for posterity and, as Divine was a member of the British actors' union, Equity, they were not in a legal position to negotiate any distribution deals without first having obtained his written agreement to his appearance in the film.

Everyone stared in disbelief. Who did this pompous person think he was to come between all these creative artistes with such business talk? I stared back and waited. They turned to the star.

'But Divi is our friend,' Logan stated. 'You would love us to have the film on release, wouldn't you?' he asked Divi directly.

Divine was now struggling to spread frozen slabs of butter on wafer-thin pieces of melba toast. He ignored us all, not looking up from this essential task.

'Sorry, Andrew,' I interjected, 'but Divine makes a living from acting and cannot afford to give away his services. You had no right to turn this into a film behind his back. You must find a way to increase your funding so that you can pay him prior to any further commitments on your part.' I was enjoying being the manager of a star. 'Or else we'll take out an injunction, stopping all further screenings,' I concluded.

Divine slyly looked towards me, winked his approval – amusement, more likely – then turned to the others to commiserate! 'I've signed a contract with Bernard to represent me,' he explained almost apologetically, 'and so I have to agree with what he says.'

Breakfast was completed abruptly. To my astonishment, Divine left with them to go shopping around Harrods – they obviously had credit cards he could use – leaving me alone.

Eventually we settled on a fee to be paid to Divine of $5,000, with no ongoing royalties.

I had started to pay my way.

'Unlike the vicious harpie he so often plays, Divine in person is a softspoken man, courteous to a fault, who enjoys the kind of personal reputation that is rare indeed in show biz circles – for unflagging consideration and kindness with friends and co-workers alike.'
(Jacques le Sourd, *GWN*, 5 September 1976)

6 Divine Does Discos

'People had been yelling at me about my weight for years, and my manager and doctor were worried about my health. But you never do anything until you want to do it for yourself. What finally happened was, I saw a video of myself and I couldn't believe it. I thought "If I get any bigger I'm going to burst." I didn't even think I looked good in drag any more – just sort of grotesque.

'Excuse me,' he continued in a low, raspy voice, remembering those multiple chins and 62-inch waist, 'but it looked as if somebody had stuck an air hose up my ass.'

The Advocate, interview with Divine, 1985

TRAVELLING WITH DIVINE had made me aware of the problems he had to cope with because of his obesity. Apart from the obvious psychological ones, there were the physical battles too. During the time I knew him, his weight varied between 240 pounds (after a rigorous summer diet) and 375 pounds; his waist – when it could be found – measured between 52 and 65 inches.

Of course, he didn't like being fat. Since childhood, he had lived with the attendant problems. 'Fat kids are tormented. Kids are really cruel,' Divine commented. 'They learn all this from ignorant parents. They run up and call people "Fatso". I was always overweight, and it made me a complete introvert to the point where I didn't go out of the house until I was sixteen years old. Wanting to date, to go to the dances, and wanting to be a teenager like everybody else. The only thing holding me back was the fat. After I lost it, I was still the same person. All of a sudden people talked to me. That was a rude awakening for a young kid. It's what you look like, not who you are. A pretty face and a good figure can open doors for you. I learned that early in life, much to my dismay. A cheap way to get in there.'

But he lost the weight only too briefly as a teenager. Then it came back with a vengeance. And it wasn't an illness, certainly not hereditary. Divine just liked to eat – and eat – and eat – and drink gallons of Coca-Cola. Not even Diet Coke. And, of course, the daily doses of marijuana only fuelled the irrepressible hunger.

'Now that the hair and waist are gone,' Divine told *Interview*, 'all I know is that I'm just one of those people who definitely have a weight problem. When I'm thinner, I feel better. You put it all on again. I don't know why. Sometimes it's scary when you question yourself and you come up with different reasons. I just get hungry. And when I'm hungry, anything that is not nailed down better watch out.'

Because of the symptoms of the sleep apnoea from which he suffered, Divine slept restlessly. Every night was spent tossing and turning, waking frequently either because of the sound of his own, intense snoring, or to catch his breath in a moment of panic. Consequently, he would lack any reasonable energy first thing in the morning and his moods would be fearful. On tour, hotel breakfasts would be a time to avoid at all costs. Divine would arrive at the very last practical minute, having thrown on his previous night's clothes from the heap on the bedroom floor and not bothered to take a shower or clean his teeth. A body that size needed cleaning regularly. Divine remained unconcerned as to the effects of his personal hygiene – or, rather, lack of it – on those around him.

Breakfast time became a routine. I would try to get through it before he arrived, making the excuse that I needed the additional time before leaving to make essential phone calls to the next venue. He would eventually arrive and go straight to the buffet table to pile a heap of food – bread, eggs, butter, ham, jams, cheese – on his plate. He would return to the buffet to pick up his cereal and juice. Once settled, surrounded by food, and having caught the attention of the waiter (whose attention was not difficult to attract – most of those in the room would by now be watching him with curiosity, or barely hidden disgust), he would order his hot dish of more eggs, baked beans, bacon, whatever. . . . Only then would he grunt some kind of acknowledgement to whomever of his travelling colleagues were still at the table. It could hardly be called a greeting.

Breakfast would then be continued in comparative silence – that is to say, not much speech – until his mood started to turn. This would usually happen once his stomach was satisfied. Burp, fart, more grunts. Then a stream of sarcastic comments about the previous evening's activities – and, to my dismay and frustration, very little interest about the next 24 hours' itinerary.

When there was no more food left on the table, it was time for Divine to return to his hotel room and release most of what had just been put inside him. To be brief – and as delicate as possible – on this particular problem, Divine appeared to have a difficulty in controlling his bowel movements. It would not have needed a 'scratch 'n' sniff' card to be able to find Divine's room ten minutes after breakfast. Indeed, we would often joke on tour that it was not necessary, at such a moment, to check with the hotel's front desk to know how to locate our star.

I had constantly to make excuses to his hosts, his work colleagues and his travelling companions about his reluctance to communicate with them and tendency to fall asleep anywhere, any time. I apologised on his behalf, always explaining that he was either extremely tired from the pressures of touring, or that he was basically very shy and found it difficult to make idle conversation. In truth, Divine was anti-social. I did make allowances for the reduced energy levels caused by the restless sleep, but it became very clear to me that his ability to close his eyes, drop his chin to his chest and commence snoring – all literally within seconds of sitting in a car or aeroplane – was sheer laziness on his part. Indeed, should one of us happen to make a comment with which he disagreed, the snoring would be interrupted by his caustic dis-approval, muttered *sotto voce*, followed instantly by an extra forceful snort in order to underline his unwillingness to take the subject any further. He just had no interest in social niceties, in being part of a group.

In any band of travelling players, all look to their leader – their star – to create the atmosphere within which they will spend their long, often weary days together. In our band, Divine, our star, provided nothing most of the time, least of all companionship. In this regard, he was using his weight in order to cover his laziness. It was my task, as his manager and representative, to make the excuses and talk on his behalf. On tour, I did one hell of a lot of talking.

Divine resented my attempts at discussing this social problem with him, denying to himself – and consequently to me – that it existed at all. It was really not in my own interest to spell out how much we all hated being on tour with him during these selfish moods, so I did my best gently and persuasively to turn the subject round to discussing the physical problems he might be suffering from his being overweight. He agreed to visit Barry Goozner, my doctor in New York.

Dr Goozner had been recommended to me on my arrival in New York. Although I had very little reason to visit him beyond annual check-ups, I had taken a liking to him and therefore trusted in his advice and care. I called his secretary and asked her if I could make an appointment for Dr Goozner to see my colleague, a Mr Harris Glenn Milstead. I also left a message for the doctor to call me at home as soon as he could.

A few hours later I was explaining to Barry that Mr Milstead was, in fact, the actor Divine. He seemed delighted – he was a fan of the movies – and asked me only one question: 'Is he taking any kind of hormone treatment or drugs for professional purposes?' In other words, Barry was politely and discreetly enquiring if Divine had any sex-change ambitions! He was relieved to hear my response. At my request, he agreed that, while he must respect confidentiality between doctor and patient, he would not have a problem with giving me 'an overview, a general report' on his consultations with Divine. He seemed to respect my genuine concern and need for basic information in my capacity as Divine's personal manager.

Divine, too, had few reasons to visit Barry Goozner over the next few years. He also liked the doctor tremendously and told me that he felt, for the first time in his life, free and able to discuss the most intimate and personal details with him. I never discussed these particular conversations with Barry, but Divine would tell me that they were very much of a sexual nature. I do know that Barry gave Divine some much-appreciated and thoughtful advice about Aids and safe sex well before it was considered necessary to do so.

On every one of his visits to Dr Goozner, I received the same verdict: absolutely no apparent health problems beyond those created by the obesity. Dr Goozner lectured Divine about losing weight, drastically. He warned him that, in ten years' time, his excess baggage could create severe – perhaps fatal – problems for him. Divine was concerned, worried; he had great respect for Dr Barry Goozner. But he was lazy.

In September 1979, I received an unsolicited request for Divine's services; this time from John Gravett, a New York cabaret agent: 'Bernard, you manage the drag queen, Divine, don't you?'

I didn't think of my star client as a drag queen – I was determined to establish him as a character actor – but I let John continue. 'My clients in Fort Lauderdale, Florida, own a highly successful gay disco and are regularly booking top disco recording stars for personal appearances,' he told me. My thoughts flashed back to the recent conversation with Scott Forbes at Studio One in Los Angeles. 'They've asked me about Divine. Do you want me to book him for next month?'

'But John, Divine isn't a disco star. He's never been near a recording studio,' I explained far too honestly. 'What would he *do*?'

'I've been careful to explain that,' John insisted, 'but they told me *Pink Flamingos* has been getting late-night screenings recently and a tremendous following has built for him. He says they'll be happy just to have him turn up in costume and *be* Divine.'

I was certainly interested. 'And they'll pay a fee of $1,000,' he added. I was definitely interested. The phone company was threatening to cut our lines off any moment now – and the rents were due.

'OK,' I agreed, without consulting Divi first. 'As long as they know there's no act. Send me a contract.'

Three days later, the contract arrived. With it came three round-trip tickets to Fort Lauderdale and a cheque for $500. Apparently the performer receives a 50 per cent deposit in advance (which is supposed to be held in escrow by either the agent or the manager until the performance is completed, although we were to exist on these advances for the next few years). I liked that arrangement. So did Divine. I had barely been given the opportunity to explain the idea to him over the phone, before he arrived on my doorstep to collect his share of the advance payment. He didn't seem at all concerned as to what he would actually do for his fee.

The contract was for Hallowe'en night, 31 October. Van Smith was asked to create an outfit for the appearance and travel with us to do his make-up. Divi offered him a fee of $75 for his services, probably the first time Van had ever been paid for this particular paint job. The three of us set off as if we were going on holiday, with curiously little apprehension as to what it was all about.

A limo was waiting at Fort Lauderdale airport to take us to the Marlin Beach Hotel on the infamous Lauderdale 'strip'. Divine already knew that the hotel had a reputation as a gay paradise of orgiastic abandon. He was greeted as a celebrity guest and enjoyed signing autographs at the pool, surrounded by bikini-clad beauties of only one gender.

At midnight the limo arrived again, this time to take us to the Copa disco. Divine had finally faced up to the fact that he might have some sort of obligation to earn his fee that evening and had become extremely nervous. He was now behaving like a spoilt brat, bitching, complaining, screaming at everyone. He had stubbornly refused to discuss any sort of detail about the evening ahead and now was ready to blame me for getting him into this mess!

At the disco, several hundred barely dressed young men were wildly gyrating on the dance floor to Donna Summer and Sylvester records. We were ushered into the makeshift dressing room and Van Smith set up the sticks of make-up to commence the frustrating task of holding

Divine's sagging chin in one hand – in an effort to stop him falling asleep, face dropping to his heaving chest – while carefully designing with the other.

The disco's resident female impersonator – drag queen in truth – improbably named Tiny Tina came to pay his respects. Divine ignored his presence, clearly uncomfortable with another oversized man dressed as a woman in his dressing room.

'We're all so excited,' Tina cooed, 'and so honoured! The great Divine is actually premiering her act here at the Copa tonight – and I get to introduce her first!' Divine had pushed Van aside and was glaring at me. 'Get her out of here,' his look clearly told me, without his moving his lips. But Tiny Tina was oblivious to the star's impatience and determined to complete this welcoming speech. He turned directly to me. 'Now, darling, tell me. What's her first song and how long is she doing tonight? Be sure to limit it to six songs. The boys get bored, you know, with us queens. The black girls are best. They usually only have one song to sing, even though they *will* stretch their way around the twelve-minute version. Ohhh!' The last was a screech of sheer delight. 'We're all waiting.'

Tiny Tina exited in a flurry of feathers, sequins and spectacular arm gestures. I faced Divine. Van hid his face behind the vodka bottle (a fairly regular sight). There was no getting away from it. Whatever John Gravett had assured me, this place was clearly expecting a polished disco act. Five minutes to go and Divine was now hurling his fright wig at me and screaming abuse. The music was blaring so loudly, we could barely hear ourselves shout, let alone speak. Divine started pushing me violently. It took a good few minutes to calm him enough to explain that he had to go on stage – he had already spent half his fee. I assured him I would remain by his side to cope with problems.

Tina made a grand announcement. We heard the word 'Divine'. The crowd cheered. I literally pushed Divine on to the area of the dance floor used as a stage. Boys surrounded him; sitting, standing, cheering, waiting for the music to start. Eventually, an eerie silence. Divine looked round at me and mouthed, 'What do I do?' Without thinking, I whispered in his ear. 'Say "Fuck you!" Just say "Fuck you!" ' Somehow, it seemed appropriate at the time. I think that huge bulk in front of me, dripping with sweat and shaking with nerves, was just so glad to receive any sort of advice at this moment that he smiled his best shit-eating grin, stretched his right arm upwards with his fist in a clench and – with perhaps more truth behind the exclamation than this particular audience ever realised – screamed: '*Fuck you!*'

It worked. The more he repeated it, the louder they cheered and applauded, blowing kisses and hugging each other on the dance floor with those looks of mutual acknowledgement that say 'I knew she'd be such a bitch. I just *knew* it!'

'Fuck you! Fuck you all! Divine was releasing all his pent-up anger and tension on the audience and they were lapping it up. Little did either of us know that at this moment he was also beginning to create the simple, basic script that would earn him hundreds of thousands of dollars in the next few years.

Not knowing what to do or say for an encore and, as it happened, acutely embarrassed at his lack of preparedness, he then stormed off stage. The crowd went berserk. This was exactly the Divine they had hoped for: way over the top – the filthiest person in the world – two stubby fingers up to convention. I followed him into the dressing room, where he burst out crying.

'You were wonderful,' I assured him, which was true (in its way). 'But you must go back on. I don't think fifty seconds is quite enough for a fee of $1,000.'

He begged me not to make him go back. Using acutely forceful words, he made it clear to me that he was adamant he had now exhausted his current repertoire for personal appearances. I advised Van to start to repair Divine's makeup while I found the manager's office to discuss the possibility of a quick finish to the act. John Castelli, the Copa's co-owner, sat behind a desk, the top of which was covered with paper money. He was flanked by three muscled minders. The scene instantly reminded me of every dreadful 'B' movie about Chicago gangsters.

Before I could speak – and I had no idea what I would say when I did – Castelli stood. I prepared for my execution: how dare I con these good people of Florida into believing that Divine was a disco diva? To my surprise he was soft spoken as he declared, 'She was wonderful. Absolutely wonderful. Did *you* create this concept for her, young man? What a sensational way to open her act. Now, get her back on stage as quickly as possible to start singing before the boys get restless.'

At this, I was not-too-gently ushered out of the room while Castelli, head almost buried in dollar bills, continued counting. The security staff 'assisted' me back to the dressing room. I realised I had said nothing to Castelli.

Divine was reluctantly and unsuccessfully trying to dry himself while Van struggled with as good a repair job as possible in this ludicrous situation. I told them that the owner was ecstatic about the performance so far, but (allowing myself the right to delete specific details) was eager to have Divine return to the stage once more to take another bow. The star seemed content with this apparent praise and decided he could pull himself together for one more round of applause.

This time he literally pushed the minders aside and threw himself on to the dance floor – was he perhaps already beginning to feel a satisfaction in the hero worship flowing from those around him? – and repeated his sacred script.

'*Fuck you!*'

More laughs. Then silence. He didn't move. They weren't applauding; they were only too obviously waiting for a song. Suddenly, appreciating the situation we were in, Tiny Tina appeared from (almost) nowhere and screamed at Divine, 'You're nothing but a motherfucker who eats dogshit!' The star of the evening, not aware that this was a colleague's efforts to save the day, took the insult personally and turned on the Tiny One with full force. 'And you're nothing but an amateur drag queen,' he retorted. 'Who the fuck do you think you are to talk to me like that?' More applause. Was this perhaps the beginning of Alternative Comedy?

From within the mass of flying feathers and falling sequins, Tiny Tina produced a horse whip and started to lash out at Divine. I could see that our star was taking all this quite seriously. Divi lunged for the whip, broke it in two and pulled a young admirer from the audience. He instantly ripped off the boy's beach shorts and lodged the two pieces of horse whip in a place (belonging to the body of this reluctant third party) that the audience truly appreciated. In mock fury, Tiny Tina grabbed Divine and started to wrestle him to the floor. Two minders joined me in breaking up the sumo-like exhibition on stage, while the spectators booed and hissed at our efforts to do so. As soon as Divine was back on his feet, stunned and still furious, I pushed him into the spotlight for the planned final bow. Reacting to the audience's cheers, he tore open the front of his dress, grabbed his sponge tits and threw them, soaking wet from sweat, into the crowd. A more suitable finale could not have been imagined.

Back in the dressing room, Divine was unapproachable and I feared the worst from his wrath. I tried to keep visitors out until he calmed down, but Castelli was too quick and he instantly moved towards Divine to kiss him on the cheek.

Divi, thinking he was about to be assaulted once again, pushed him away. Castelli fell onto me and we both fell to the floor. Divi thought this very funny and started to laugh hysterically. Castelli, Van Smith and I joined him in laughter from the floor. Heaven knows what we were all laughing about, but one thing was sure.

A new disco star had been born.

Too wet—and nervous—to change, Divine wanted to leave in costume to return to the hotel. Castelli handed over the second half of our payment, in cash, and declared that, although the 'act' was not what the agent had promised, it was truly memorable. I think he might have also used the word 'unique'.

On his way out of the club, Divine was mobbed by fans wanted his autograph. Eager to savour his success—and to meet some members of the audience on, perhaps, a more intimate basis—he decided to stop at the bar for a drink. Suddenly the bar was packed and doing tremendous business, with Divine sitting on the counter, signing anything and everything offered him and willingly answering questions of his past. He was in his element and those in the bar were getting a second show. Castelli forced his way to the counter and offered us drinks. I started to relax for the first time that day and joined my two confederates in a heavy session. On the house.

Divi managed to persuade an especially cute Copa beachboy to drive us back to the Marlin Beach Hotel. It was 3 A.M. My last memory of that extraordinary night was of our willing chauffeur, sitting totally naked in the driver's seat of his convertible Cadillac, with Divine, wigless in the passenger seat next to him, waving the driver's shorts in the air and screaming at whoever could hear: 'I'm a star! I'm a star!' Van, meanwhile, was sitting in the back, similarly waving Divine's soaked blonde wig, which was perched on the bottle of vodka he had just persuaded our friendly club owner to donate to him. I was hanging on to the $500 cash. At least the phone bills could be paid when we got back to New York.

Back home after the Fort Lauderdale event, Divi and I spent our spare hours—of which there were many—planning, scheming, dreaming. We began to build the trusting relationship that was to continue for years to come. Why did he trust me when his previous representatives had let him down? I'm certain, in these early days together, it was simply that he knew I respected him as an actor. Not a drag queen, a freak, a demi-celebrity good for an immediate entrance into the latest fashionable disco. I had come across Divine as an actor. He knew I admired his natural comedic talent.

He was similarly impressed with my legitimate theatre background. He would take great joy in introducing me to his friends. 'Do meet my new personal manager from England,' he would say boastfully. 'He's just left Glenda Jackson and Douglas Fairbanks to look after me.'

Divine wanted to be a film star—a *rich* film star—more than anything else in the world. He joined the Dreamlanders because he saw in it an opportunity to get into films—albeit through the basement door—and he took the risk of taking over the lead in an off-Broadway show because he saw the potential, should he succeed, in bringing his acting abilities to the notice of others in his chosen profession. Then, going to London with *Women Behind Bars,* despite the indignity of taking second billing to the most famous pair of tits in Britain, was a dream come true for an American underground actor.

He was aware that his had been an impressive discipline throughout the on-again, off-again year's run of *The Neon Woman.* 'Theatre people are very dedicated,' Divine told a journalist. 'When I work I am very professional and proud of the fact; there are too many people out there who want your job. There is no need or time for tantrums and all those ridiculous displays of emotion.' He was satisfied. He had paid his dues. He now had all the proof *he* needed that his career as an actor could be taken seriously.

However, through his excursions into the realm of celebrity status, he seemed to have achieved only just that. Friends connected with the entertainment industry were keen to be seen with him—as long as he was in drag, looking and behaving as outrageous as his screen/stage image—but did not talk to him about potential work. John Waters and Divine were in touch from time to time and Divine had heard many rumours of a new film being planned, but no one had yet approached him formally. Certainly, casting agents were not calling to meet him.

Divine and I talked of theatre, of the Broadway musical that I would produce for him, of his being able to act in men's clothes in the not too distant future. He was at his most attentive and co-operative during these discussions. I talked to him of the meaning of—and potential work for—a character actor in our trade. I encouraged him to watch the TV screenings of Sydney Greenstreet's old movies and assured him that it was a good idea to model himself or someone who had succeeded in the very roles Divine longed for.

We started to approach every contact either of us had in the world of theatre, asking them to think of Divine's potential for casting – and not just as a female character. Most thought we were crazy. Many of his closest friends warned him that I could be ruining his career by taking this route: Divine was an adored, worshipped cult drag queen. That's what the public wanted, they would insist. But that's not what *he* wanted. And certainly not what I wanted for him; after all, what did I know about managing a drag queen?

It was a difficult, uphill struggle. Always. It never changed. I would meet with agents, producers, writers. I looked up all my previous business contacts. Most of the time I received reactions of considerable astonishment: how could I possibly be risking my entire career on this oddball? Why was I putting so much into this particular one project? Yes, they would love to help me, but surely this Divine character is an overnight joke, a transvestite, a cult figure for the gay audiences? I sat in the Russian Tea Room, Algonquin Hotel, Plaza Hotel's Oak Room – all those same locations where I had previously discussed the next production possibility for Douglas, for Sir Mike, for Glenda – and, time and time again, witnessed the looks of bewilderment when my colleague opposite me realised I was there only to represent the notorious Divine.

Divi would wait patiently for me to return to his apartment, getting himself stoned in preparation for my usual report of no interest. Often, in these times, he would only respond with a comment such as 'Why bother, Bernard? They'll never accept me, the bastards. They can only see me in wigs, bras and heels – and in someone else's show.'

Was it the challenge that kept us together at these times? Was it sheer determination? Or was it really that we were both so hungry and in need of each other's potential for earnings? For, just as he could sit on his bare wooden floor for days waiting for the phone to ring, neither was I – even with all the personal meetings I was having in New York – being offered such wonderful opportunities as to be a producing partner with Jimmy Nederlander or The Shuberts.

Whatever the reason – and presumably it was a combination of all – Divine and I seemed by now locked into an effort to turn the most unlikely actor in the business into a commercial success. We surely must have been mad.

I presented to Divine my basic, logical plan for him to achieve his ambitions:

1) *Work*. Gain the attention and respect of the powers that be in the entertainment industry by always giving first-rate performances.

2) *Expose*. Receive good reviews from media critics, thereby spreading the word to the public.

3) *Exploit*. Generate as much personal publicity as possible from the reviews in order to become box-office potential (therefore very employable) and a household name.

But what to do while we waited for offers? We needed cash badly. Divine had no other source of income to speak of. And with his celebrity status and extraordinarily recognisable figure, he could hardly apply for a job as a waiter at Studio 54. I couldn't stop thinking of the fee from Fort Lauderdale and the potential of this, for me, previously untapped area of our industry. The discos.

In the late seventies, it seemed that a gimmick was more of an essential attribute in order to achieve overnight recording stardom than a vocal talent. I remembered a 1976 disco hit, 'More, More, More,' by Andrea True, an infamous X-rated movie star. As far as I could tell, all Ms True did on her record was a lot of heavy breathing; a clever gimmick, as it surely would not have been very difficult for her to distinguish between her song lyrics and her movie scripts. Surely, if a porno star could have a hit record, then Divine could too? All we needed was a record producer and someone to foot the bill.

David Plattner was in his early twenties. Divi and I had first met him when he was producing a dreadful stage tour of a melodrama. Max Hager, the costume designer on the show was a friend of Divi's and he introduced us to the young producer after a performance in San Francisco. David and I exchanged cards and we were pleased to meet him again when he visited us briefly in Provincetown. He was pleasant, charming and enthusiastic to become involved with us. But we already had a theatre producer on our team of two.

I now recalled he had mentioned that, prior to his recent, disastrous attempt at producing in the theatre, he had been a record producer. It didn't take long to persuade him that he might become famous through Divine if he could create for him an instant disco hit. He threw himself into the project. Divine's eyes sparkled when I relayed this latest idea to him.

'What do you think, man?' he asked me in his inimitable, direct fashion. 'If they paid me $1,000 for *not* singing anything, how much can we ask for with a hit song in the act? Hey, we'll be rich,' he concluded. 'Yeh, great, tell Mr Plattner I'll be his new star.'

Nobody gave a thought in these discussions as to whether Divine could actually sing or not. In fact, I don't recall that particular question ever being asked of him. He would, however, willingly list his own wide-ranging musical tastes whenever asked. 'I love Diana Ross, black music, soul music,' he would begin. 'I used to adore The Supremes, then I lost interest for a while. But eventually I realised what a great entertainer Diana Ross is. I also love Tina Turner, Aretha, Frank Sinatra – I don't necessarily agree with his politics, but I love to hear Sinatra's voice.' I rarely ever saw Divi sit quietly and listen to music, but his list would certainly be influenced by a current boyfriend's choice too. 'I also like classical and opera, especially Wagner – a little bit of everything,' he would continue. 'I'm not really crazy about Liza. Barbra Streisand has a great voice, she can really belt it out, but she doesn't thrill me.'

Divine signed endless pieces of paper – he was now a recording artist under contract, having not yet ever entered a recording studio. On our newly acquired producer's suggestion, Divine started to look for a suitable song with which to make his recording début. The only writer he knew and trusted, Tom Eyen, had recently teamed with the composer Henry Krieger, and they quickly penned the witty ditty, 'Born to be Cheap'.

Cheap. Cheap. I was born to be cheap. Cheap.
A child no mother could keep. Cheap.
As sure as there's trash, I was born to be cheap.

Perfect!

At 11.30 p.m. on 24 November 1979 (less than four weeks after our Hallowe'en experience), Divine was summoned to his first recording session, at Right Track Studios in New York. He was in a state of great excitement over this new career move and had proudly talked of it for the past few days to his friends and followers, who sat neatly at his feet in a haze of marijuana while he held his Buddha-like briefing sessions. We had all read the exotic tales of the Beatles' all-night recording sessions. Colleagues had eagerly reported dropping in on Elton John or David Bowie while they buried themselves in studios for days – weeks – on end, creating masterpieces of music in 'drug-crazed, liquor-filled' recording binges.

Divine was determined to come prepared. He brought the dope. I supplied the tequila. Divine's 'personal assistant', Jay Bennett duly accompanied his master with toothbrushes and changes of T-shirts to allow for a prolonged first session. We were all eager to meet the fine rock and jazz musicians that David Plattner had surely lined up to accompany Divine.

At 12.17 a.m., 47 minutes after arriving at the studio, the three of us were in a yellow cab on our way back to 58th Street, clutching clean T-shirts, unused toothbrushes and full liquor bottles. In that brief time, Divine had successfully laid down his vocal tracks, not only for 'Born to be Cheap', but also for a B side chosen by Plattner, Shirley Ellis's famous 'The Name Game'. He was joined in the studio only by David Plattner, his partner Joe Beck, and the engineer. There were no musicians for Divine to be buddies with. The music tracks had already been completed and Plattner played a synthesiser just to guide Divine. Although this session proved to be an anti-climax after all Divi's anticipation, a record had been made.

Naively, we thought that that was all there was to it. Divine could now be sold as a recording star. On the way back from the studio, we joked about Andrea True; and as we passed a porno movie theatre, with its marquee proclaiming *Debbie Does Dallas*, Divi grandly announced, '. . . and Divine Does Discos!'

'"I'm not Leontyne Price but I'm working on it," admitted Divine. "Maybe I'll do the trampoline or something. On TV I could do a show like the one Cher used to do, wear fifteen dresses and have guest stars who never get to be by themselves."' (The *Philadelphia Enquirer*)

7 Fuck You Very Much!

'"What do you want for Christmas, Divine?" I asked. "Actually anything expensive, anything very expensive — yachts, planes, Rolls-Royces, servants twenty-four hours a day, unlimited funds," he replied. "I'm not too far away from the American Dream."'

In Touch, December 1982

AS DAVID PLATTNER BUSIED HIMSELF trying to get a distribution deal for 'Born to be Cheap', Divi and I spent our time doing anything we could to keep him in the gossip columns and to let word spread that he was available for bookings. We even printed a rather classy, black-and-white glossy folder promoting his services:

HAVE A DIVINE EVENT!

Have Divine host your party; have photos taken with Divine; Divine will sign anything as a personal souvenir! Have Divine judge your costume contest or announce your cabaret performers. Please note that Divine does not perform a cabaret act or any pre-rehearsed show at these events. Divine attends only as a celebrity host.

What a nerve we had! I thought it couldn't have been plainer or spelled out more clearly, but our attempts to earn a buck anywhere, anyhow, brought problems of their own. Even though I would stress the limitations of my artiste's contribution to the contracted event, there seemed to be no assurance that the promoters would then pass on this information in advance to those they wished to attract. How naive of us to even think they would.

Word did spread quickly, however, and we started to discuss various potential projects. Or, rather, I discussed them. Divi continued to have virtually no interest in the details, other than the amount of the fee and the date on which the deposit would arrive.

In 1977, Divine, under Ron Link's direction, had participated in a concert in Toronto to promote the band Rough Trade and its lead singer, Carol Pope. The event had been given the meaningless title

Restless Underwear. Jonathan Scharer, a young impresario, and Carol Pope's manager, Vicky Wickham, now wanted to bring the event to New York as a showcase for the band and were very eager to use Divine once again. They had rented the vast Beacon Theatre, on the Upper West Side, for 14 February 1980.

We signed a contract guaranteeing Divine a fee of $2,000 in exchange for his 'appearing on stage for a maximum of seven minutes to sing two songs, together with ten male dancers'. It was agreed that Divine would be billed as 'Special Guest Star' under the title and that David Rubin, our stage manager from *The Neon Woman* tour, would be asked to direct Divine's appearance in place of Ron Link. Divine received his $1,000 advance on the fee just in time for Christmas.

At about the same time, Betty and Phyllis from Provincetown had called, this time from Key West, Florida, where they were wintering and planning a season of cabaret at the island's historic, but recently unused Opera House. Things, apparently, were not going well. 'Would Divine please, please help us out by doing a week early in the New Year?' they cried in unison down the phone. As *The Neon Woman* was no longer in production, I suggested a week of 'The Best of New York Cabaret', with Divine appearing only as the compere. We agreed to a week in early February and that Divine's fee would be $1,000 plus all expenses.

It was obvious that these two tough business ladies intended to sell the week on Divine's name—which I knew was likely to work, as Key West was another popular holiday paradise for gays—and so I wanted to ensure that his public would not be misled. Again, the contract stipulated 'Divine's name to be billed at the bottom of the poster and clearly indicated as Compere.'

A popular but oft-abused theatrical phrase employed in connection with my star was 'You were simply divine, darling, simply divine!' So, I invented the title for Key West: *Not Simply Divine—An Evening Of The Best Of New York Cabaret*. I thought I had spelled out the limitations of our agreement by using the word 'Not.' The names of the cabaret performers would be billed *above* the title on the posters. His $500 advance added to the upcoming anticipation of Christmas.

The most important event of the year for Divine was approaching fast and he needed to concentrate his entire energies on it. Nothing could ever interfere with his preparations for Christmas. If Divine has left just one indelible personal memory among those who knew him well it would certainly be that of his Christmas times. He practised no religion, but to him Christmas was a wonderful excuse for buying, buying and buying. He was extravagance personified, but, on seeing the result each year, who could blame him? His trees were legendary, covered in exquisite baubles, lovingly collected over the years from the very best stores in the world. How often in the future was I to follow him on to crowded 747 jumbo jets, laden with carrier bags from Harrods, Bloomingdales, Hong Kong or Australia, full of decorations for next year's tree? These were among his most precious possessions and he wouldn't dream of allowing them to be packed in his luggage and thrown into the plane's underbelly.

Divine would spend all year choosing superb and unnecessarily expensive gifts for friends and acquaintances. At Christmas time his generosity was overwhelming. Silk scarves and shirts from London's Turnbull and Asser, cashmere sweaters from San Francisco's Wilkes Bashford, overflowing seasonal hampers of gourmet luxuries from Fortnum and Mason – all would be charged to ever-increasing credit accounts and then wrapped carefully, lovingly, in the most exotic and expensive Christmas paper. It mattered little to Divine that most of the recipients had no idea of the special – and considerable – value of the store labels sewn inside their gifts. He had achieved his joy and happiness in choosing each item and being able to present them from under the tree.

At his annual Christmas reception at home, he would offer the very best candies from Belgium, a choice of finest British teas and only genuine French champagne. Dainty chocolate-covered strawberries would be laid out on antique lace doilies and served on Harrods' china. The Madison Avenue penthouse would be transformed into a grotto of fairy lights and candles to delight any child's heart.

Christmas Day itself would be Open House. Come at any time. Stay until bored. John Waters would arrive with a gift – to the great additional pleasure of those few of Divine's young fans whom he had befriended during the past year and were now invited to attend his Christmas at home. 'Divine valued his privacy and entertained at home often; we will all remember the parties, the teas, the flowers, and at Christmas ... God, Santa himself was never so upstaged,' John recalled.

Pat Moran and her family would come from Baltimore and leave with arms full of valuable gifts. Mink Stole and, of course, Van Smith would be there, but, by 1979, Divine had drifted away from most of the original Dreamlanders. Hangers-on, cadgers and genuine friends would mix together, gossip as at any other party and pay homage to their host, our star, who would rarely move. He would be stoned out of his mind by the time the first guest arrived, squatting on the floor on huge cushions in one corner of the room. Those arriving would kneel and kiss him on the cheek, then wait for him to point his finger at their particular gift under the tree.

Willing minions, with whom Divi constantly surrounded himself, would run for him, laugh when he did, share his joints (if offered) and show the necessary disapproval of a guest should Divine have reason to signal his own displeasure. These acolytes were reigned over by the aforementioned Jay Bennett, who may have finally switched off the spotlight at the end of *The Neon Woman* tour, but made certain the specific spotlight in his master's life that was directed at him never diminished. Jay had various ambitions – to be a photographer, to be an actor – but appeared mostly to enjoy the position of subservience in which he catered to Divine's every whim. At first, he washed, cleaned, fetched, carried and said 'yes' when required. However, like many personal adjuncts, he could be demanding in return, accepting more and more money and other favours from his employer and taking further and further liberties in his home.

Jay Bennett's greatest fault was his love of gossip, however malicious and distant from the truth. Jay was a stirrer and I was frequently at the top of his list of victims. He was yet another of the pre-Bernard Jay followers who now deeply resented the closeness – and privacy – of my working relationship with Divine. Jay and I lived in an accepted state of truce most of the time, for our mutual friend's sake, except when, every two years or so, Divi would decide he could take no more of Jay and would instruct me to fire him. I would accept this task, admittedly with relish, but Jay always returned, smirking with glee and satisfaction.

Christmas for Divine was an excuse to live in his dream world, shutting out all reality. I was happy to be a part of his extended family in 1979 and to see him at this time of year. His gentleness, generosity and obvious pleasure at giving to others was a surprising, but most welcome contrast to the other extremity of mood I had experienced from him since we worked together. That Christmas I began to see another side of Divine's character and, while not yet understanding why it couldn't display itself more frequently, I had much respect and love for this new friend, as he was on Christmas Day.

However, I was, as always, aware that, immediately after Christmas,

Divine would be in urgent need of cash again and there was nothing planned until February. His advances on February fees had already been over-spent in December. Then, lo and behold, a Christmas miracle! My phone rang early on Christmas Day: a charming Frenchman was calling from Paris. My schoolboy French was brought into service instantly and, from what I could understand of the conversation, Fabrice Emayer, the owner of Le Palace, Europe's most fashionable disco, would like Divine to host his upcoming New Year's Eve celebrations. In Paris. In six days' time.

The evening's festivities were to be broadcast live by Radio Luxembourg and also featured on French television news. It seemed like a wonderful opportunity of European exposure for Divine and all he would be required to do, I was assured, would be to walk around the venue in female costume, greeting the customers and, at one point, appear on stage to sing the now obligatory 'Born to be Cheap'.

Our negotiations were completed by phone between breakfast and lunch on Christmas Day. Divine instantly threw aside the idea when I whispered it to him later at his home, not wanting to talk about such a depressing subject as *work* on this of all days. I told him the fee agreed. He changed his mind.

Divine, Van and I flew overnight to Paris, arriving at seven in the morning of 31 December 1979. We were waiting in the customs hall for our luggage when a smartly dressed, very attractive young man introduced himself as the chauffeur from Le Palace. He was there, he said, to assist us in any way we wished. Divine took the offer literally. I left them alone for a moment to check the baggage carousel, turning round to see to my horror our chauffeur holding a tiny silver spoon under Divine's nose—in full view of the other passengers and not twenty feet from the customs officers.

After breakfast at our hotel, I met Fabrice at his stunningly beautiful vaudeville theatre turned disco. He was a fan of Divine's from the movies and was thrilled that the star would be there to welcome in the eighties: 'A Divine Decade of Decadence', he had advertised it. All entrance tickets had been pre-sold for that night, but there were already people waiting outside at 10 a.m. in the hope of last-minute, additional tickets going on sale.

Once again, Divine had left all details to me. Fabrice was already asking more and more of my star. He explained that, since announcing

Divine's participation to the French media, attention had increased considerably and 'It was most important, for Divi's sake,' as he so discreetly put it, 'to be doing his best to impress.' In other words, he wanted more for his money than a three-minute appearance singing 'Born to be Cheap'. I returned to the hotel, but was annoyed at not being able to discuss this problem with Divine as, it seemed, our chauffeur had continued to offer his 'good services' to the star and the 'Do Not Disturb' sign was clearly in position.

Divi started getting ready in his room at 7 p.m.—the venue was due to open at ten—and, while Van assisted by shaving Divine's back, shoulders, arms, legs (many disposable blades were needed) I patiently tried to teach him, phonetically, a simple speech I had written in French. I had agreed that morning that he would be the voice heard live on radio all over Europe, ushering in the decade. I felt—and he agreed—that it was only polite to attempt it in the host country's language.

From 10 p.m. to 6 a.m. he never stopped. Divine earned no end of respect from me that night. How on earth he managed to get through those eight hours—on five-inch heels and in and out of costumes—I'll never know. He was an absolute joy to work with. I was discovering that this born performer could have great fun as long as he was kept busy; it was in times of waiting that boredom, fear—and the frightful moods—took over.

I had still not had the opportunity to advise Divine of the preparations I had been making for him all day. He seemed content to trust me and follow my minute-to-minute instructions. At the required hour, he was placed on a ten-foot model of a spaceship, holding precariously on to the side by one hand and one foot. The music started, the stage curtains opened, the stage floor was lost in dry ice and, on cue, the top-heavy spaceship started to rise to the top of the building, with its out-of-proportion passenger hanging on for dear life. The cheers from the audience were deafening. Divine was extraordinary, waving from this dangerous piece of stage scenery and grinning wildly, acknowledging the tremendous response and waiting for the set to return 'to earth'.

Something had gone wrong. The spaceship seemed about to enter orbit. It wouldn't come back down. From way above, he looked at me, standing in the wings. I shouted at him, 'Smile, Divine, just smile.' He kept smiling. The audience continued to cheer and, after what seemed like twenty minutes but was more likely only two, our spaceship suddenly jogged into motion, almost throwing its passenger into the arms of the observers below. As it descended, the stage was once again buried in dry ice. Divine could not see when to step off his prop but was aware that the familiar intro to his song was already blaring through the mega-speakers on stage. He gingerly stepped on to what he thought was the stage, but he was actually still two feet above it and he fell in a heap, losing his shoes in the machinery of the stage set. Before I could rush to his side to assist, he had gamely picked himself up and was now busy swaying away from side to side, on stockinged feet, slapping his thighs and screaming 'Cheap. Cheap' for all his life was worth. But of course it was not enough. The crowd was not willing to let him go. He was now stomping across the stage, screaming his familiar script – in English, but the limited number of words employed were well understood by these European fans.

Behind the spaceship set and another curtain, a group of trampoline artistes were busy doing warm-up exercises, five agile young men bouncing up and down on the huge trampoline, ready for the curtain to open, the spaceship to fly away, and to start their act. In a flash, I screamed across the din to the stage manager, who, like all of us, was now wondering how to move on with the planned show while our star was having such a good time on stage, delighting his audience with the unscheduled 'Name Game'.

'Open the curtains,' I instructed. 'Open the curtains and fly the spaceship.' The trampoline artistes heard my instruction and positioned themselves on the stage floor. The curtains parted behind Divine, who was totally oblivious to what was going on. The spaceship, behaving perfectly this time, disappeared. Alone on the front of the stage was a gyrating Divine, behind him a badly mangled pair of high heels – and behind them, five young men and a giant trampoline.

I ran to him, took him by the arm and led him upstage to the waiting support act. Joining in my fun, all five of them together heaved this huge object in a red-sequined miniskirt from behind and threw him on to the trampoline. Without hesitation, my star picked himself up and started bouncing up and down, losing his wig in the process, his miniskirt riding up to his polystyrene tits. The audience was adoring every minute. The five experts joined Divine on the trampoline, clearly astonished by my star's agility. They had obviously never seen *Female Trouble*.

I yelled at the stage manager to close the curtains slowly. On seeing that his act was now coming to an end, Divine shouted at me, above all the noise, 'How do you say "Thank you very much" in French?' But he couldn't hear my reply. So, he improvised with the only word he already knew they understood:

'*Fuck you very much! Fuck you all very much!*'

Fabrice Emayer was literally crying with joy at my side, raining kisses on my cheek in grateful thanks. His idea to use Divine had been a great success.

The good-hearted trampoline team had awkwardly managed to get their new star off the equipment and were preparing to recommence their act, while Divi was now standing next to me in the wings, sweating profusely, his dress soaking wet, his shoes still on stage, his wig still on the trampoline. 'What's next, boss?' he asked, with a grin.

Rehearsals started in New York for Divine and his dancers, in preparation for Valentine Day's *Restless Underwear*. There was an instant rapport in the rehearsal studio and it was clear that Divine was loving being the star with his chorus boys, likening himself to 'Ann-Margret in an Elvis Presley movie'. David Rubin and the choreographer invented two clever dance routines for Divine's songs and, content with our advance work, we left for Key West and what we thought would be a fun week in the sun.

Not Simply
DIVINE

screamed the poster greeting us at the tiny airport. Nowhere was there any mention of the cabaret performers involved. I immediately attacked our employers and wondered how the hell I could have allowed Divine to work for such people again, after all our problems with them in Provincetown. In their defence they mumbled something to the effect of having lost the contract and therefore not remembering what I had said about billing. However, as if it would instantly dismiss my problem, they assured me that tickets were selling very well.

Divine was concerned about misleading his loyal gay following and we spent the day, in intense heat, dreaming up any sort of gimmick that could involve him in more activities on stage. That night he made every sort of camp entrance possible, including being carried on stage on a stretcher by six musclemen, and dancing on roller skates (the only idea he made me swear I would never repeat again; he was terrified). But the audience, most of whom had been in P-Town that previous summer, clearly expected a theatrical comedy such as *The Neon Woman*. They were restless and unappreciative of all Divine's special, last-minute efforts. There were boos and catcalls at the end of the show.

The next morning, with Divine's unhesitating agreement, I cancelled the rest of the week's performances and we left town. Unpaid, of course. Betty and Phyllis gave an interview to the local newspaper, claiming it was totally Divine's fault as he had 'promised them a play'.

We flew to La Guardia airport and took a taxi to Manhattan. I dropped a sulking Divine (because I had no cash to hand him) at East 58th Street and continued on to my home on West 71st and Broadway, passing the Beacon Theatre on the way. And there it was, the poster:

DIVINE

in

RESTLESS UNDERWEAR

Once again, we had to realise that they all knew that, if anything, it was Divine's name that would sell the 2,000 seats of the Beacon Theatre. And they were out to sell seats. For the third time in six weeks, Divine was forced into a situation where he had to take emergency measures in order not to disappoint his fans. David Rubin brought together a few of the New York-based actors he knew and Divine started to rehearse a series of comedy sketches that we all took turns in rewriting just for him – a sure sign of panic.

Restless Underwear was a gigantic disaster in New York. The theatre was full of gay men, all of whom had obviously come to see this new comedy Divine was starring in, with its camp title. The sound system installed for the evening was totally inadequate and the audience couldn't even hear the feeble attempts at sketches (which, thinking back, was probably for the best). They booed and hissed at poor Carol Pope and Rough Trade, who really didn't stand a chance of success after the way the promoters had advertised the event. When, in the second part of the show, Divine performed his two songs with his male chorus line, he received a standing ovation, which only made things worse as we had nothing to follow it with – and the audience's frustration, quickly turning into anger, was therefore increased. The promoters were swamped in the intermission with demands to return ticket money. Many of the audience had left before the final set from Rough Trade. Divine fled back to his home; me to mine. We didn't dare speak that evening about what had happened.

The next morning, Divine called me early. 'Hi, it's Divine. Phillip says you've totally ruined my career and that he'll never risk going to see me in a show again. He was attacked by our friends last night for letting me be part of such a dreadful evening. They all blame you.'

I started to find excuses, listing the problems. But Phillip was right: I knew and accepted it was my fault. I should have controlled everything with more strength – or advised Divine to back out the moment I'd first seen the posters. 'But you needed the other $1,000 desperately,' was my lame offer.

Divine immediately interrupted me. 'We sure have a lot to learn together, man, don't we?' he gently suggested. 'I think I better stay away from a New York stage for a while and learn how to do these things in Idaho or somewhere. Let's have lunch. We need to start planning my future as a disco star.'

I appreciated his generosity at this moment. It was clear to me that he was accepting equal responsibility for our teamwork decisions, whether good or bad. But there was no doubt at all that Divine was hurt by the public's very vocal reaction to this fiasco. 'There have been a couple of shows that I regret doing,' he told the *Detroit Metro Times* in a 1981 interview, 'but I was broke at the time and they were waving money in my face, so I did them. But then they flopped. And it all came back on me. The public usually forgets about it but I never do.'

Indeed, we had a lot to learn. Most important of all, we learned that Divine could not be 'sold' just as a celebrity, for the simple, but very acceptable reason that his fans wouldn't allow it. They knew, they were telling us, that he had so much more to offer. It was all very well for Divine to adopt his 'signature' line, *'Fuck you very much'*, which the fans adored, but they weren't going to be 'fucked' that easily.

Something we had already learned, however, and with great interest, was that his name *could* fill a 2,000-seat theatre in New York.

'I've never had anyone say they were disappointed in me. I can stand on stage and do nothing, and people will write "Divine was outrageous".' (*Los Angeles Times*, 24 February 1985)

8 Briefly Not the Bitch

'"Don't ask me why they like me so much," Divine said. "There must be some need out there."'

Washington Post, 25 June 1981

I T WAS BECOMING OBVIOUS that David Plattner couldn't get a deal to distribute 'Born To Be Cheap'. Despite hiring music lawyers to send out cassette tapes, the responses he was receiving were negative. We began to realise the problem ourselves: while the song's lyrics were a fun gimmick and the audiences enjoyed them at personal appearances, the beat was standard rock 'n' roll and therefore totally unsuitable for the DJs in the dance clubs. Record companies, although realising there just might be some potential in a single by the notorious underground film star Divine, were not going to invest any money in pressing, printing and promoting without being able to achieve sales through plays at the discos.

Finally, David seemed to give up on placing the single and we stopped hearing from him. I had been given a direct copy from the studio master-tape for the purpose of making a performance dub of the songs. Wax Trax Records, a small label based in Chicago, was keen to press and merchandise, but without having to pay any advances. Glad to have any sort of opportunity to hold a completed record in his hands – rather than just talk of having made one and singing it in clubs – Divine agreed to hand over his tape to Wax Trax. We did make an attempt at the time to inform David Plattner of this deal, but our letter to him was returned and we knew of no forwarding address.

Wax Trax, in turn, licensed the single to the Beggars Banquet label in England. They both eventually released it, with very limited pressings, and the record quickly disappeared into history. Of course, any copies now found are collectors' items; Wax Trax even paid for a small marketing campaign after Divine's death in an effort to finally get rid of the boxes they had been holding in store for about eight years.

When David Plattner eventually read about his record being on sale, he commenced a lawsuit against both Divine and myself for $15 million. We were quite flattered; how exciting to be thought worth that amount of money. The case never came to court. In the pre-trial hearings, we offered Mr Plattner twenty per cent of Divi's royalty receipts on the record (which at that time – almost two years after the long-forgotten release – were in the region of $400), but the case was dropped.

I spent much of the summer of 1980 in New York, attempting to raise monies to produce *The Thorn*, a musical I had specially commissioned from writers Steve Brown and Alan (*Little Shop of Horrors*) Menken. Described as a show about 'A Rock Star of the Highest Magnitude and the Lowest Morals: Her Fight to get to The Top', Divine was to star in this parody of Bette Midler's film *The Rose*. Although we gained a tremendous amount of publicity by announcing the project, the funds were never found.

While I concentrated on this task, Divi was overjoyed at being invited by Andrew Logan to attend a screening at the Cannes Film Festival of *The Alternative Miss World*. Andrew and Michael, Richard Gayer and Divine shared a rented villa outside Cannes and, according to Divine's eager and enthusiastic stories on his return, created no little havoc with the paparazzi when he posed in several inches of the Mediterranean for the 'typical starlet's bathing picture' dressed only in the 'typical startlet's bikini'. Once again, although still relatively unknown in Europe, Divine attracted the media like a magnet. He loved this experience.

Divine was also thrilled to be invited as a celebrity guest to a screening of Andrew Logan's movie at the Chicago Film Festival in November 1980, and then travel to London twice in the future to attend yet more 'première screenings'. I was amused to read his own summing-up of this entire experience in an interview with England's *Face* in 1981:

When they filmed it, in fact, there was no producer, nothing. They just wanted to make it and see if there was anything they could do with it. And all of a sudden they brought me over to London again for the opening at the Odeon in Leicester Square. Then they took me to Cannes. Plus, they gave me money for being in it. I said, 'This is the greatest movie I've ever made.' I've got money in the bank from it, I've been to Europe four times! I'd never been to Cannes or St Tropez or Monaco. I loved it. I'd made this movie and I didn't know I was making it.

Despite the lessons we had learned recently in Key West and New York, it was still essential to earn cash and continue to expose the work potential of Divine. At this point, the two songs were all Divine had and – we now knew – this did not constitute a disco act. However, the club world is a small and competitive one and club owners, having heard about Divine's success at the Copa in Fort Lauderdale, were beginning to contact me in an effort to book him. We couldn't afford to turn down these offers, so we came up with a formula which we hoped would not only be acceptable to the owners, but also not disappoint the fans.

Divine would only accept a club booking if there was another featured attraction on the same night, such as a theme costume contest, a special anniversary party when drinks would be either discounted or given away, or even a Divine Look-a-Like contest. Divine would not be promoted as the *only* attraction to bring in the patrons; and there would also be some validity to using the word 'host' in advertising: Divine could host the party, or compère the contest. Although we agreed that he could sing his two songs, this would not be advertised ahead of time so that his fans would not come expecting a regular disco act. In addition, the contract would stipulate the number of hours that Divine would agree to mix with customers – in full drag, of course.

We first experimented with this formula at the lavish and hugely successful Limelight in Atlanta, Georgia. The Sunday afternoon gay tea-dance was mobbed and Divine was billed, correctly, as the Tea-dance Host. Disco Divas were rarely featured at tea-dances – consequently no one had any idea what to expect of him. Van prepared Divi at the hotel and a suitably outrageous entrance was arranged from the limousine. The boys greeted Divine as if it was Elizabeth Taylor herself visiting their hedonistic weekend partying. The more Divine created lewd and indecent poses, the more the crowd waiting outside the club cheered.

Inside the expensively equipped dance palace, Divine was ushered to a private champagne booth, where two scantily dressed young boys were introduced as 'our personal staff' for the rest of the day. Champagne flowed and the disco guests soon began to line up outside our booth, waiting for Divine's autograph.

Divine enjoyed the flattering attention and the fact that it didn't seem too difficult to sit and drink champagne for a living, surrounded by sexy young men. He signed anything on offer: the invitation cards printed for the event; the back of personal ID cards; pages in notebooks; old photos and magazine articles; dollar bills; twenty-dollar bills (not yet $100 bills – that was to come later, in Texas); bare chests; bare arms and bare legs. The magic marker had never been put to such versatile use. Eventually, a young man, clearly high on whatever was his personal escape for the afternoon, stood in front of Divine, turned around, dropped his shorts and bent over. Divine obliged, carefully dotting the two 'i's in his name on particularly tender skin. Of course, this created hilarity with those standing watching Divine's every move. Immediately, the line for autographs grew longer, but the search for suitable items to sign was now over. It seemed that every boy in Atlanta wanted the – albeit temporary – souvenir of meeting Divine, penned on pure white skin.

Inevitably, the heady mixture of amyl nitrate, alcohol, speed and non-stop Hi-NRG music was enough to encourage further exhibitionism. John Carmen, the Limelight's press representative, brought another young man, dripping with perspiration and wearing only a white jock strap. 'Tim would like an autograph from you, Divine,' John announced. Once again, Divi, well into the merriment and voyeuristic satisfaction of this unusual (but paid) task, obligingly picked up his magic marker from the drinks table and looked up. Tim stood facing Divine, grinning from ear to ear, jock strap by his ankles and his not-unworthy erection proudly pointing directly in our star's face. The penis joyfully bobbed up and down. Divi looked at me, sitting by his side. I was about to say, 'Perhaps we've gone far enough for today?', when he cut in with his instruction: 'Hold it still please, Bernard, while I sign it.'

I hasten to add that I did call it a day after that one particular effort by Divine to please everyone. But the moment was caught for posterity by a photographer from Atlanta's gay newspaper and news of the deed circulated, seemingly, overnight. It took years for us to live down that moment and I recall many light-hearted arguments with club owners when I refused to allow Divine to repeat that specific exercise in 'hospitality'. However, Divine adored telling this story to journalists whenever they would ask him, 'What exactly does your manager *do* for you on tour?'

Our new formula was a success; everyone was satisfied (to say the least). We took the show on the road.

Zoogies presents The Most Outrageous Social Event Ever . . . The Valentine's Day Empress Ball featuring the One and Only Divine, the World's Biggest Celebrity . . . at the Hyatt Regency Grand Ballroom, Minneapolis.

(The *Minneapolis Tribune* heralded this event with 'Wednesday night in the Twin Cities, we have the choice of seeing three great ladies of the stage: Lena Horne, Laura Branigan or Divine.')

Coming to Duffy's, Dayton, Ohio . . . Divine at The Prom . . . Banned!!

For the first time in Boston – Divine at The Metro – Divine will choose the Hottest Person in Boston . . . Divine will bring a Representative from the Ford Model Agency in NYC . . . Divine will spend four hours driving you crazy.

The Club San Francisco in Coconut Grove, Miami, presents An Autograph Party. A special party in Honor of the One And Only Divine . . . 'His charm and wit have made him one of the most popular and requested personalities.'

Just in time for Hallowe'en . . . A Treat for Patriotic Tricks . . . A Real Piece of The American Pie . . . Wrap Yourself in the Flag and Salute the new Ms Liberty – Divine – at the Limelight, Chicago.

Modern Enterprises presents An Evening Hosted by The Most Glamorous Being In The Cosmos – Divine – at Washington Hall Performance Gallery, Seattle.

We moved across the States, our little team – Divine, Van and I – zigzagging our way from town to town, wherever there was a venue bold enough to risk hiring Divine.

'What do I do?' Divine would explain. 'People find it hard to believe. I sit there in a dress and have drinks and sign autographs. I don't have any sort of act. It's just me. As if it were *my* party. And I make an entrance. You have to look good, at least, if you're not going to do anything else. They're fun, and people enjoy them. I never really wanted to be a cabaret artiste. What am I going to do? Go to the piano and sing love songs? People would throw tomatoes at me.'

Most of these engagements were gay-oriented; not because Divine happened to be a gay person himself (at this stage of his career he was still reluctant to talk about his personal life in interviews), but because it was the gay community that openly and proudly identified with the determination of the *female* character Divine to be, to do, to say exactly what she wanted: nothing, nobody, was going to stop her, to put her down.

As the sexual revolution of the seventies spread to mid-America, gays were finally coming out of their closets and, in a curious way, looking on Divine as one of their leaders. And not because he was in drag – it is, of course, a tiny minority of gays who actually identify with female impersonators or transvestites – but because 'she' had no shame, no compromise. When Divine was on stage, in character, they could cheer and respond to something larger than life, someone their own day-to-day convention, with which they were often still forced to live, couldn't touch. He was their idol; their hope for a more extrovert, freer world for themselves.

'If it weren't for them,' Divine acknowledged of his gay fans, 'I doubt I'd be here today. They were the first people to give me support and to give the character Divine a big push.'

As there was so much uncertainty about exactly what the promoter would get from Divine for his money, it seemed that, more often than not, the club owner was really paying just to be able to meet – and show off to his friends – this infamous star of underground movies. *Pink Flamingos* was a highly popular video rental by this time and late-night screenings, when the bar staff finished work, were a regular occurrence. On being offered the opportunity actually to import this unbelievable person to their home town, club owners just couldn't turn it down – for the sheer hell of it. But was it Divine they wanted to meet? Or Dawn Davenport? Or, most likely, Babs Johnson?

We would arrive at the local airport early in the day of the scheduled appearance. A stipulation of our contract was that a car and driver would meet us and go immediately to our hotel, where Divine would catch up on the sleep he'd lost the night before. As much as I would try to dissuade them in advance – 'Wouldn't you prefer to meet Divine when he's rested and at his best?' – it was almost always the club owner himself who would come to the airport in his car.

Divine, in the late seventies, lacked any sort of sartorial taste. He was content to dress in dirty, baggy black draw-string trousers; tent-like, stained T-shirts; a scruffy, worn pair of beach slippers on his otherwise bare feet, and then cover himself in a much-abused red-and-grey-striped wrap-around coat. Whatever the weather or temperature, he would then don a pair of sunglasses before exiting the plane. Although I could never quite understand it, I really believe most of these local bar owners across America really *did* expect Babs Johnson, 'the filthiest person alive', performing goodness knows whatever atrocious extremity as she walked off the plane. I dreaded their initial reactions, but began to anticipate them; enormous disappointment, then shock, then disbelief, then anger as they stared at this shapeless, ageless, shabby-looking individual, who, to make matters much worse, would sulk and be almost totally incommunicative, despite his host's strained efforts to please.

In the car, Divine would sit in the front passenger seat – where he had more leg room – and instantly fall asleep, snoring aggressively and, every now and again, falling sideways on to his driver/host for the day. Van Smith would either fall asleep too, or stare out of the window as if nothing was unusual. It was left for me to improvise on those nightmare car journeys from airports. Forever conscious of needing to speak well of my client (and knowing that, whatever I was to say on this ride, would be heard – and later commented upon – by the half-awake lump in front of me), I would attempt some sort of cheerful small-talk, asking questions about itinerary, ticket sales, *anything* to keep the driver from questioning me about Divine's current state.

I recall several direct threats at airports, when the club owner would, on being presented to Divine, take me aside and say something like 'I don't want some old, tired faggot impersonating Divine. I've advertised the real thing and I want *Her*. Make a phone call. Do something. My customers will never accept *That*!' Then, often, as an afterthought: 'What's his problem anyway? He looks like he's about to die.' I just had to get us to the hotel, pack Divine off into his room as quickly as possible, and then fast-talk our host into trusting me. 'Honestly,' I would plead. 'Believe me. He *is* Divine. He's just very tired from touring. Wait until you see him on stage tonight. You won't be disappointed.'

And, God bless him, they never were. If it was a constant wonderment to me over the years, it must have been like a minor miracle to many of our hosts – how that impolite, selfish old man they had met a few hours earlier, stepped on to a stage when his music started and, 'Wow! She's unbelievable, Bernard. She's fucking unbelievable.' And, with those words of reassurance – and forgiveness – they would put their arms around their lovers, or their favourite customers (often one and the same, I noticed) and excitedly, contentedly watch the show. I would have my first drink of the day.

Getting through those days was often horrendous. I frequently had to cope with making our hosts cancel cocktail or dinner parties because I insisted Divine would not – could not – socialise prior to an appearance.

In truth, it would have been difficult because of the amount of time needed to prepare, but, in any event, Divi would flatly, firmly refuse any invitations, no matter how much I would try to explain to him that it was often his attendance at these private parties that was the host's priority. I soon learned that, on stage, he would never let me down: Divine was certainly a pro. But Divi never saw any reason why he needed to be anything but himself off stage – as ugly as that might sometimes be. He put himself out for no one. But he always earned his money and the club owners always invited him back. On a return visit to a venue, I would be relieved to see that this time it was a hired limousine and chauffeur meeting us at the airport. Divine would not meet his host until after his stage appearance that night.

In July 1980 we were back in San Francisco, where the fans were wonderful and Divine at his happiest, renewing old friendships and being toasted by all and sundry as the city's favourite star. I was in my hotel room when I received a phone call from John Waters, who I had met only once, briefly, at Divi's 1979 Christmas celebration. Indeed, it had been six years since the making of *Female Trouble* and Waters himself had made only one other movie, *Desperate Living*, in 1977. Divine had to turn this down, as he was busy appearing on stage in *Women Behind Bars*. 'Bernard, what's the problem with Divine and *Polyester*?' John asked.

I was embarrassed suddenly to be speaking directly with him and with no warning of the conversation. New Line Cinema had been having brief conversations with me over the past few months about Divine's participation in John Waters's next movie. Of course, Divi was thrilled to hear there was another film on the horizon – he was aware he needed this career move badly – and he had kept me informed of several chats he had had with John about his possible role and other creative aspects. There was certainly no lack of excitement from either of us about this project, but, with his usual professionalism in such matters, Divine had insisted to John, who of course was the film's producer as well as writer/director, that all business conversations were to be had with me.

Until now, however, John had made no effort to talk with me, but left such conversations to his co-producers, New Line. Divi thought that John was reluctant to have to discuss business with me as the director felt there should be no barriers between him and his star. John knew as well that Divine urgently needed the exposure of another leading movie role. This was planned to be John's breakthrough into mainstream film-making, with New Line and others providing a $300,000 budget. No less impressive, and intriguing, was the gossip around that John had engaged Tab Hunter, 'Hollywood's golden boy of the fifties', to play a leading role. John Waters seemed to accept Divine's participation as being inevitable.

While making every effort to reassure New Line that Divine did indeed want to be in a new movie by John Waters, no commitment could be made until we entered into detailed negotiations regarding his fee, profit participation and billing. In addition, we needed a firm decision from the producers as to the dates required for Divine to film, as he was beginning to be very busy on the road and would not automatically be available. So far, no firm dates had been offered.

New Line had suggested a fee of $5,000, with no profit participation for Divine. I was told that no actor was being offered a share in the film's profits. The last conversation I recalled – some weeks before – was when I had informed New Line that their offer was totally unacceptable to Divine and that I would await further contact. I had the impression from our phone talks and from hints Divine had received from John Waters, that the producers were not only shocked by my attitude, but also blamed me entirely for the hold-up. So be it. Divine deserved a better deal. That's what a manager is for.

Or, to be precise, that's *not* what a manager is for. It's what an agent is for. At this point, I truly wished that we had a suitable agent to represent Divine on such matters, as my experience in negotiating a film deal for a star was nil (with the very limited exception, of course, of a heated breakfast at Harrods). But we had not been able to interest any reputable, well-connected agent to take Divine on as a client, so both Divi and I accepted my playing the dual roles in his business life. Divine was even further content, knowing that my handling such negotiations on his behalf saved him an additional ten to fifteen per cent of his earnings, which he would have had to pay to an agent.

I turned to my considerable experience on the other side of the table, negotiating as a producer to employ the services of actors. I recalled the frustrating times when agents would hold out on my offers and make us sweat, knowing that we needed that one particular actor. At that time, Divine and I were in just that fortunate position with regard to *Polyester*.

Not long before, on a brief visit to London, I had met with a former theatre colleague, the producer Michael White. Michael had recently had enormous success as the originating producer not only of the stage version, but also of the movie of *The Rocky Horror Show*. Eager to build his experience as a film producer, he had joined New Line Cinema and John Waters as a third partner on *Polyester*, investing a considerable amount of the required capitalisation. On learning, at our meeting in London, that I now represented Divine, he had become quite excited, telling me of his own involvement with John's film. 'I would never have invested without knowing Divine would be playing Francine Fishpaw,' he declared. Of course, we did not tell either New Line or John of this meeting while we were negotiating, but we now had the advance knowledge that they had committed Divine to the project without his deal being finalised.

'The problem is that no one seems to want to discuss details,' I gently responded to John. 'We need to talk business. Is the movie definite yet?'

'We start filming in five weeks' time, on September 1st,' he astounded me with this news. 'What is it you want?'

'What *Divine* wants,' I stressed, 'is a fee of $15,000, a minimum of two per cent of the movie's profits, first star billing above the title. And . . .' a pause, no reaction at the other end of the phone, '. . . a firm commitment to dates, including overtime pay for any additional filming required beyond the agreed dates.' Fair enough, I thought.

John's reply surprised me. 'Right. I've noted all that. Someone will be in touch,' he stated, matter-of-factly. 'We must get this sorted out immediately.'

Divine was ecstatic on hearing my news. Neither of us had believed that the film was coming this quickly. He also was extremely satisfied with my demands and agreed – with relief, I think – with my advice to him to continue to have creative discussions with John, but refuse to talk business. I believe he was on the phone to John in Baltimore within seconds of our conversation, discussing costume designs, make-up, who else was in the cast, where would he stay in Baltimore during the filming, anything and everything, like the excitable, enthusiastic actor that he was.

I was delighted; I wanted John to be reassured of Divine's personal longing to make this film and knew I could trust Divi not to get into business talk, although both John and Pat Moran tried to approach him on such matters during the forthcoming weeks. Divine would take great joy in relating to me their anger in having to deal with me and my demands.

In *Polyester* (1981, 35mm, Colour, 86 minutes), Divine played the role of Francine Fishpaw, an overweight housewife married to Elmer, a faithless purveyor of pornography. This was the first time Divine had played the role of a victim in a movie.

'That was a challenge,' said Divine later. 'It was a nice change because of being typecast – the bitchy, over-the-edge, glamorous-type figure. All of my parts were very similar to that character. So I was dying to get my teeth into something different. And to play the victim, instead of the person who was victimising. At times it was scary because I didn't know if I was doing it right, to be the underdog, when you are used to being on top of everything. It was strange.'

Francine's daughter trucks around with vicious punks (including former Dead Boy, Stiv Bators), her son is a criminally insane foot fetishist, her former cleaning woman and now best friend, Cuddles (Edith Massey) is a middle-aged debutante, her mother, LaRue, filches money out of Francine's purse, Elmer leaves to spend erotic times with his secretary (Mink Stole) and Francine's dog commits suicide by hanging itself from the refrigerator door, leaving the message 'Goodbye Cruel World'.

Francine is plagued by ingrate kids, obesity, alcoholism and French provincial furniture. Until she sees her Polyester Prince, in the form of Todd Tomorrow (Tab Hunter), her dream lover – handsome, slim, roughly debonair, and the owner of an art drive-in that shows Marguerite Duras triple bills. And he's in love with her . . . or so it seems.

'Not Since Davis! Not Since Crawford! Not Since Stanwyck or Hayward! Now . . . Divine plumbs the depths of a woman's heart,' screamed New Line Cinema's press release.

Divine started filming *Polyester* in Baltimore on 1 September 1980. His detailed Agreement with John Waters was signed on 25 August.

Our demands had been met, but only just in time. We were both delighted that this engagement would enable Divine to become a member of the Screen Actors Guild; indeed, a formal Guild contract had to be signed prior to his commencing work. This contract was brought to Divine for his signature thirty minutes before his first appearance on location. Divine was already in Baltimore having costume fittings and make-up trials, but would not have started work on location on 1 September without a signed contract. I don't think the producers believed this ultimatum, but it didn't need me to instruct my client. Divine was adamant.

'Tab Hunter's back – and a transvestite's got him,' was a New York *Daily News* headline on 23 April 1981. 'The first day he walked on the set of *Polyester* I couldn't believe it. I lost my voice. I thought, "Tab Hunter. Here." ' Divine told *People*.

'He enjoyed working with me, more than he did with any of his previous leading "ladies",' said Divine. 'He thought I was easy to work with, I didn't give him any attitude – there was no sort of "star trip". We had a wonderful working relationship. He was only in Baltimore for two weeks of filming, he was so professional. I was a fan of Tab's when I was growing up. His experience with making thirty-seven films was helpful to us. He helped me with our scenes together. He had tips for the cameraman and the lighting man, even for John. He knew little shortcuts because of his years in the business. His help was unbelievable, it saved a lot of takes. I think my best scenes in the film are with him.'

'He's super. He's like Annette Funicello gone bananas in a pasta factory . . . Divine is in a class of his own,' Tab would say of his co-star in many interviews. 'Of all the leading ladies I've ever known – Natalie Wood, Lana Turner, Rita Hayworth, Sophia Loren, Geraldine Page – Divine's got more on the ball than any of them. Who knows? Divine and I could end up being the William Powell and Myrna Loy of the eighties.' And then, as if that wasn't enough of a compliment, he would often add, 'Divine is not at all the way people think of him. He is thoroughly professional, very hard-working and a really nice man.'

They adored giving interviews and the media lapped it all up. It was a great story – the antithesis of Hollywood – although it wasn't only gay magazines that tried hard to make something more than just a professional relationship between Divine and Tab. And we were amazed that the second most frequent question that ever came up in all the disco appearances Divine would give in the years ahead was 'Did you and Tab Hunter get it together?' Divine never joked about the subject, and never lied. He adored Tab and was sincerely flattered by his genuine attention. Their relationship, however, was never more than one of friendship.

'It was great,' he told the press. 'We became good friends and went off and made another movie. I didn't go off with *him*. I went off and made another movie with him, *Lust in the Dust*.'

With its gimmick of being filmed in Odorama – as audiences file into the theatre they are handed special 'Scratch 'n' Sniff' cards with numbers keyed to scenes in the film, allowing them to experience some of the same, sometimes revolting, smells as the characters in the movie – *Polyester* opened in May 1981 in 50 United Artists theatres across America.

In Santa Barbara, California – a wealthy, conservative town full of retired folk, well-to-do students, surfers and a few Chicanos ('All of Tab's friends live there,' Divine pointed out) – the local newspaper wrote, 'With the première of *Polyester* Friday, Santa Barbara is opening a window on a strange and wondrous cinematic world – the world of director John Waters, and his substantial star, Divine. Hailing from the bowels of suburban Baltimore, these fellow outcasts exhibit a kinky twist on the Midas syndrome: everything they touch turns to disease.' And some accused them of 'selling out' with this movie.

John Waters then presented *Polyester* at the Cannes Film Festival, from where Rex Reed reported 'The hottest ticket in town is an invite to an orgy of shylock and trashy tastelessness called *Polyester*.'

Most of the critics liked Divine. Vincent Canby in the *New York Times* praised his acting abilities and said, 'He looks like Elizabeth Taylor if she'd been locked up in a candy store for three months.' Kevin Thomas in the *Los Angeles Times* decided that Divine was, 'a ballooned-up cross between Elizabeth Taylor and Miss Piggy . . . not just an overwhelming presence, but a skilled performer'. The *Washington Star* commented, 'Divine has come into his own as a character actor . . . Divine pretty much runs this show. With verve, perfect timing and an over-the-edge affection for the beleaguered appeal of poor Francine, Divine confers a measure of sweetness on the production.'

There were some who were not so keen. David Denby in *New York*: 'Divine doesn't have a trace of delicacy – she's a squalling big mama with a bullhorn voice, wallowing in put-on degradation.' Archer Winsten, who doesn't like John Waters and didn't like *Polyester*, wrote in the *New York Post*: 'His heroine-hero, Divine, is in a class by himself.' And that wasn't a compliment.

However, a sweet surprise for Divi was to read in the *New York Times*' 'overview' of the season's best female movie performances: 'A film season in which one of the funniest woman's performances is being given by a female impersonator (Divine in John Waters's *Polyester*) . . .'

'I was typecast until *Polyester* came along,' Divine commented. 'I played bitchy Bette Davis/Joan Crawford-type roles. Thank God John Waters had the guts to write a different type part for me. I wanted a challenge and *Polyester* is certainly the best thing I could have done – particularly from the critics' point of view. I think it's the first time I've been taken seriously as an actor.'

All in all, Divine had a good time making *Polyester*, but it was also a learning experience about himself, how far he had come—matured—since the last time the Dreamlanders worked together, six years earlier. Living in a comfortable apartment in central Baltimore, Divine took his work very seriously. Pat Moran and her family would be welcome visitors after a long day's filming, together with Mink, Van and a few other Baltimore friends, such as Bob and Judith Pringle. Tab would often join them, which pleased Divine, and John might call by briefly. They would eat together, talk of the day's work and gossip. But nothing much more than that. Divine didn't care to have a wild time when working. Francine Fishpaw was a demanding role and he had to concentrate each night on the next day's lines. Divine the Actor would certainly not have lived up to the image his recent club audiences had of him. But he was content.

He called me in New York nightly. I was impatient for his calls, feeling a long way from the action, but there was virtually no need for me to be by his side during the filming—he was surrounded by willing staff and friends to cater to him—and, having earned the reputation of Big Bad Manager over our negotiations, it seemed best that I did not hang around the producers each day. But I was pleased to learn how Divine needed to have these nightly chats with me, sometimes lasting over two hours. It was apparent that he was having trouble accommodating to some of the Dreamlanders' style of 'non-acting' now that he had developed his own standards and technique. Edith Massey, with her need to do takes time and time again before getting them right, was obviously annoying him.

'It got to the point where you had to realise that you just can't use people because they are your friends,' he said. 'Some of our friends were really bad actors—to the point where it's not even funny. Edith has her own style of acting. I did read one article that said that none of us could act, but we all "had large personalities". Maybe that's what it's all about—who knows?'

And he was having his own problems with John Waters. He had articulated to me a few times before about how he feared working with John when filming. He found his director very short-tempered, very impatient. 'He makes me so nervous,' Divine would tell me night after night. 'He shouts and wants everything to be exact the first time. I know I'm quick and rarely need to do a scene more than twice, but I wish he'd give me more help, more advice. I do think John takes me for granted.'

I visited him on the set only once and it was a gratifying experience. Clearly, this cast – amateur and professional – had tremendous respect for Divine and it showed in the way they greeted me too. Probably because Divine was doing such a good job as Francine, the producers put aside their grudges and took pains that day to tell me of their optimism and excitement, not only for *Polyester*, but also the offers of work Divine was sure to receive from it. John Waters was courteous and even invited me to be an extra in the scene they were filming that day – my screen début is as a doorman at Todd Tomorrow's drive-in; don't blink or you'll miss me – and I returned to New York the same evening, satisfied that Divine was held in great esteem and that I was not needed in Baltimore.

As always, I did need to plan his immediate future. $15,000 didn't go very far over a nine-week period and, whatever might or might not come to Divine as a result of this movie, it wouldn't be until at least the middle of next year. Time to start calling the clubs again.

' "John knows he can write any part for me and I can play it," Divine said. "Producers look at me the wrong way, though – to some of them I'll always be that fat drag queen, the oddity. But people are willing to take a second look." ' (*TGIF*, Chicago, 26 February 1988)

9 The First Lady of Filth

' "Yes, I'm always single. I think I always will be . . . I get letters from people all the time, and some of them are very suggestive. . . . I don't think I want to be in love again," Divine confessed. "I've been in love. You end up—at least with me it's always ended up this way—you know, not quite right. I become very possessive and jealous when I'm having an affair. One little scene after another. It makes you crazy. So I actually hope it never happens to me again. I'd rather decorate or something. Anything. You're just setting yourself up to be hurt or rejected." '

The *Advocate*, 1988

LEE WAS A FRIEND FROM DIVINE'S PAST. I was never certain if they were lovers in that earlier period of friendship. I think Divi told me they were. However, one day in New York, I was visiting my star at his home and he introduced me to his friend. Lee, Mediterranean in his dark, handsome looks, was charming, polite and about ten years Divi's junior. Divi explained that Lee would be staying with him for a while. He also told me that Lee was a French Canadian and lived with his wife, Mandy, in Key West, Florida. I noted that Lee's suitcase was already unpacked next to Divi's mattress in the only bedroom.

In the few years I had known Divine I had not been aware of his having a lover. This gave us the freedom to develop our own close relationship without the inevitable interference from those with whom one shares pillow talk.

Divine had seemed basically content with the friendship he had with his room-mate, Phillip. As with his childhood, he was reluctant to look into even the most recent past in any great detail; it was as if the past—any part of it—was long-distant history to Divine. He thought only of the future, and, when he had cash to spend, the present.

He had given me reason to believe that his friendship with his Dreamlanders co-star, David Lochary, had been, at times, a very intimate one, but his rare public mentions of him were guarded. David Lochary had died in 1977 of complications caused by an angel dust overdose. 'He was the closest friend I've ever had,' Divine would say. 'The closest friend I've ever had has passed away, and everybody else is still here.' He would pause, clear his throat, and continue. 'He was like the brother I never had. In Baltimore, when we were younger, I saw him every day. He was either at my house or I at his. As I get older, I miss him more.'

Divi's phone book was peppered with first names and phone numbers from his recent travels – Lance and Michael in Los Angeles, Rick in Houston, Kevin in San Francisco, Johnny in Miami. Names I couldn't identify and so I presumed that these were his late-night contacts or, to be more direct, his 'quick tricks'.

When on tour Divi was very secretive with me about these extra-curricular meetings. He would instruct his personal assistant to make arrangements for him and have his date come to the hotel once I was back in my room and he had showered. I did, though, know the next morning if it had been a successful encounter as I would see the trays of dirty crockery outside his door, waiting for room service to take them away. Divi loved to eat after sex and, if his friend was still fun to be around, would invite him to stay for food. The contents of the tray on the floor could give away the degree of fun my star had achieved just a few hours earlier. However, I would never meet the extra hotel guest; he would be bade farewell and furtively rushed out of the hotel before Divi made his entrance into the breakfast room.

I don't think it was embarrassment that was the reason for this secrecy. I believe it was more to do with shame. Divi didn't like my knowing of his need for sex in this manner and he was far from comfortable with these liaisons himself. He was beginning to make use of the power of fame and wallowing in his recent discovery that the benefits of such fame – even though limited and created by a grossly over-weight (and therefore generally considered unattractive) man dressed as a woman – could include an exciting accessibility to young fans who desired a more intimate, closer moment with their idol. Of which, presumably, they could brag to their friends. 'Starfuckers'.

Divine was finally satisfying his insatiable appetite for sex, although he wasn't fooling himself. He knew these hitherto unavailable bodies were using him, so why shouldn't he use them back? But Divi was an extreme romantic by nature, his heart longed for much more; on tour, he was experiencing a loneliness – a singleness – like never before. So he took enjoyment in playing lust games, but he knew it wasn't 'proper behaviour' and therefore always presumed I wouldn't approve.

Back in New York—and bored—he would often vanish in the afternoon for a few hours, feeling it necessary (it wasn't) to make me some
excuse about where he was going. I certainly didn't control his every
movement, but our day-to-day relationship at this stage seemed to include my knowing of them anyway. I soon learned that these afternoon
sessions were spent at The Gaiety, a long-established male burlesque
showroom in Times Square. Between the screenings of the latest gay
porno movies, sexy young boys would dance suggestively on a tiny stage,
in intimate proximity to the audience. After some applause, each boy
would return on his own to the stage to strip—completely—to a second
song. The highlight of these shows was their finale, when some fourteen
boys would appear together on stage, naked and with erections firmly in
place.

Of course, there were strict house rules forbidding any customers to
visit the boys in their tiny, cramped dressing room, but Divine, being a
most popular celebrity at this venue, was invited (or, if not, he would
then invite himself) to join them just as they were preparing for their
'exposure' (for want of a better word) in the finale.

Years later, when he finally discovered that I had known of these
exploits all along, he cheekily explained, 'I felt they needed my assistance
in preparation. It's the only time in my life, Bernard,' he admitted with
a sly wink, 'that I wished I had more than two hands and one mouth.'

I got to know Lee a little and started to like and feel comfortable
with him. At first it seemed as if he had just renewed his friendship
with Divi, but, after some weeks, the tell-tale signs of romance started
to show. Divi would go nowhere without Lee. I would visit them at
the apartment to discuss business matters and Lee would be allowed,
encouraged, to stay in the room—something I wholeheartedly disapproved of. But if Lee left the room, Divi's concentration would wan-
der until he returned. It was obvious. Divine was in love. Or, at least,
he thought he was in love.

Some amount of irritation on Phillip's part showed itself to me; he
frequently told me he was not happy with Lee's seemingly permanent
status in the home. Jay Bennett, too, was miserable about this intrusion
into his master's life. Lee was beginning to look after Divi with care and
attention, giving him much greater pleasure than Jay could in his method
of service. It wasn't long before Divine was having heart-to-heart talks
with me and asking for my every possible assistance in helping it 'work
out' between him and Lee.

After some weeks, Lee had to return to Florida and his work as a bartender in the Monster, a popular gay disco on the island. Divi was devastated and became impatient, more selfish than ever. I was seeing for the first time – there would be many more – how painfully jealous and possessive he was with lovers. He had no self-confidence, no sense of security in his relationships. He needed constant reassurance of commitment. And this was difficult when Lee was in Key West (with his wife) and Divine was in New York, bored and restless – and fairly broke – between engagements.

We continued to tour the States. In early 1981 our calendar included two return stops at the Limelight in Atlanta; for the second we brought Edith Massey with us and re-created on stage a brief moment (no – not *that* moment) from *Pink Flamingos*.

Then a surprise for Divine: a show at the Monster in Key West; Lee was proving to be useful too – he arranged this booking personally. I started to place stories with the national press and was delighted to see their enthusiasm. The *New York Post*, for instance:

> Divine, the 300-pound transvestite entertainer, is a bit snappish these days about Pan Am. It seems the airline lost one of Divine's pieces of luggage on a flight to Key West via Miami. Divine was to do a show that night at the Monster in Key West but when the party arrived Divine's valise containing dresses, shoes and falsies was nowhere to be found. Divine eventually got the show on with the aid of a borrowed bra (the big, economy model) and some size 10 EEE shoes. Where is the missing bag? Pan Am told Divine: 'It could be in Caracas.' Let's hope there's someone in Caracas who's Divine's size.

A short tour of Texas followed ('Do you have any idea of what to expect in Texas?' enquired a reporter. 'No, but things are big here,' replied Divine, 'and I am too, so I figured the two of us would get along'), Seattle, Boston and, of course – although he still didn't have the required disco act, but Scott Forbes was getting impatient – Studio One in Los Angeles. *Frontiers* reported:

> The line outside West Hollywood's Studio One disco looked more like the midnight-movie line-up at a showing of *The Rocky Horror Picture Show*. . . . One brave Divine fan went as far as he could to mimic his idol. Six-foot-plus, a head-to-toe reproduction. His blonde fright wig was the first to go. 'Who is that bitch?' Divine demanded. 'Bring her here!'

Everywhere he triumphed. The audiences just seemed to adore him and, the more crude and trashy he was on stage, the more they cheered and screamed in delight. Divine was learning fast. He could now pad his stage appearance to over twenty minutes, by introducing what can only be described as 'scatological Divine chat' around the two songs. In truth, by this time, his act was becoming downright filthy. In defence, Divine always insisted that his act was not intended to make any kind of socio-political statement about women, men or anything else that humans may agitate over. 'It's just good, dirty fun,' he said, 'and if you find it offensive, honey, don't join in.'

He dealt with hecklers brilliantly. The inevitable 'Show us your tits!' would be shouted from the audience. 'Show us your willy, first,' would come Divi's instant response. But also, his order. He wouldn't let it go. He discovered that the kind of guy who shouts such a boring and, in this case, meaningless request was also content to remain anonymous in his public bravado. Divine would stop his act and insist, repeatedly that the lad come on to the stage to show his 'willy' first. Of course, the audiences lapped it up, by now trying to encourage the reluctant heckler to accept the star's instruction. But Divine would also know instinctively when to drop a particular line and move on. They would rarely heckle Divine again after that experience.

'How much did you pay to get in tonight?' Divine would ask of his eager spectators. 'Ten dollars' might be the chorus back in unison. 'Well, now,' he would continue, 'that's eight dollars to see the show – ' a pause – 'and two dollars to fuck me right after. All line up outside the dressing room and I'll be here till Christmas!'

His repertoire increased at an astonishing speed. Soon, he was relating incredible, but hilariously funny anecdotes about Britain's Royal Family, which I was certain would eventually get us both thrown into jail. 'I like to pick on the Royal Family because people seem to like that, as long as you don't pick on the Queen or the Queen Mother too much,' Divine commented. 'You can say anything you want about Margaret or Anne, especially Anne . . . Princess Michael, she's fair game. But the Queen is very popular. And rightly so.'

'I just got back from England,' Divine would advise his audience, rubbing his mike under his armpit. 'And I wanna tell you about the Royal Family. There's Princess Margaret the dyke. I know, I had her last week. And the newest, most hated member of the family, Princess Di – the royal nit-wit. She's the one who fucked Charles and had the baby, right. Now they are so afraid that the baby will fall out of the crib and one of the Queen's Corky (*sic*) dogs would come along and think that it was a dog yummy and eat it up. And they'd be looking everywhere for the crown prince and where is he? Out back in a pile of dog shit and they're gonna call me up to come and find him!'

No one wrote this material for Divine – no one would have wanted the credit! It was his own judgement as to what his fans craved from him. He just made up these stories himself. It wasn't, as many suggested, just filth for filth's sake, however; rather, he was catering to his audiences' own inabilities to say out loud the things we all think at some time or another. So, just as in their adoration of the star's extremes of visual image, they came to enjoy being shocked by what he might say. The attraction of Divine seemed to lie in his colourful parody of rigid gender roles and conventional sexual morality. Even the idea of being both fat and sexy was used as a vicious vehicle of satire. He gave them Trash.

It was not without some considered thought that highly respected writers often referred to Divine as 'the modern-day Lenny Bruce' and 'the forerunner of punk'.

He quickly constructed an answer to his critics. 'I mean, it's only stuff I hear every day. Outrageous is like the Jonestown massacre, I find that outrageous for all those people to drink poisoned Kool Aid and kill themselves for who knows what reason; who will ever know? That's outrageous; and for someone to murder somebody is outrageous, I think; to take someone's life. But to walk around the stage in a dress and spout a few dirty lines, most of them very funny – I don't see what's outrageous about that.'

On stage: 'They dress me up like this, push me out on stage and make me talk dirty . . . *I love it!*' he would scream. But off stage he was more serious about it all. 'I know I possess an underlying goal to shock,' he admitted. 'I never mean to offend anyone, but rather I set out to shock people. Shock in this case isn't something bad; rather, I view it more as a new, different type of experience.'

I always felt a review of his act in the *Ann Arbor News* summed it up:

Throughout, Divine lived up to the legend if not the name, with a scatological, sexual, Anglo-Saxon barrage that, depending on your point of view, either strained the First Amendment to the bursting point, or was a real hoot. . . . Now would you call *that* the harbinger of a successful evening's entertainment? Yes, yes, a thousand times yes! Will we burn in hell for this?

Van Smith was tiring of his work. Certainly, he didn't feel challenged by the thankless task of painting Divine's face late at night. And he was specific about not accepting any other duties on his travels with us. He was only there as a make-up artist. The now frequent departures from New York were interfering not only with his social life, but also with his freelance opportunities as an illustrative designer. I don't think Van approved of the disco shows and the exploitation of the Divine character in this way. It was becoming clear that Divine needed to make new arrangements, however reluctant he was to lose Van's services. Divi was adamant that he would not accept the task of preparing his own make-up, which would take Van about one hour, and he was very nervous of trusting this essential, vital part of the nightly metamorphosis to a newcomer, a stranger.

Another problem had arisen on tour with Van. At Atlanta airport, on one of our short tours, Divi had bought a huge, fresh ham to bring home. It was heavy and would not fit into his hand luggage for the plane journey ahead. I had little hand luggage with me and happily offered to carry it for him. While Divi browsed around the airport shops, Van and I visited a bar for a drink together.

'Why are you carrying this for him, Bernard?' Van asked me, with anger. 'I'll not carry anything for him. If he wants it, it's his job to carry it. We're not his servants. You're just spoiling him. He's going to believe he's some sort of star, if you keep on like this!'

'Van,' I carefully responded, 'I don't think my offering to carry this item makes me his servant. But I do believe Divine *is* a star, or I wouldn't be risking my own career on managing him full time. And I think my job is to help persuade the public that Divine is a star. But I also believe that, in certain respects, the public want their stars to behave like they think stars should, with glamour, with magic, with mystery. Carrying a bulky, heavy ham around with him while he's recognised in the airport is not very magical. I don't think Divine can totally succeed until he actually has the confidence in himself to know he's become a star.' Van looked shocked and bewildered. 'And so, yes,' I continued, 'if you want to say I'm spoiling him, so be it, but I am quite purposely encouraging him to believe he is something special.'

Van disagreed with my methods totally. This conversation turned into a fairly ugly row between us. I understood Van's problem. The Dreamlanders was a group of equals with one leader, who encouraged them all to believe in their own importance to the group's development. To date, with the exception of the director himself, there had been no star treatment within the Dreamlanders. Now Van was having to accept that his colleague, whom he had helped create, was the star of this tiny band of entertainers on the road. Van was afraid and unhappy that he was just becoming an adjunct, a useful person to have along. As much as Divi tried to reassure his good friend of how much he truly valued his special talent, Van was clearly uncomfortable with the plans and ambitions that the performer and his manager were chasing. The Dreamlanders had always been a group, now it seemed Divine was going his separate way.

For a while, Jay Bennett had persuaded Divi to let him come along on some of these engagements with us, receiving a fee from Divine for his services as a personal assistant. Although I was still having my own problem with Jay's frequent outbursts of hysteria, he was certainly proving to be a good companion for Divi and helping to relieve his boredom with the long days on the road. Divine and I were never close buddies sharing the same interests, and in any case I was busy all the time attending to details; I was, of course, doubling as his road manager as well as personal manager. Van did not chose to socialise with Divi during the day, preferring to stay in his hotel room and to venture out on his own after the late-night shows to have unencumbered fun.

'Sometimes on the road they put you in a beautiful hotel suite with all these rooms,' Divine would say, 'and you're wandering around by yourself and you think "what fun is this? Now, if Boo-Boo and Fifi were here, wouldn't this be fun?" Sometimes I fly people in and get people to stay with me and you can sit around and laugh and have a good time and fool around with room service. Status is no fun by yourself.' In short, Divi was lonely and bored. Jay helped to fill the gap for a while. And, of course, Divi loved the constant attention his assistant would show him. He became used to having absolutely everything done for him on tour; Divine's only task was to perform. But Jay could not – and nor would Divine even contemplate the thought – do the make-up.

Van, although not wanting to let his friend down, was by now urging Divi to find a replacement, generously offering to instruct the new person in this particular make-up design. Divi knew the combination of Jay Bennett and me on tour was not a good one, and, moreover, I was spelling out to the star as often as possible that he could not afford to employ two staff on the road at this stage. For months we argued. Divi insisted that Van was irreplaceable and that he needed the services and companionship of Jay. Suddenly, a solution to the dual problem presented itself.

Lee jumped at the idea, immediately gave his notice at the Monster, flew to New York and started taking lessons from Van. Lee had a natural artistic talent and quickly completed the task to his new employer's satisfaction. Divi was happy. He now had, in one person, a touring companion, assistant and make-up artist. And lover. I was content. Lee was fun and helpful on tour, he was satisfying my client's needs (and considerably improving his moods), and we could reduce our number again to three.

In June 1981, John Springer Associates – once again hired by New Line Cinema, who were doing a great job promoting the current openings nationwide of *Polyester* – arranged for John Waters and Divine to appear on *The Tomorrow Show* with Tom Snyder. I insisted – fighting all the way with New Line Cinema – that Divine should dress as himself, not in costume. As I kept trying to explain to the unwilling marketing department at New Line, Divine was an actor, and other actors currently starring in movies, such as Robert Redford or Dustin Hoffman, would never be expected to wear their movie costume on a TV talk show. With great reluctance – and once again blaming the entire problem on me – they finally agreed.

Divine and I were delighted. It was the most important decision we had made together about his career, and, for the record, we were in total, one-hundred-per-cent agreement with each other on this matter.

'What was Tom Snyder like?' Divine would later be asked.

'He's an all-right guy until the cameras start. Like that S and M woman that was on before us, and he said to me, "She's the first person I ever met who made sado-masochism sound boring." Which I thought was a funny thing for him to say. And the camera started, and he said, "And what about the draaaag" and everything. . . . He wore more make-up than I ever wear. . . . And he was so hung up with this whole gay thing. I said, off screen, "What does this have to do with anything? We're here to talk about movies. A lot of people in this industry are gay. When they get on your show you don't bother them with all these banal questions." He was more or less out to get me after that, I think.'

Other TV talk shows followed and, together with the ever-present press attention and gossip-column coverage, interest in Divine's career was growing – sometimes from surprising, but most welcome sources.

I was discussing with an important casting agency the possibility of

Divine playing a role in an upcoming movie, *Blade Runner*, to be directed by Ridley Scott, one of Hollywood's new 'darlings' since his success with *Alien*. Divi was invited to give a private reading for the director at his Hollywood office. We flew to the West Coast – at Divine's expense – and worked solidly together for many hours on the brief pages of filmscript provided. Divi was terrified. It was the first time he had ever had to audition and, although it had been arranged in privacy and with great courtesy by Ridley Scott's office, he was a nervous wreck.

He spent the best part of an hour alone with the director. I waited outside and became as nervous as my client. Divi wasn't offered the role, but told me Ridley Scott had spent most of their time together talking of the John Waters movies and how great a fan of Divine's he was. He also asked him to read from a completely different filmscript than the one we had prepared from. Divine was immensely flattered to have been approached and humbled by this experience. Once again, I was impressed and proud of the way he had dealt with it – and delighted to note that he was beginning to be taken seriously within his own industry.

Divine attended several screenings of *Polyester* during the summer of 1981: in Baltimore, New York, San Francisco, Los Angeles and Washington DC. At each, whether in drag or not, he was greeted with huge acclaim. These openings were wonderfully orchestrated by John Waters, New Line and John Springer. They were old-fashioned movie events – and Divine was, without doubt, the modern equivalent of the Great Movie Star. The crowds offered him adoration and, in return, he gave them what they wanted: the Image.

One particular event during these opening nights remains in my mind. The movie was scheduled to première in a small, but popular art theatre in Washington DC. As the seating capacity was limited, the producers decided to have two screenings on the same night, with a break of about two hours between them. Klieg lights, lines of hopeful ticket buyers and press photographers made the evening memorably exciting. Divi entertained the first audience of the evening by making a personal appearance at the theatre in full drag.

We then hastened to his hotel suite – Divine, John Waters, Lee, Van, Pat Moran and myself – to order room service before returning to the theatre for the second screening. The waiter took our order – with Divine sitting on the floor in costume and make-up, but no wig or heels – and we waited for ages. Finally the food arrived, the room service waiter full of apologies. Our steaks were passed around and the waiter left the room. We then realised he had brought no cutlery.

We were fearful of another hour's wait for him to return and we needed to leave the hotel in twenty minutes. Divi went to his bedroom and returned with a smart, black leather hold-all. He emptied it on the floor and well over two hundred pieces of silver cutlery fell out. Some of us collect the free shampoo or matchboxes provided in hotel rooms; it seemed that Divi collected cutlery. We all laughed, helped ourselves to knives and forks and started to eat.

Immediately there was a knock on the door. The room service waiter, realising his mistake, had hurriedly returned with a tray full of silver cutlery. He seemed more than confused at the sight of us all eating. 'Never mind,' Divine reassured him. 'Just leave it all here and we'll be fine.' Divine had no shame. His collection increased.

News was spreading fast and offers for Divine's celebrity appearances were beginning to arrive unsolicited. A British promoter, Kevin Millins, called. London's most popular gay disco, the cavernous Heaven – operated by Richard Branson and his Virgin Entertainment – wanted to fly Divine in for a PA in September. They offered £500 plus all expenses, and Kevin would organise a few additional gigs, in the north of England, if we wished. Again, I explained the limitations of the act, but Kevin already was aware of the details and was extremely enthusiastic. Divine accepted.

On 24 September 1981, Divine made the first of many personal appearances in London. Heaven was mobbed. His unique notoriety had certainly spread to England by this time. But Heaven was strictly a palace of High Energy and they weren't even interested in his singing his rock 'n' roll repertoire of two songs. The manager, David Inches, informed me he wanted Divine to eat. On stage. With his friends.

An outside caterer was engaged to provide a lavish, excessive gourmet Italian meal and have it served on Heaven's stage at midnight. Divine was to invite his friends to join him. Shortly after midnight, a long, grand table, exquisitely set under blaring spotlights, was occupied by Zandra Rhodes and various other celebrity friends of Divi's. Then the Guest of Honour arrived to sit at the top of the table. *She* was dressed in a bright red, heavily sequined miniskirt. Hundreds of London's boys stood gawping, patiently waiting for something to happen. Divi talked with his friends, sipping wine and virtually ignoring his audience. The lights shone mercilessly and the Guest of Honour soon achieved what must have been a record-breaking volume of perspiration.

I watched all this with amazement. What was it about my star that would amuse and entertain all these people, just by his being there, dressed as a woman and eating? Such was his attraction; such was our peculiar ability to earn money.

There was a full hour's wait until the first (of five) courses arrived; a heavy, greasy pasta. Divine started to earn his fee by grabbing hands full of the food from the perfect china serving dishes and chucking it on to his plate – without, of course, offering it to his guests first, and then forcing it, still with his hands, into his welcoming mouth. The pasta covered his face, his hands and the miniskirt. The crowd roared, applauded, screamed with approval. And then Divine stood, burped, farted and addressed his guests loudly, so the audience could hear: 'I'm soaking fucking wet and need to shit,' he politely informed them. 'I'll be back in a minute.' I forced my way through the crowd and followed him, surrounded by bodyguards, to his dressing room. The boys reached out to touch his sweaty, clammy body as if he were royalty. I was bemused.

In the dressing room he looked at me and said, 'Right. That's enough. I've earned my £500. Now let me get out of these stinking clothes and we'll leave and go to eat somewhere together!' And so we did. Quietly, without the management becoming aware, we left through the back door. And his audience, and guests, waited patiently under the glare of the spotlights for his return – and the next four courses.

Divi started to see what a hoot his new-found career was. But we were still very aware, even though there were no longer complaints from unsatisfied customers or venue owners, that we were basically conning everyone. And how long could it last? Divine knew he was capable of giving more. But what was it, exactly, that he should give? He appeared to be very much in a field of his own. Who should he emulate? What was the next step?

We returned to the States and I continued to fill our date book with enthusiastic offers to engage Divine.

A friend introduced me to the owner of New York's La Cage Aux Folles, the travesty nightclub that had been through a period of trendy and profitable success, but was now fading. A three-night engagement was negotiated for Divine, in an effort to renew vitality in this venue. The same friend brought a young record producer, Mark Bauman, to see Divine's act, which now included three boy dancers and lasted about thirty-five minutes. Mark was impressed and told me Divine must make a Hi-NRG record to add to his act. I related to Mark our recent history of attempting to do just that.

He introduced me the following week to an associate of his, an even younger, Italian American named Bobby Orlando. I think Bobby was 21 at the time. Mark assured us that Bobby O, as he liked to be known, was already a success in the business of producing Hi-NRG records. On 9 November 1981, Divine signed an agreement with Bobby Orlando and Mark Bauman, representing 'O' Records, guaranteeing the commercial release of a minimum of two master recorded tracks.

On 24 November 1981, Divine spent a brief time at a recording studio in New Jersey, having no idea at all before he arrived as to what he would be doing. Bobby and Mark played him what they called a good, solid Hi-NRG backing track. It just sounded like a basic beat to us. Bobby scribbled some lyrics on a piece of scrap paper; he seemed to be dreaming them up as he wrote. Divi and I looked at each other, furious with this lack of attention to the recording artist and wondering, again, what the hell we had got ourselves into.

Bobby gave the lyrics to Divine and told him to start speaking them as he played the prepared music track under Divine's voice. As Divi spoke them, bewildered by what they meant, Orlando encouraged him to begin to sing them to the beat, rather than speak. Divine, in his usual, professional, eager-to-please-and-get-it-over-with way, complied to the best of his ability.

It didn't take long. Perhaps one hour. Divine had recorded 'Native Love'.

Divine's recording of the Bobby Orlando/Mark Bauman production of 'Native Love' was to become one of the most successful and popular singles in the brief but immeasurably important history of dance music in the eighties. All over the world.

' "Don't you find it bizarre that people will come along and pay money to be abused?" I asked Divine. "Oh, a lot of comedians abuse the audience completely, *horribly*, and the people love it," he replied. "They pay a lot of money to sit there and take the abuse. These are people who should probably get chained up against the wall and be beaten by their wives or husbands – but they're not capable of seeing that far, so they go and get abused by a comedian and everyone laughs at them and they love it . . . I don't understand that mentality at all, but it does exist so I take advantage of it." ' (*New Musical Express*, 12 March 1983)

10 Divine the Disco Diva

'The time is right, Divine's prime time is now. For those who want to miss his fifteen minutes, duck and cover . . .'

The *Face*, September 1984

I
N THE WORLD OF POP MUSIC, I suppose we were innocents, an eager pair of babes in the wood. Or just stupid?

Whatever, we chose not to commit ourselves to the luxury of consulting experienced music attorneys to represent Divine. My star was satisfied with my personal representation. He trusted my own qualifications to negotiate on his behalf. And he trusted my loyalty to act only in his best interests. As for me, my own experience in the theatre world with entertainment attorneys had been disillusioning. I had long ago learned that a contract is only a guideline to principles which both parties should more or less follow; that, ultimately, it's as good as the piece of paper it's written on. Engaging the services of an attorney to negotiate and prepare a contract is time-consuming, expensive and often leads to misunderstandings and tension between the two contractual parties, even prior to the commencement of their working relationship.

Divine had signed a simple, two-page document with a short-term commitment on either side. As his new record producers were not prepared to discuss any sort of advance payment against future royalties until Divine could prove his sales potential to them, I wouldn't allow him to sign anything more complicated. The Agreement was even non-exclusive; Divine was free to record for anyone else at the same time, should the opportunity arise.

He returned to the studios shortly after and recorded a second track penned for him by Orlando and Bauman, 'T-shirts and Tight Blue Jeans'. Divine had now fulfilled his commitment and we waited to see what would happen.

Orlando handled his own business negotiations and appeared also to be the more active of the two partners in the studio. His own sensibilities stemmed from an Italian culture that was distant from our own and we quickly found that we had little in common with this aggressively heterosexual, smooth-talking kid with the strangely out-of-place fifties hair quiff. We were told that he had already earned some respect in disco circles with some Hi-NRG tracks produced for a three-girl vocal group, the Flirts. He also boasted of his having been responsible for the initial successful tracks of England's Pet Shop Boys, but we gathered there had since been a falling-out with this fast-rising duo.

Bobby Orlando explained that he owned his own label, 'O' Records, and therefore he would not have to shop around for a deal, but would be releasing a single immediately. Remembering the frustration of the David Plattner efforts with 'Born to be Cheap', this news delighted us and we entered into the new recording deal with optimism. Divine had dollar signs in his eyes when advised he would receive six per cent of the wholesale price on all records sold under this Agreement.

Divi was asked how he happened to branch out into music. 'Well, I always wanted to do everything,' he would answer. 'The problem was just convincing other people to take an interest in it – producers, money people. It seems, in showbiz, if you do one thing, everyone becomes convinced that you can't do anything else.'

'Then why do it in drag?' would be the inevitable follow-up question. 'Well, drag is a secondary gimmick – it's what I started off with and it seemed to catch on,' was his careful response. 'And, in the beginning, I didn't care if I was dressed as a man or a woman or in a collie outfit. I wanted to make people laugh so hard they'd never forget me. So we did it for the shock value. Putting that image on me grabbed a lot of attention and it also seemed to click – and when something works you don't fix it. If it takes heels, a wig and a dress to do it, I'll go with it.'

As much as he hated the transvestite label and wanted nothing more than to escape from it as quickly as possible, Divine was no fool. He was astute enough to realise that he had no great singing voice. Without at this time understanding the overriding importance of the producer and production in dance music, Divine felt that it was the successful public image – the visuals – of the female character that was most likely to give him the chance to succeed in the music field. From our first day in the record business we had the good sense to insist on total control over the choice of materials and designs used on his record covers. Apart from the many pirated and unauthorised Divine singles that appeared around the world, we retained this control together and remained convinced that the colourful and often outrageous sleeves – to which Divine paid much more attention than he did in the recording studio – were responsible for at least as many sales as the record productions themselves.

'Native Love' was packaged, with an instrumental version on the B side, and Bobby Orlando's one-room New York office was crammed full of boxes of 12-inch singles. Orlando appeared to be a one-man operation, so volunteers were brought in to mail these promo discs to the DJs and clubs across the States. As he explained to us, he had to get club play started before any thought of retail store sales. It made sense to us and Divi realised he could do a lot for promotion by immediately adding 'Native Love' to his club act.

'O' Records did not appoint a press agent, but, with the media's current interest in Divine, it was not difficult for us to place our own items in the columns regarding this new aspect of his career. The *New York Post* of 29 December 1981 obliged with a headline 'Disco Disc':

> Simply Divine. In this case it's a single record, 'Native Love,' introducing the 300-pound star of *Polyester* into the recording world. Divine has signed a short-term contract with 'O' Records, a small label, and plans to do two more singles, including a disco remake of an old Dusty Springfield hit. 'Native Love' will be released late in January.

And John Springer Associates were delighted as this news certainly helped boost publicity for *Polyester* and a renewed interest from television shows in featuring Divine. On 30 April 1982, Divi appeared on the ABC network's *Good Morning, New York* at 8.20 a.m., performing 'Native Love' in outrageous drag in front of the studio living-room set of potted plants and breakfast table! He certainly had guts. The show's announcers and crew gave him the most surprising and welcome applause at the completion of his song, something very rarely heard on live TV without a studio audience.

The introduction of the song into the club act was also a revelation to Divine and a complete breakthrough for his young audiences. It was clear from the very start – although neither of us had any creative knowledge at the time of what makes a successful disco record – that Divi had a potential hit. Everywhere we went, the DJs praised 'Native Love', reporting the success they had already had in playing the song each night. Frequently, in these early months of 1982, the crowds attending Divine's shows on the dance floors would break into wild cheers as the intro to the song started on Divine's specially prepared performance dub and they would be screaming the lines, 'Step by step, slowly I turn. Step by step, come on' as he sang them. It took no time at all to learn that Divine needed to finish the act with an encore of

'Native Love' before leaving the stage. His act was now running over forty minutes.

'Native Love' instantly brought about another major change of Divine's popularity as a club act. Its success as a dance music single brought the name Divine to venues throughout the country, whether gay or not. Suddenly, the invitations to perform in principally hetero-sexual venues were arriving. Whoever this Divine person was, the club owners wanted the singer on the record to perform live. Their cus-tomers – the young, wired-up, all-night dancers packing the floors until the early hours of each morning – were demanding to see him. Booking agents we had never encountered previously – in his tours of the gay clubs – were calling and making offers. They didn't know if Divine was a man or a woman. They didn't care. They certainly had never heard of *Pink Flamingos*. Most of the time, they didn't even make the current connection with *Polyester*. They just wanted the vocalist on 'Native Love'.

The same night as the *Good Morning, New York* TV appearance, Divine was booked to appear at the Funhouse in the Chelsea area of downtown Manhattan. This particular venue was renowned for its huge, loyal support from very young Hispanic and Latino dance music lovers; its patronage was often called 'the bridge and tunnel crowd' – kids travelling in to New York for the night from New Jersey or Long Island. Although run with an iron fist by an adorable middle-aged queen called Ronnie, whom all the kids accepted and loved, it had that *anti-faggot* feel about it when throbbing with thousands of boys and girls for the night. The Manhattan police were regularly outside at 5 a.m., when the excited, energised kids spilled out into the streets, still high on the music and the night's exploits. The Funhouse had a very tough reputation. In truth, we were both very nervous of how this over-weight, trashy drag queen would be received by such an audience.

The show was scheduled for 2 a.m. We arrived at 11 p.m. for Divi and Lee to start the make-up and other preparations which, all in all, took a good three hours to complete each night. However, 11 p.m. was early for this venue and there were few on the dance floor, which was the size of a football field. The stage was placed in the centre of the floor. Access wouldn't be easy once the floor was full and, it immediately occurred to me, a hasty exit, should one be necessary, would be even more difficult. We were shown to the dressing room by a burly bodyguard, who stared in obvious disbelief at the balding, now shapeless man carrying his fright wig ahead of him.

I opened the door to find the club's DJ in a passionately intimate and totally exposed erotic liaison with a very young and beautiful blonde whom he introduced, with no apparent embarrassment, from their horizontal position on the dressing-room floor, as the opening act to Divine for that night. We hadn't been told of an opening act, but were delighted as we thought this gorgeous young female might put the young boys in a better humour for the night's star attraction. Divine and I enjoyed telling friends the story of this chance encounter as we watched our two dressing-room companions of that evening become major music superstars in the coming years.

The DJ suggested – having seen Divine's act elsewhere – that he only sing 'Native Love' that night. No 'Born to be Cheap'. And definitely no trash. Divi was happy to comply, with his simple logic of 'as long as they pay me the same fee, I don't care how quickly I get to go back home'.

Our opening act performed her one song and received a good response. The dance floor was indeed mobbed. It took four of the bodyguards to physically force our way through the youngest crowd Divine had ever played to. As he was trying to keep up with his minders – and already profusely sweating from intense nervousness and the overwhelming body heat on the dance floor – his intro to 'Native Love' started over the giant speakers. By the time he was pushed from behind on to the high stage, the crowd was already singing along with the words and waving their arms jubilantly in the air. Divine grabbed his mike and joined in. There was an audible gasp as they fell silent. These kids could not believe their eyes. They stared in shock.

Then Divi's particular magic took over. He had them spellbound, completely under his control, within seconds. He performed just as he always had done, gay club or not. The Funhouse's microphone had never been so abused, his tongue never so exposed. Even 'Native Love' that night included improvised additional lyrics from his usual trashy asides between songs. If they didn't want him to do his entire act, he was determined to pack everything he had learned from club gigs into the one song.

The cheers at the end of the song were deafening. Divi looked at me from the stage as the minders tried to help him down. 'Go back and do it again!' I screamed at him. But our DJ had already decided that. The intro to the song was back, blaring through the speakers. The noise of approval from the dance floor seemed louder, if that were possible. Divine gave even more the second time around, but you couldn't hear him screaming his lyrics through the live mike (he never, ever lip-synched). 'Native Love' had only been in the clubs a couple of months; there wasn't a single copy yet on sale in the shops. And yet these kids knew every line. No doubt about it, Divine had a disco hit.

But we had begun to worry. Exactly why wasn't the record in the shops? The clubs were certainly playing it; the DJs reporting excellent feed-back. We were even hearing of a limited amount of radio play on dance-music-oriented stations, and regional disco charts were seeing 'Native Love' climb with astonishing speed. But the disco hit wasn't much use without record royalties to follow. Everywhere we went, DJs and customers would be asking why they couldn't buy the single in the local record stores. We didn't have the answer and Divi was getting furious about it. He had demanded that I have a meeting with Bobby Orlando and Mark Bauman to discuss the situation – something I had been trying to do for some weeks now, but Orlando would avoid the issue with one excuse or the other.

However, Bobby Orlando was as aware as we were of his record's success in the clubs and he, in turn, was getting requests for more Divine product. Not keen to release 'T-Shirts and Tight Blue Jeans', he had to bring Divi back into the studios to make another record. And quickly. The life of a disco single is ephemeral. The dance-floor habitués quickly move on to the next batch of singles delivered freely by every record company to every DJ. A follow-up to 'Native Love' was urgently needed, but there was no existing contract with Bauman and Orlando. Bobby asked Divine back into the studios. Hesitantly, we decided to call his bluff and hold back until our producers talked about the distribution problems they were obviously having.

Pressed by the urgency, Orlando admitted that there was a 'legal problem' with his distributors and, as he couldn't solve it instantly, he was in negotiation with New York's Vanguard Records to handle all future 'O' Records products, including Divine. We quickly did some homework on Vanguard, finding that it was a highly respectable label making its profits from a considerable classical music catalogue. The last contemporary success Vanguard had was with Joan Baez in the sixties! However, I insisted on a personal meeting with the Vanguard chiefs and I was assured by them that they were eager to update their own image (considerably, it seemed) and would put everything they had behind Bobby O and Divine. We were satisfied.

They too put on the pressure for a follow-up single, so, with this information in hand, I agreed for Divine to go back into the studio pending the drawing-up of a new, long-term Exclusive Recording Agreement.

'Shoot Your Shot' was recorded by Bobby Orlando on 30 April 1982, the same day Divine sung 'Native Love' on live, morning TV and appeared at New York's Funhouse. The ball was rolling with speed.

Bobby Orlando briefly mentioned at the studio that Mark Bauman was no longer involved with production of Divine. Despite our questions, we were never offered an explanation. On meeting Bauman personally some months later, I discovered that it had been a one-sided decision and that Bauman planned legal action against Orlando for excluding him from a new contract. We never heard anything further of this dispute.

With the sexual implications of its lyrics and its repetition of the Donna Summer-like pumping bass, 'Shoot Your Shot' was greeted by DJs and clubgoers as a kind of sister record to 'Native Love' and immediately began a similar speedy climb to club success. The new song was greeted with unanimous approval by those coming to see Divi perform, although we noted that the small number of music journalists who bothered to notice Divine's growing popularity on the disco charts – mainly magazines specifically written for Hi-NRG enthusiasts – were commenting on the extreme similarity between Divine's two recordings. But what did we care? Unlike the reviews for his movie roles, Divine had never given a thought to being reviewed in the music press. He wasn't thinking of achieving legitimacy, respectability, in the world of pop music. He just wanted to earn a fortune from it. Once Vanguard started distributing 'Shoot Your Shot', he thought, the money would start arriving. Why, however, was Vanguard taking so long?

Lee had kept his home in Key West and would stay with Divi in Manhattan only when another club gig was imminent. If there was a break of more than a few days, Lee would return to Florida and Divi would provide yet another air ticket for him to travel back north when next required. Principally because of Lee's presence, but also from his newly created cross-over status from freak gay club attraction to genuine disco star, Divi was enjoying touring a great deal more and was a little more fun to be with.

The tours of the States – I would usually try to arrange batches of six or seven engagements within a ten-day period – were hectic as we still needed to limit our little team to three in number. Lee doubled as personal assistant to Divine and sound technician, working alongside the club's DJ (or, when we were really fortunate, a professional sound engineer) in operating the all-important backing tape we provided in its carefully planned order of songs. Lee knew when to stop the tape for Divine to launch into one of his trashy monologues, and soon learned regular cues from Divine as to when the next number should start. Most disco artistes only sang and therefore just required their tape to play from beginning to end, without any breaks. The club DJs would have no idea how to control Divi's particular act, which he performed with his usual talent of split-second comic timing. The job of our own sound technician had therefore become more and more essential as Divi introduced further recordings into his act, and Lee became reliable in this additional task.

I was now working full-time as Divine's career manager, booking agent and, when on tour, road manager.

Divine performed at night and concentrated the rest of his energies on catering to Lee's every need. It was odd – and embarrassing – to see Divi struggle up from his seat as our plane came to land in order to get Lee's jacket from the overhead cupboard and help him into it, prior to any other move taking place. And heaven help the club owner from Divine's wrath if Lee's bottle of bourbon was not clearly on display as we arrived at each dressing room. Daytimes were now frequently planned between them for any potential sightseeing Lee might enjoy, something Divi had previously had absolutely no interest in doing. Although I found his displays of romanticism touching, and was of course delighted to see how his love affair gave him this increased enthusiasm for touring, Divi conducted this area of his life with his regular selfishness and lack of sensitivity towards others. I was now excluded from all but essential conversations and meetings. Divi was friendly and co-operative as long as my requests – his commitment to earn his fees – did not interfere with his spending time at Lee's side.

Lee appeared to be absolutely genuine in his affection for my star (I felt a parental protectiveness in this regard) and certainly went out of his way to please Divine. They shared a hotel room each night; other late-night visitors to Divi's room were, for the time being, a thing of the past. The only immediate difficulty this caused was Divine's lack of interest in spending any time after his shows in greeting his fans. I realised that his previous enthusiasm in doing so was principally to allow him the opportunity of meeting someone for a sexual tryst later in the night. Now this was no longer necessary, his patience for what I considered to be a major part of his contractual obligations was thin, whatever he might claim. 'Let's face it, you've got to keep the fans happy,' Divine would always tell journalists. 'I've heard actors say "I don't owe them anything." It's not true. You owe them everything.' Fortunately, Lee would assist me in encouraging–sometimes forcing– Divine to practise what he preached.

Matters played perfectly into Divi's hands when Phillip Miller invited a new roommate, Ed, to share the apartment at East 58th Street. Divine immediately announced that his continuing presence there would be an imposition and that he had therefore decided to move– lock, stock and barrel, and therefore at considerable expense–to Key West, Florida. It seemed that Divi was not yet content with his share of Lee's attention.

A suitable apartment was rented, Divi's worldly goods trucked to the Keys, and, soon after, Lee and Divine became room-mates. Predictably, Jay Bennett followed to take on the paid position of home help; cleaning, cooking and shopping–and once again offering his master the luxury of doing virtually nothing but share lazy, sweaty, romantic times with his love. It should have been ideal, but, as always, Divine did not count the expenditure. That was left to me and Divi wanted no conversation about it.

On 12 July 1982, a new Agreement was signed between Divine and 'O' Records and Visuals Ltd, giving Bobby O an exclusive deal with his vocalist for the next year, plus four further one-year option periods under specific conditions. This time the document was nine pages of close typing and we still chose not to use the services of an attorney. In fact, the reason it had taken nearly three months to complete is that I had to renegotiate–and subsequently rewrite–almost every clause of the ludicrously one-sided and irrelevant 'standard contract' Bobby had initially presented to us.

By the end of the summer, 'Native Love' was disappearing from the disco charts and 'Shoot Your Shot', backed with the fabulous 'Jungle Jezebel' on its B side, was riding high, but still no records in the stores. I became convinced that Vanguard Records had no interest whatsoever in this controversial new recording artiste they had recently inherited. Whatever the excuses, an important clause in our new Agreement with Orlando was that Vanguard would *guarantee* distribution and I needed to excite the ageing, conservative bosses; get them out of their stuffy offices and into our real world.

In September 1982, Divi and I agreed he should take a calculated risk. Since the 1980 Valentine's Day Massacre of his career at the

Beacon Theatre we had avoided any overt exposure in Manhattan, limiting appearances there to discos that didn't undertake major advertising campaigns, thereby only relying on their regular patronage to attend a Divine appearance, involving little risk.

We decided to play the Ritz, a 2,000-capacity hall in the East Village, noted for its rock 'n' roll concerts by the famous and not so famous (and had-been-famous), and the only suitable venue for rock bands to play in Manhattan before they graduated to the arena status of Madison Square Garden. We would go all out with an advertising and promotion campaign that would let his New York fans know that, without doubt, their star was back again.

It was unheard of for a disco singer to appear at the Ritz. We engaged a musical director, who brought together a band of musicians to replace the backing tapes for the occasion. We hired a team of male disco dancers and female back-up singers. With all their help, Divine and I directed, choreographed and designed his first rock concert, albeit with Hi-NRG music as the content. And, as far as the word can be applied to his particular material, we *refined* the anecdotes and monologues to pad a fifty-minute show. 'Born to be Cheap' and 'The Name Game' were brought back, to join 'Native Love', 'Shoot Your Shot' and 'Jungle Jezebel'. And, for the first time and out of necessity, he performed 'T-Shirts and Tight Blue Jeans'.

The promoters at the Ritz would not guarantee Divine a fee as they had no confidence that he would draw, so we reluctantly had to agree to accepting a percentage of the door receipts. The Ritz office noted on its staff advisory sheets an estimated attendance of 300. I carefully prepared and mailed out VIP invitations to those for whom we were doing all this: Bobby Orlando, the Vanguard Records executives and a few other important people we knew within the music industry. Just over 1,500 fans turned up. The Ritz was taken by surprise. Divine was magnificent, giving encore after encore. The show lasted just over one hour.

Bobby Orlando failed to attend. No one came from Vanguard Records. What the hell was going on? A show-down was called for.

However, Divi had made a triumphant return to New York. The risk had paid off. Even Phillip Miller loved it and praised Divine. Television's popular, off-the-wall TV talk show, *Late Night with David Letterman*, was eager to interview Divine about his new recording success. Divi had previously appeared on this show, with John Waters to promote *Polyester*, but had been overshadowed by his director. The opportunity of this exposure was indeed timely; if our record label would do nothing to promote its star, then we would just have to do it ourselves.

'Good afternoon, Mr Jay, my name is John Seine,' announced the soft, accented voice at the other end of the phone. 'Would Divine consider coming to Holland in the near future to promote his current chart hit here? I'm a booking agent and would be happy to arrange a few shows to make the visit worth his while.'

Mr Seine then offered me the unexpected news that 'Shoot Your Shot' was climbing fast up the club charts in Holland and was about to break into the regular pop charts. In his exclusive recording agreement with 'O' Records, Bobby Orlando had the right to licence his product as he wished to overseas territories, despite the lack of developments in the home country. It seems he had successfully negotiated a deal in Holland. The Dutch distributors were most eager to use Divine for a few days for press interviews and television appearances. They had approached John Seine to contact me with an offer.

As soon as I was off the phone with Holland I called Key West. 'Do you fancy going to Holland for a few days soon?' I enquired nonchalantly, without explaining anything.

'Holland!' Divi growled. 'Where the fuck's Holland?' I believed his ignorance. I don't think geography was his strong subject at school. 'It's a small country near to England,' I heard myself rather stupidly explaining 'And it seems that you've got a hit record there and they'll pay you to do your act.' A few minor details were discussed and he asked if he could call me right back. I understood – although he wouldn't actually say as much to me – that he wanted to consult with Lee before making a commitment.

Ten minutes later: 'Yeh, great, man. Let's go!' was his decision. 'And Lee tells me they have a queen there too.'

I couldn't resist it. 'Actually, Divi, they've got lots of queens there. You'll love it.' And off Divine and Lee went to Holland for five frantic days of interviews, TV spots and live shows, promoting 'Shoot Your Shot'. John Seine provided a Dutch road manager. They were based in Amsterdam, where Divine quickly discovered that smoking pot is legal.

His hosts, Break Records, the booking agents and the enthusiastic boys and girls of Holland treated Divi as pop star royalty. He loved it there and couldn't wait to go back, as John Seine had suggested, early in 1983. 'I could live there happily,' he told me on his return to the

States. 'They're all so liberal, so switched on. And those guys who look after you. They're the best.'

Of course, he couldn't have foreseen how useful and what a turning point this charming little country would prove to be for his career. Or how much he would hate going back there within the next three years.

'Divine doesn't care about the "sexual preferences" of his audience as long as they enjoy the performance. In Holland, he explains, the majority of the fans waiting at the backdoor are young adolescent girls, "they scream and giggle at me like I'm Barry Manilow or something". In places like Britain the following is much more cult . . . half gay, half "post punk" underground.' (*Gay News*, 12 August 1983)

11 Spend . . . Spend . . . Spend

'Today Divine is dressed like a banker in dark suit and striped shirt.
"Well, I was on a big chat show in the States and he said, 'You're a
transvestite,' and I said, 'I'm not, I'm an actor and entertainer,' and
he said, 'So, if you're not a transvestite, why are you sitting here in a
cocktail dress?' and I thought, well, he's got a very good point there.
It was the last time I made an appearance in drag that wasn't my own
show." '

Time Out, 6–12 June 1985

OR THE NEXT FIVE YEARS Divine would be one of the world's most
travelled entertainers. 'With the record career, he was in the air
more than an astronaut,' commented Pat Moran.

He took Divine the Female Character around the world
and achieved fame—sometimes respect, almost always notoriety—but
certainly fame. His dance music recordings were to become either
hits or curiosity items in places Divine had often never heard of and
undoubtedly never dreamed of visiting. His passport (which when
renewed in 1985 contained both names: Harris G. Milstead and
Divine) was crammed full of entrance and exit visas and work
permits.

As promised, John Seine's company, Europop, brought Divine back to
Holland early in 1983 and the enthusiastic recording artiste launched
into two months of touring—performing every night—that was very
quickly to turn into a wearisome chore. The itineraries were mind-
boggling. Divine soon became Europop's most sought-after client. Neither John nor I could resist accepting the offers. Divine had waited for
this all his life. He was in demand. Reasonably good fees were being
negotiated for his disco act. He took on everything, with no idea of the
amounts of energy, concentration and discipline that these tours would
demand from him.

Lee accompanied Divi, together with Hans, the Dutch road manager
who soon became a friend and enthusiastic supporter of his highly
unusual road companions. I turned up every now and again, commuting
between Europe—to keep a personal eye on my star and try to unravel
any complications he had involved himself in since my last visit

– and the office (my home) in New York, which, by now, was a full-time operation looking after Divine's interests.

The trio was again based in Amsterdam, from where they would travel by car each day to that night's performance venue. Often the car journey took over three hours in each direction, entailing an 8 p.m. departure from the tiny hotel (no luxury yet for Divine) and a drive in darkness along never-ending, flat motorways until they would arrive, either in a tiny village where the one disco would be the only sign of life around, or, more often than not, at a huge car park in the middle of nowhere. If access through the car park could be negotiated, in the middle of it would be found a throbbing, pulsating warehouse. The noise would be deafening.

Hans, who spoke only limited English, did not provide detailed itineraries such as Divine was used to receiving in the States. The lists from Europop would itemise only the date and town for appearances. Despite many requests from Divi and Lee – and angry demands from me – no further details were forthcoming. They were in the dark both literally and metaphorically on these long, tedious car journeys. When asked how long the drive would be for that night, Hans would give his stock response. 'Not too long. Two hours. Perhaps three.' 'What time is the show scheduled for?' Divi would ask, being used to performing on time in America and believing the answer might give him a better idea of the journey time ahead of them. 'When we get there,' Hans would reply. 'Shows go on once the star is ready.'

Divine preferred to prepare his make-up back in Amsterdam, so these car journeys offered the Amsterdam tourists the bewildering sight, as the boys left the city each night, of a huge, grotesquely painted face with bobs of white hair on an almost bald head, body wrapped in a dirty blue cotton robe, eyes closed and snores drifting through the open car window (to allow any breeze to blow on the heavy make-up). Frequently, when the car came to a halt at a red light, those in the car at their side would stare in curiosity and take photographs. Divi couldn't have cared less. He just had no concern about his public image when not on the stage. He seemed to take a perverted delight in displaying his boredom and intolerance with this method of going on the road.

Very little conversation would take place, even on a three-hour journey. Hans played his choice of music on the cassette deck and Lee would drift into sleep or stare through the window at the cruel, bleak, infinite darkness surrounding them. Again, Divine's own lack of leadership was responsible for these being unhappy times. He never changed this attitude prior to shows.

The reaction to Divine in Holland was a revelation. The shows in Holland were mobbed with adoring kids. Divine was given ovations every night and the lines outside his dressing rooms would seem endless.

Within a few days a decision had to be made to limit autograph signing to thirty minutes after each show. Divi would quickly change out of the dripping, skin-hugging female clothes into his loose-fitting slacks and T-shirt, wipe off the now ruined, running mess of colours on his face, place a filthy towel around his shoulders – to soak up the sweat – and position himself in a safe corner of his room, protected by a table. He would never greet fans in costume. 'I'm not a transvestite,' he would time and again insist. 'A transvestite is someone who wears women's clothes all the time. My favorite part of drag is getting out of it. Drag is my work clothes. I only put it on when someone pays me to.' Now the 'second show', as we called it, could begin.

Of course, fans expected the Bitch, the over-painted exaggeration of humanity. They would burst into his room, screaming their own ideas of suitable obscenities and throw themselves at the star, hugging, kissing and releasing all the extrovert, exhibitionist energies within them. Naturally, the previous forty minutes of stage performance had encouraged this behaviour.

It's understandable why they assumed Divine would want them to behave like this. But, in his laid-back, anti-social manner, he hated these raucous displays. Lee and Hans would restrain them as much as possible, reassuring them that the gentle, quiet, shy man behind the table was indeed the one they were waiting to meet. Divine would quietly ask their names. With hardly a glance in their direction, he would write the names on a photo and sign it 'with love'. The next two would then be ushered in for the same process. Photographs with their star – often pleaded for – were definitely not allowed.

Back in the car for the return drive to Amsterdam, his mood would gradually change. Now work was over – and his ego suitably boosted – he was the livest wire in Holland. No one slept on the return journey, whether they wanted to or not.

We came to look forward to these good times. And – I suppose partly from sheer relief – we would adore those moments when Divine's mood dictated that we must all share in his happiness and battery-charged enthusiasm for life. Divine had a way of making people laugh, when in private, that was infectious. He would tear people to pieces in a caustic, but hysterically funny manner. Usually, on these long return car trips in the early hours of the morning, he would choose to criticise those he had just worked with – the club owner, the DJ, the doorman, even some of the fans – and would astonish me by the explicit and impeccably judged detail with which he could dissect them, even though one would have thought he had hardly noticed them to judge by his behaviour only hours earlier. This particular brand of his humour wasn't cruel. It wasn't even bitchy. It was his way – through laughter – of perceiving those around him. And, more often than not, he was right on target.

I recall with fondness many long rides when Hans would find the local late-night music stations on the car radio and we would all sing along to the latest chart hits, waiting, hoping that a Divine record would be played. And sometimes they would be. Then Divine would open the windows, sing in full voice with his own recording – and repeat all those body and limb motions of his act that it was possible to re-create in the tight seat-belted restraints of Hans's car. Now Divi was out of costume and make-up, it was so wonderfully inappropriate to watch this bulk come to life in this way, and we would all be in tears of laughter before long. Should we pass a motorway service station that still served hamburgers at this late hour, the cafe's patrons would be treated to the most extraordinary display of excessive campery. These private shows were great fun to observe and I often wished those who had caught a glimpse of him early in the evening, asleep and disdainful, could see him now.

If only Divi could have tried more to share others' moods, to adjust to his companions' needs. He was the most wonderful company to be with when he wanted to be. But, sadly, only when *he* wanted.

The success of 'Shoot Your Shot' spread quickly to Belgium, Germany and Switzerland. And everywhere the record went, Divi soon followed. It seemed that wherever there was a discotheque playing Divine's records, John Seine would arrange for him to appear. For a fee.

Within no time at all, Europop was sending itineraries with two shows on the same night, in different venues. Although Divine had always refused to do this when asked in the States, he took on the task in Europe, and Lee had to quickly devise a means of patching up the make-up for the second show of the night.

On one such hectic occasion, Divi had played an 11 p.m. show at a club in Holland. The second show, scheduled for 2 a.m., was at a venue in a village in Germany, about 150 kilometres' distance from the first. Divine was rushed into the car without signing autographs at the Dutch club and, while Hans was driving, Lee desperately tried to repair Divi's face, knowing there would be little time once they had arrived. Divine was sitting in the back of the car, dressed in a chartreuse-coloured miniskirt and with a freshly painted face, his wig and heels held by Lee at his side. Hans approached the Dutch–German border and Lee handed his passport to him; they had been through this routine several times now and were used to the formalities involved. At this moment, Divi realised he had forgotten to bring his passport from the hotel in Amsterdam, many hours away.

Hans explained to the officer at the border gate that they were in a terrific rush to get to the next venue and that they were only going to be in Germany for a matter of a few hours. Couldn't he just allow them to go through? Divine was doing his usual escape from this bothersome reality of life by sleeping and, of course, snoring.

'It's Divine,' Hans said, hoping the officer might recognise him from the television and press publicity he was receiving in Germany. The officer peered through the back seat car window and shook his head in confusion. Divine, without opening his eyes or moving his face, which securely rested in its usual position on his chest, grabbed his fright wig from Lee's lap, placed it precariously on his head and continued to snore.

'Ah, yes. Divine! Divine!' the officer delightedly exclaimed, now recognising the more familiar image of the passenger from his recent TV appearances. The car was waved on royally with no further trouble. Divine, cunning as ever, knew the answer, but had no intention of getting into social conversation. On their return, however, at about 4 a.m., with Divi in his fun mood, the same gate officer was patiently waiting, with about a dozen autograph books at hand. Divine immediately got out of the car, in blue dressing robe and clean face by now, and signed everything with personal inscriptions.

He told me that it was this experience that persuaded him he was now a star in Europe: a famous face. But, it seemed, only with his wig on.

Back in New York, I had been receiving nightly calls from Divi complaining bitterly about the endless car journeys and the packed schedule. He was exhausted after two months of being on the road. He begged for a break, a holiday. But he was getting deeper and deeper into debt and I knew he couldn't afford to stop working while the offers were there.

Divine had not had the luxury and convenience of a credit card since those times when, as a teenager, he used his parents' cards. I had had no choice but to apply to American Express for a credit card in his name now he was on tour without me always by his side. In America I had taken care of the bills on tour, carefully allocating him a reasonable amount of cash to spend on himself. But these current European tours were so full of last-minute problems and hiccups that it was essential that Divine should have his own way of charging an expense, should a hotel or an air ticket not be prepaid as instructed. On receiving his first American Express card he also received a firm lecture from me about using it only for genuine tour expenses – and keeping the receipt slips carefully so I could be aware of any expenditure involved. He agreed politely and thanked me for my concern and assistance in establishing his credit.

Then all hell broke loose. Divine was truly the proverbial bull in a china shop. The little boy in the toy store. Divine finally had the one accessory he cherished; the ultimate proof, to him, that stardom had arrived. The credit card.

And his first task was to clean up his image. At the age of 38, Divine rediscovered the sartorial elegance and expensive tastes that his mother had described his having as a child. His ability to purchase what he desired quickly led him to London's Savile Row and the famed English tailor to the stars, Tommy Nutter.

'I was in England a lot, touring and doing records and things,' he explained. 'I needed a suit and I hadn't worn one in ten years or so. I went to a couple of people who wouldn't fit me because of my size. I went to Tommy Nutter who does all of my friend Elton John's clothes. Now, my men's clothes are traditional. I don't buy trendy clothes. I buy updated classics – double-breasted, three-piece suits, slacks and either T-shirts or regular shirts,' Divine would love to inform reporters. 'Everything is monogrammed. I used to hate that more than anything. Now there are Ds on everything. It started out as a joke and now, if it doesn't have a D on it, I wonder why.'

Divine also discovered sales counters in Harrods he had not dare go near before. And the joys of Bond Street. 'And what does Divine do when he is in England?' a journalist enquired. 'Shop,' was Divine's instant response. 'I like to cover the area between Harrods and Fortnum's. All over Bond Street. My feet just take me there. The first time I went to Fortnum's, I thought there was a wedding party in there. Then I realised they were the salesmen in tailcoats.'

He became a regular and welcome visitor at Maud Frizon Shoes. 'I was behind Imelda Marcos one hundred per cent,' he would declare. 'I don't know what the big deal was. I have forty-six pairs of shoes and I'm quite proud of it. That's just men's. I didn't even count the heels. I guess I have a dozen pairs of those.'

However, Tommy Nutter charged about £1,000 for a suit tailormade to Divine's requirements. And Divine ordered five at a time. His Maud Frizon shoes were never less than £250 a pair. The tailored shirts he was now ordering from Bruce Cameron Clarke by the dozen – suitably monogrammed, of course – were averaging £150 each. Not to mention the silk scarves and handkerchiefs from Turnbull and Asser, the XXXL silk boxer shorts from Crolla, the fifty or so bow ties from Harrods. And the £10,000 black mink, floor-length, wrap-around fur coat he had recently commissioned in New York.

He would establish a store credit line by paying an initial deposit with his American Express Card. Then he would instruct the store managers to forward future invoices on a regular basis to his personal manager in New York, handing them my business card. It was some months before I became aware of this spending spree and then it was too late to avoid it. He had carefully instructed both Lee and Jay to hide these new purchases from me if I visited him on tour or at home. He had thrown away the receipt handed at the time of purchase to the customer. By the time American Express's brown paper parcels started to arrive at my office (their usual envelopes not being large enough to contain the number of dockets he had signed that month) and I received the stores' invoices, accompanied by charming letters confirming the credit line and thanking Divine for his patronage, he had run up tens of thousands of pounds' worth of shopping bills.

John Seine was negotiating the top fees he could for Divine, but the clubs in Holland and Germany knew the performer also needed this exposure to boost record sales and therefore would not pay any additional expenses above the gross fee agreed. Therefore, from such fees, Divine would have to pay my commission of twenty per cent, Europop's commission of ten per cent, Lee's weekly salary, Hans' fees, including the use of his car, the hotels bills, the transatlantic air fares, and his own day-to-day living expenses. These, of course, were all in addition to the basic costs involved – new dresses, wigs, make-up, heels, tights, photographs, etc. – in just *being* Divine.

I calculated that, on these early European tours, he should net about 40 per cent of the gross fees, after touring expenditures. This was not considered at all unreasonable as these personal-appearance tours were principally to boost promotion for record sales. They were not intended to be the performer's sole method of making a living, and certainly not the instrument by which the performer could instantly and dramatically improve his lifestyle. From this 40 per cent for personal use, Divine had to put aside funds for his rent in the States, his huge long-distance phone bills and his living expenses when out of work. Not to mention the US taxes payable on his income.

I soon learned that, despite my urgent and desperate efforts to get Divine to understand and acknowledge the details of the essential expenditure, his basic philosophy was that, if his contract stated Europop was guaranteeing total fees for the current tour of, say, $75,000, then he had $75,000 to spend on himself. He could see it no other way. Even the fact that he would commit over $100,000 during that period didn't seem to disturb him. That was for his manager to take care of, was his attitude. But he wouldn't listen to his manager.

Of course, we were waiting for the record royalty cheques, a common problem for recording artistes. Financial statements, together with relevant payments, were due every six months, based on the previous six months' sales. Since it was November 1981 when the first contract was signed with Bobby O, we had every reason to be surprised when, by January 1983, we still had not received any sales figures, let alone money, and we learned of a dispute with Vanguard Records that, much to our frustration, was holding up any sort of distribution in the United States. We were now travelling through Europe, seeing the records on sale in the stores and high up in the charts. This must translate, we reasonably supposed, into money.

In early 1983 Divine and I flew into Katwijk aan Zee in Holland to receive his first Gold Record, for sales of over 100,000 copies of 'Shoot Your Shot' in Benelux. It was an exciting and memorable moment for Divi, but, as he walked off the stage from collecting his treasured disc, he whispered to me, 'Now let that bastard in New York tell you we haven't sold any records.'

During the time we had been spending in Europe, both Divine and I had become friendly with the two Pieters of the Company of Two Pieters, the publishing company in Holland to which Bobby had licensed the product, and with Jan van Nieuwkoop and Gert Van De Bosch from Break. They had worked resourcefully and enthusiastically on the promotion and marketing of their new artist and we had appreciated the teamwork – together with that of John Seine and his colleagues at Europop – that we had not experienced, but had so often longed for, in the United States. They were obviously all having success with Divine and needed to retain his friendship and our loyalty. The Two Pieters insisted, on my questioning, that they had some time ago paid a good advance to Bobby and had since then provided him with up-to-date sales figures and payments when due.

It was clear we were in a classic chicken-and-egg situation. Divine's sole income was from these disco appearances. The demand for him could only stay at this current level if further successful recordings followed. Break was already screaming for a follow-up to 'Shoot Your Shot'. We could not afford to refuse to go back into the studio, as Divi was in need of a new hit. So, while I met with 'O' Records' accountants (who declared they themselves were having difficulty in securing the relevant figures from their client, in order to supply them to us), Divine had no choice but to return to the studio in New York and record yet another totally unprepared single, 'Shake-It-Up'.

If 'Native Love' was considered to be the sister record to 'Shoot Your Shot', then 'Shake-It-Up' was incestuous. Bobby O assured us that his licencees in Europe were requesting exactly this similarity in new product. That was not what we were hearing or reading on our travels. The European music journals were frequently critical: 'A series of forgettable, grunting Plain Joke workouts written by Bobby O', was how one described Divine's records. 'The illustrious "Shake-It-Up" adds a richer mayhem to the well-trod "I Feel Love" bassline formula. The triplets are identical in all but name: why compose a dozen unique tunes, when one unashamedly unoriginal idea may achieve a finer bouquet?' was the sarcastic question posed by another.

On being interviewed, Divine openly admitted, 'I think Bobby's music is more or less the same. And this was a complaint that I was constantly hearing from fans. "Shake-It-Up" sounds like "Native Love", which sounds like "Shoot Your Shot", and I got sick of hearing it, you know. Running around apologising for my music – I don't have to do that.'

'Shake-It-Up' was delivered to Holland and quickly released. Divi did more TV promotion, lots of club dates and the record appeared in the charts. But sales were not as good as the previous two and the chart positions didn't climb so high. It was a success – the third in a row for Divine – but everyone was complaining of the identical nature of the songs. The Dutch team insisted that Bobby O quickly bring Divine back into a studio to produce something original and contemporary, or, they confirmed to us in unison, it was unlikely that Divine's recording career in Europe could continue its current momentum.

Divine's boredom and frustration were showing in his work and his attitude to those working with him. I was receiving gentle, but repeated complaints from Europop about lack of co-operation and shows that were being 'walked through'. Divine had started to refuse to do TV promotion on the same day as a club appearance. TV promotion was, of course, an essential priority in record marketing. Therefore, quite correctly, John Seine had decided to cancel the club engagements. Divi was now furious with him because it meant a reduction in his fees.

Additionally, the previously friendly and pleasant working relationship with Hans was now showing strain due to Divi's insistence that Hans give him more and more cash to spend on tour, contrary to my instructions to Europop – on behalf of, and having been agreed with, my client. In turn, I was now complaining to John, with whom I valued an excellent business relationship, that his monthly transfers of money to me in New York were seriously under expectations. Each time, when presented with detailed figures from John, I was to discover the sole reason: Divine had demanded cash from Hans that he knew should have been returned to the office to cover expenditures.

Divi's overspending was getting very serious and, at this rate, would get him into deep trouble in no amount of time. I needed time with him to talk about it. And he needed a rest from the tough schedule in Europe. But I knew I had to approach this subject carefully and when his own humour had improved. Moreover, he couldn't possibly afford to take the requested two-month holiday just now, without any income during that period.

I hurriedly arranged a working visit to South Africa, accepting an offer from Patric van Blerk for Divine to be the star Easter attraction for five nights at his disco, Zipps, in Johannesburg. In addition, Patric would arrange a few other disco appearances in other cities, allowing a two-to-three week holiday in South Africa for Divi and Lee together, with all expenses paid. It seemed like a good compromise.

Patric was an owner of Principal Records, a small South African label that had recently licensed Divine's recordings from Bobby Orlando – for an advance payment against royalties. Another fact we had not been aware of. How many other territories around the world had bought the product too?

I insisted upon – and immediately received – confirmation that Zipps maintained a multi-racial policy in its staffing and membership. I joined Divi at the end of his tour in Europe and flew with them overnight to Johannesburg, stopping for a brief 45 minutes in Nairobi, where Divine bought four shopping bags full of tourist souvenirs at the airport's only shop. It was no surprise that they eagerly pinned his signed publicity photo on their wall as he left, although, in truth, they had no idea who he was. Except a Big Spender.

Patric van Blerk and his partner Charles Coetzee established an immediate rapport with Divi. His Holiday Inn suite included a refrigerator stuffed full of two-litre bottles of Coca-Cola. Supplies of marijuana were his for the asking. They even planned a hash cake for tea the next day. Divi relaxed and began to enjoy the additional comforts available. And, once again, the intense media interest in him.

A press conference was held prior to his opening night at Zipps. 'I don't mind being here in South Africa,' he replied to the obvious question in those days of performers boycotting the country. 'If politics dictated, no entertainer would be able to perform anywhere in the world. Just show me a single country in the world that does not have political and racial problems.' Somewhat naive, but at least he was facing it head on. 'In my act I knock these sacred cows of society. I make people laugh at them and also think about them,' he continued. 'I'm an entertainer, not a politician, but that doesn't stop me from making comments in my show.'

The club appearances were packed and received with the customary wild and energetic enthusiasm by Zipps' mostly gay clientele. Johannesburg's *Citizen* noted that:

> . . . as the ads for this Easter package of vast quantity and variable quality insisted, this is *Afrika*, and if Divine don' lay no claim to the thrones that thrust way above the groping masses of disco souls, then she surely deserves to be denoted the Diva of Disco Drag. . . . Looking like a bloated Anita Ekberg out of *La Dolce Vita*, the definitive Dame of Dirt's act indicates an almost paranoid mixture of influences – from conventional pub drag with its sexual *entendres*, through the mimicry of Danny La Rue, the social observations of Dame Edna and a variety of High Camp goddesses, from Sophie Tucker to Bette Midler.

Well, that just above covers everything, I thought.

Our brief South African tour was virtually without incident, with the exception of an amusing moment in which Divi was photographed backstage at Zipps with a former Miss World, Anneline Kerzner. Ms Kerzner adored Divine and, being a major celebrity herself in her home country, it made for an excellent piece of promotion in the next day's *Star* newspaper. We learned, however, that Ms Kerzner's husband, a rich and highly influential businessman, spent most of the night attempting, in vain, to have the photo banned from publication. He most certainly did not approve of the one beautiful female being associated with the other. That was a shame, as the gentleman was also the impresario behind Africa's Vegas-style Sun City entertainment complex and this minor incident would likely put a stop to any possible future appearance there by my star.

Divi and Lee arranged a two-week holiday at one of the internationally famous game reserves in South Africa. They received first-class treatment and the rest achieved its purpose. They returned refreshed and full of animated talk, not of the usual animal attractions on this type of vacation, but more of the obvious crush they both had on their personal six-foot-three, blond, muscled guide. From all accounts, the three were inseparable. Divine and Lee conveniently forgot to also tell me at the time of the dozens of African wicker baskets, tribal jewellery, voodoo dolls, zebra rugs, elephant feet and other assorted junk they had purchased during their visit, leaving their South African hosts to arrange the sea freight back to Key West. When the freight bills finally were forwarded to my office, they were way in excess of the actual cost—and value—of the contents.

Before they had departed on their holiday, I had tried again to sit with Divine and talk of the financial problems he was creating for himself. Once again, he had listened attentively, responded apologetically and thanked me for my concern and advice.

Nothing had changed.

On my return to New York, I received promotion copies of *The Simply Divine Cut-Out Doll Book,* starring Divine, with designs and illustrations by Van Smith, and published by St Martin's Press.

'I had talked to different publishers about doing a book,' Divine said. 'I thought it was too early to do a book on myself; I mean, the career is just starting to get good. Up until now, it's been hell and nobody wants to read all that shit. I think maybe in about thirty years I'll want to write about all the things that have happened. So, we finally came up with the idea of a paperdoll book because one had come out on the Reagans and that did very well. They approached me and in the

meantime, one came out on Elvis and on Marilyn and on Prince
Charles and Lady Di.

'So I got Van Smith,' he explained. 'He was the only one who could
do it, because he's always done my costumes and knows them better
than anyone. I think it's very good. The colour in it turned out really,
really great.'

This promotional gimmick for Divi received much media attention.
In San Francisco a journalist wrote:

> You can dress Divine up, if you really insist, as a dominatrix, as a
> Jungle Jezebel, as a glamor girl – and other heretofore undefined
> manifestations of couture. You can send this oversized collection of
> merry-widowed maiden and Frederick of Hollywood rejects to your
> high school sweetheart (the one who married the milkman), or to an
> unmarried aunt. You can take the pages out of the book and repaper
> your bathroom. You can decopage an old lamp shade. You can . . .

Opening the vast quantities of mail and packages that had arrived
from all over the world while we visited South Africa, I also became
aware that Divine had become, in his own, unique way a sort of pin-up,
a highly desirable image to grace the front and centre pages of respectable and not so respectable magazines. A four-page colour feature
appeared in England's revered *Illustrated Homes and Gardens*, featuring Divine as the model for The Bathroom Theatrical, dressed exoti-
cally by Zandra Rhodes and bejewelled by Andrew Logan. His was the
front-cover full-page photo on Spain's *El Mundo De Las Candilejas*,
and similarly on London's *Gay News*, Germany's *Inter View* and
America's *In Touch*. Divine was the 'Creem Dream', spectacularly
photographed by Robyn Beeche, in England's *Face*. *After Dark* printed
a three-page centrefold of Divine, photographed by Bill Bernardo,
whose own company, Exposed Cards, was now distributing a series of
Divine Greetings Cards.

Exhibitions and photo compilations now regularly featured Divine
in portraits by such luminaries as Francesco Scavullo, Andy Warhol,
Christopher Makos, Marcus Leatherdale, Don Bachardy and Richard
Bernstein. David Hockney had painted a portrait of Divine, which was
featured in a worldwide touring Hockney exhibition and would eventually be purchased by the Carnegie-Mellon Institute.

Most interesting of all to me was that Divi's recent sartorial
extravagances were even proving to have some benefit. At long last,

the wonderfully supportive Page Six gossip column in the *New York Post* had noticed Divine the Man:

> . . . the rotund star of *Polyester* looked divine the other day in a well-tailored man's summer suit (not polyester) and huge pink sunglasses with an enormous rhinestone earring in one ear. He came into Serendipity 3 with his business manager and was surrounded by fellow diners and employees begging for autographs, usually a no-no at the restaurant. But Big D loved it.

Yes, this busy career was certainly not without its attendant problems and inconveniences, but Big D had come a long way.

'The obvious question here, of course, is whether Divine is going respectable, and, to Divine, the answer is equally obvious: "I think I've *always* been respectable. What I do onstage is not what I do in my private life. . . . It's an act," says Divine. "It's how I make my living. People laugh, and it's not hurting anyone." That is to say, the outrageous behavior is a joke, folks, a joke, even though viewers who would never assume John Wayne shot Indians every day don't hesitate to picture Divine parading around in tawdry clothes committing anti-social acts. "A lot of critics can't get past the wigs and the dresses," Divine sighs. "I wish they would, not only for me, but because some of the movies and plays I've been in are actually quite good."' (*New York Daily News*, 17 May 1983)

12 Welcome Home, Baby Glenn

'My parents were the sort of people who thought you should only be in the newspapers three times: when you are born, when you marry and when you die! It was bad enough when I became a hippy during the '60s. When they found out I was doing drag! That was the icing on the cake! We didn't speak for nine years. Then I heard my father was very ill and I got in touch: the growth we've made in the last few years is phenomenal. We were always a very close family before, so it's sad we've wasted all those years. My father now is a very sick man. I'm glad I've had the chance to tell him I love him before he dies. My stage persona did bother them initially, but then they discovered I didn't wear dresses all the time. My father looked over some of my bank statements and said "If I'd known this much money was in it, I'd have worn a dress myself." '

New Musical Express, 25 May 1985

BY THE SUMMER OF 1983 we were unable to avoid a more formal conflict with Bobby Orlando. Our frustration was at boiling point. He had taken up his option to renew Divine's exclusive recording Agreement on 12 July 1983 by paying the required advance against future royalties due of $3,500. To date, that was the only amount we had received from Bobby Orlando. It was not possible to continue in this way and I approached a New York attorney, Jim Mosher, on Divine's behalf. He heard our story, read the relevant papers and advised us that in his opinion Bobby was clearly in breach of contract; that Divine was legally entitled to look elsewhere to record, once 'O' Records had been served notice of its breach.

But that's not what we wanted as Divi was afraid of losing Bobby's talents as a record producer and not achieving another success. We just wanted to receive certified sales figures and other information relevant to our being able to calculate royalties due.

Our attorney contacted Orlando, which, of course, gave the producer confirmation of our unhappiness with our relationship. A furious Orlando suggested there was nothing untoward and that his accountants, a most reputable New York firm, would answer all our questions to our satisfaction. A meeting was arranged immediately with a senior partner of the accountancy firm. Jim Mosher and I arrived on time, eager to peruse the financial statements we had been promised by Orlando. We didn't get the information we wanted.

While Jim Mosher prepared the next step—to issue a writ against 'O' Records—Divine once again went back to the studios with his producer in an effort to provide another single to satisfy the European demand. As absurd as this situation might seem now, at the time we really had no choice. Jim explained to us that the alleged breach might have to be proven in a Court of Law, should Orlando challenge it, and it could therefore take ages, perhaps years, before Divine could make another record. We just had to hope that our newly appointed attorney would find a satisfactory way of solving this issue and, meanwhile, swallow our pride and continue to let Bobby Orlando and Divine use each other in this manner.

He recorded 'Love Reaction' and two other hurried and meaningless tracks—'Kick Your Butt' and 'Alphabet Rap'—that Bobby explained would be added to the existing Divine catalogue to form a first compilation album, titled 'Jungle Jezebel'. Bobby recorded the vocals—usually in one take—and did the rest of the production behind closed doors. He was, in effect, the record label, producer, writer and sole owner of the copyright to these tracks.

Within days, 'Love Reaction' was rushed to Europe and I received a frantic call from John Seine, on behalf of the Dutch team working with Divine. This time they were distraught and John informed me that Break had formally rejected the new single as it was, as far as they were concerned, an almost exact copy of 'Shoot Your Shot' and the others. They were furious that Orlando was taking no notice of their comments and suggestions, just as he was ignoring Divine's.

In the heated conversation between the Company of Two Pieters and Bobby Orlando, it was suggested to the record producer that something along the lines of a fast-rising British chart hit, 'Blue Monday', by the Manchester-based band New Order, might be perfect for Divine. Bobby called me immediately to ask if I knew the record. I didn't. Nor, it appeared, did he. He went that day to an import record shop in Manhattan and bought New Order's single.

The following day, Divine returned to the studio to re-record 'Love Reaction' with its brand-new backing track. Within a week, everyone was receiving calls from Holland congratulating Orlando and confirming their delight in the new track. Divi and I were relieved that our colleagues in Europe appeared to be confident that they could achieve even greater success with this one.

We were even happier to hear the news from the two Pieters that they had licensed Divine's records to Design Communications, a small, independent record company in England. The British label's two owners, brothers Nick and Ian Titchener, were planning to start marketing Divine's singles through the clubs as soon as 'Love Reaction' was ready for them.

The Titcheners released and promoted the new single with a similar vigour and determination to our European team. The single was all over England and, for the first time in that country, clubgoers were beginning to accept Divine as a recording artist and not just a foul-mouthed tart.

Within a few weeks, the British newspapers were reporting that New Order's record company, Factory Records, was threatening to serve a writ against Bobby Orlando, claiming that our producer had lifted 'Blue Monday's' all important bass rhythm line and that 'Love Reaction' was therefore not an original record.

Although I do not believe any writ was ever served by the British band or its record company, it was clearly the last straw for Divi. Divine agreed to my instructing Jim Mosher to serve the breach of contract writ against 'O' Records, due to the record company's failure to provide financial statements as provided for in our Agreement.

While we waited for 'Love Reaction' to bring Divi back to Europe, we continued to accept offers of club dates in North America. Although his singles were still not available in the shops, the DJs were buying European copies from the local import shops and all the records were receiving requested dance-floor play and turning up on the DJ's personal charts. This of course only added greatly to our frustrations and anger, but at least it kept the offers for appearances coming Divine's way. And the additional attraction of the club chart placings meant an immediate increase in his fees.

Lee accompanied Divine to a club gig in Canada and I received a series of phone calls the following morning from Toronto Airport. Lee, a Canadian national, had been stopped at US immigration control, Divine having already completed the formalities and now in fear of returning to the desk to assist Lee and thereby run the risk of involving himself in any problem. Despite Lee's marriage to Mandy, his US resident's papers had not yet been finalised. My mind flashed to all those recent trips from Europe and the problems this could have created for Divine.

Divine was in a state of sheer panic. I insisted he travel on to Key West and not try to contact Lee at the airport, knowing Lee would call me as soon as he could. This he did about an hour later, confirming that the US Immigration Services at Toronto Airport refused to let him back in the country. I arranged to wire him some cash. Two days later, Lee arrived in Key West. To my relief, Divi decided Lee could no longer risk travelling with him outside the United States, at least until his papers were finalised. He would continue to be Divi's personal assistant for American gigs, but Divi and I would immediately discuss replacements for Europe.

Throughout these two days of panic from Divine, I sensed that he was not totally disappointed about being without his 24-hours-a-day companion on all his travels in the future. They certainly still seemed to be contented lovers, but I think that home life with a steady partner was now enough to satisfy Divi's romantic needs. Perhaps he could have a great deal of fun on tour with his European fans, some of whom had been pointedly indicating their availability in recent months, and then, having satisfied his lust, return regularly to domestic bliss?

German hotel room service was about to get busier in the early hours of the mornings. Divine would have his cake and eat it.

Back on the road, satisfying the renewed club demand in the States—and earning some much-needed cash to appease Divine's recently acquired British creditors—I travelled once again with Divi and Lee, principally to get my hands on the nightly cash payments before the star did.

One afternoon Divi and I were sitting together in his hotel room in San Francisco. He seemed morose, more thoughtful than usual, and I sensed something was wrong beyond the usual apathy created by the effects of the marijuana. We chatted for a while and Divine suddenly burst into tears. Between sobs and explosive clearing of his nostrils, he explained that he had been missing his parents. I listened patiently. Here was my defensive bully of a friend, opening his heart for a change. He was sitting on the edge of his bed, his tattered and much abused black telephone book thrown on the floor.

I tried to remember the rare snippets of conversation we had had about his parents. I knew they lived in Florida. How many years had it been since they last met? Nine? Ten? Why now?

He had always been so cautious when asked by journalists about his family, telling of how his parents refused to speak to him or see him. 'My mother used to say, "If you wear a toupee and come at night when no one will see you, you are welcome." I would just answer, "Well, then it's not me you want to see," and I'll just stay away until they welcome me as I am.'

Divi grabbed my hand. He was not a person given to physical gestures with his friends. I'm a tactile person; I hug, I touch. I frequently hugged Divine, my arms reaching half-way round his body, but the gesture was rarely reciprocated. I picked up the phone book, found a Florida phone number under Milstead and gently asked if he wanted me to dial it. He nodded in agreement, still sobbing. He tried to break away from me. I forced him to stay where he was.

'Hello?' A woman had answered. 'Hello, who's there?' I handed the phone to Divi.

'Mummy, it's Glenn.' I started to leave. He wouldn't let me. I found it embarrassing. 'How are you? How's Dad?' the hoarse voice enquired.

Frances Milstead recalled this incident in a letter to me. 'Then one day, nine years later, he called. When I heard his voice, I broke down and cried for joy. And he cried and Harris had to calm both of us.'

The phone conversation must have lasted about five minutes. When it finished Divi started laughing. I waited for an explanation, delighted to see the change of mood. 'It seems like they've been following my career closely in the newspapers,' Divine told me. 'But Daddy wouldn't acknowledge the fact that his son dressed as a woman to make a living. When Mummy put him on the phone just now he was quiet and then suddenly blurted out, "I've just been clearing out the garage, son, and I've found some cheap, gold earrings of your mother's from years back. I suppose they might come in useful to you. Should I send them on?"'

After the call from San Francisco, Divi started to send his parents postcards from his global travels. They were brief, joyful, reporting his success, but never with a return address. It was, for him, a cautious one-sided attempt to come back into their lives and it slowly became clear to me why he had chosen this time.

I was convinced that Divine's neglect of his parents for all these years stemmed from his belief that they were ashamed of him. He had been waiting for the time when he could return, confident that his own past decisions and the avenues he had subsequently taken — of which they had so strongly disapproved — could negate this shame. His success in

Polyester, together with all the publicity he was now receiving as a recording star, had finally given him the courage to present himself to them again as the man he believed they always wanted him to be.

We were on one of our frequent and much enjoyed return visits to play the Copa in Fort Lauderdale ('the scene of the crime', I suppose it could be called). Out of the blue, Divi declared his intention to visit his parents, who lived in Margate, about twenty minutes' drive north. It appeared he had already warned them that he would visit on this day, although he hadn't explained why he was in the area. He implored me to drive him there, insisting that he was far too scared to go on his own. I believe I was a fairly loyal friend to Divine, but this was taking loyalty beyond reason. I really didn't think it was my place to be by his side at the family reunion.

We drove together in complete silence and in intense heat. In the effort to present myself as the kind of manager he thought they would like, I sweltered in a thick, woollen suit. Divine, however, had made no such effort and was in the usual baggy cotton pants and sloppy T-shirt. Where was Tommy Nutter when he could have been useful?

South West 9th Street in Margate epitomises Florida's suburbia. Our mutual nervousness and silence was suddenly and hilariously broken by the sight of pink flamingos planted in the Milsteads' front garden. I'm sure they couldn't have appreciated the weird interpretation we gave to this fairly standard middle-class effort at prettiness.

What was not so amusing to Divi – in fact, downright scary – was a small banner hanging over the front door proclaiming: 'Welcome Home, Baby Glenn'.

To my astonishment and relief, I was dismissed, as if I was the chauffeur, and told to pick him up in thirty minutes time. I wasn't introduced to the family, nor, I gathered from later accounts, even explained. I supposed Divine had suddenly decided that the possible oncoming humiliation for him shouldn't be witnessed by one so close.

Frances's memory of the prodigal son's return was one of absolute joy. 'He asked us if he could come back home and we could be a family again,' she told me later. 'I waited and prayed and here he was coming home once more to the parents who missed him and his love. I went to bed that night and thanked God for returning my son.'

So Baby Glenn began his return to the bosom of the family – and one more step towards the comforts of middle-class respectability and security from which he had so willingly escaped all those years ago and now so desperately needed to have again in his life.

'Love Reaction' became a hit all over Europe and Divine was more in demand than ever before. John Seine and I were constantly on the phone, attempting to fit into an already hectic schedule further requests for TV appearances, press interviews, radio shows and, of course, the essential club gigs.

Divi took Jay Bennett back again on the trips outside the United States and, by doing this, finally had to accept that he could indeed prepare his own make-up each night. Jay reverted to his role of servant-to-the-star with joy and his usual possessiveness. Flight itineraries were becoming more and more involved and John Murphy, our friendly travel agent in New York, had become as important a member of our team as anyone else. I believe that in 1983 Divine must have become one of the most widely travelled performers in the entertainment industry, commuting between North America and Europe and travelling by air almost daily within the two continents.

The record was selling in the United Kingdom and Divi's popularity spread throughout England and Scotland. The British journals adored him and he soon had daily interview sessions. He returned their adoration with just the kind of quotes they wanted. 'I'd love to live in England; my dream is to live in a little cottage with a thatched roof and have afternoon tea at four o'clock,' he told England's *New Musical Express*. 'Right now, if anyone asks me where I live, I say on British Airways! If my performing career fails, I can always be a stewardess!'

And Divine was capable of sending himself up in his own particular style: 'Actually my whole career has been amazing. At times it amazes me,' he told *Gay News*. 'I mean, I did four records last year and every one is gold . . . and my voice is horrible I think . . . luckily they have machines that can make even me sound good.'

Our team in Holland was so delighted with Divine's continuing success and genuinely grateful for the almost unbelievable effort and co-operation Divi was now putting into promotion and publicity, that they thrilled him with a gift of a bulldog puppy, extending their generosity a year or so later by providing Divi with a playmate for the first puppy. Divi proudly named his bulldogs Beatrix and Klaus – after the Queen of the Netherlands and her husband – and brought them back with him (at considerable expense of course – they travelled first class) to reside in Key West.

He became extraordinarily fond of his two dogs and they of him. He always cared for them with tenderness and concern and loved playing with them on his infrequent sojourns at home. They, in turn, displayed their sadness in his leaving and their overwhelming joy (they were growing into big dogs and their enthusiasm could sometimes be quite frightening) on his return. In Beatrix and Klaus, Divi found his children, and he showed them off proudly to his fans. They were featured on record covers and posters, written about in magazines worldwide and they even received fan letters from Divi's most earnest followers.

Divine's touring itineraries extended into Scandinavia, where, again, we were pleased to see that his audiences were mixed and very young. It was vitally important to Divi not to desert the loyal gay fans who had allowed, through their enthusiasm and early support, this star to cross over into a mainstream following, but we were only too aware how limited his career would be if it couldn't move further afield. The teeny-bopper adoration he was now receiving in Norway, Denmark, Sweden and even Finland (journeys to the Land of The Midnight Sun to do 3 a.m. shows in full daylight – a weird and wonderful experience) was yet more proof that the man not so long ago dubbed by the American media as the celebrity least likely to succeed – a fifteen-minute flash-trash in the pan – had earned his place of respect in his profession. Even if most of his peers were still reluctant to offer such respect.

In August 1983, England's *Record Mirror* published its new charts. 'Love Reaction' was Number 1 on its Boys Town Disco Chart, Number 25 on its Night Club Chart and Number 42 on its Disco Chart. Another sure sign of the legitimacy Divi was now establishing in Britain was the company he was keeping in the media: 'Prince and Divine are part of a group of rock stars currently riding high in the charts – they include Michael Jackson and Frankie Goes To Hollywood – who are flirting with sexuality,' wrote the *Daily Mail*. 'In their diverse ways they're all saying: "The gender doesn't matter."'

The press was not always kind to him, however, as a performer. With this recent success as a recording artist, the media had decided to cover his act as if it were a rock concert. We felt it was unfair for him to be judged as if a fortune had been spent putting a road show together in order to promote new recording product. We knew well by now that what delighted the fans in the clubs was the down-to-earth, direct personal touch with his audience; the impression that anything could happen – and usually did. But we accepted that, by his inviting so much self-publicity, we couldn't avoid exposing him to the critics. Sometimes it was painful to read.

'Camp Artiste Divine Was A Real Drag,' was the headline in one paper following Divine's appearance at a university rag ball. 'How could they enjoy the absolutely awful Divine? . . . A few years ago real students would have shown the camp cabaret artiste the door in no uncertain terms. . . . He was just plain bad.'

And after a much-heralded show at London's famed Lyceum rock venue: 'Ugly is a word that assumes new proportions with Divine around,' wrote the *Melody Maker*. 'Super-fruit extraordinaire, his gross frame and catty repartee are his only saving graces. . . . See Divine once and that's all you need – the first belly-laugh soon gives way to boredom.'

Britain's gay press, however, remained as faithful as ever: 'Between a selection of well-known and much loved disco ditties recorded over the past years, we were kept in stitches by the vulgar exchanges between star and audience, including tasteful references to the private portions of a young lady to his left who foolishly engaged in a shouting match with the rotund performer,' reported *Gay News* of a hugely successful appearance at London's Camden Palace. 'It's very odd, but the evening was a delight. . . . Ms Divine has not, as far as we know, been invited to the Royal Variety Performance, but times are changing, and if he's good enough for the inhabitants of one Palace, surely he's good enough for the residents of another?'

Bobby Orlando was issued with his writ. He responded with a counter-suit claiming Divine had failed to return to the studios when requested to make further recordings. Indeed, by this time, with a lawsuit pending and no royalty cheques arriving, we had no alternative but to put a stop to this ludicrous situation. We were extremely sad as well as angry. The relationship with Bobby in the early days had been a friendly one. Both Divi and I were quite fond of him – as a team-mate – and recognised the undeniable importance of his efforts to bring Divine's fame to its current level.

Jim Mosher advised us to look around discreetly for other producer/label possibilities, without, of course, committing ourselves to anything prior to a settlement – in or out of court – with 'O' Records. We had no doubt that we should start looking in England. I made appointments with various record labels. There was indeed interest; doors were opened easily, for a change. Although we couldn't provide sales figures, it was obvious from the record charts listings and the huge club demand for gigs that Divine could be a money-earner for a British label. And, of course, the ongoing love affair between the British press and my star didn't hurt at all.

However, I was obliged to advise any company with which I was meeting of the pending lawsuit with 'O' Records. Time after time, I was politely asked to return to discuss possibilities further once all was finalised with Bobby Orlando. Understandably, they just didn't want to risk getting involved with potential litigation pending.

They also voiced doubts as to who might be the right producer to work with Divine if Orlando was no longer part of the team. One record company even suggested they approach Bobby to produce new Divine product for their label while matters were pending between us. Divi was horrified at the suggestion, having visions of being asked to record the next single in a New York studio with Bobby at the controls, while I waited in a downtown court for the producer to attend the trial.

Divi and I knew it was essential to be planning ahead, even if we couldn't formally agree to his actually recording until matters were settled in the States. The minute this was achieved, however, Divine would need a new single on the market – and one that was better than ever. His biggest hit yet.

Nick and Ian Titchener were aware of the situation with Bobby Orlando and sympathetic to our problems. They too had now put a fair amount of time and expenditure into promoting Divine and were nervous of losing any future benefit beyond 'Love Reaction', should he sign with a major British label. Although the Company of Two Pieters was still promising them another single in the immediate future, stating that Bobby Orlando had other tracks ready to release, we had assured the Titcheners that this was not the case and there just wouldn't be another Divine record until the lawsuit was finalised. They became very angry with their licensors and nervous of their investment. They asked me if Divine would be interested in signing a direct recording deal with them, at least for the United Kingdom. We had both enjoyed our working relationship to date with the two brothers and I was happy to encourage them to present an offer to us, subject to one specific condition from the start: *guaranteed* distribution in the UK.

Nick and Ian Titchener introduced us to Barry Evangeli, a charming Greek Cypriot who controlled Proto Records, an independent British label with guaranteed distribution deals. Proto was currently having considerable success with its sole exclusive artist, Hazell Dean.

They proposed forming InTune Music Limited, a partnership which would then sign Divine to an exclusive recording contract. Design Communication would continue to market and promote Divine's records; Barry Evangeli, through Proto Records, would handle all licensing and distribution deals.

Divine and I eagerly met the three and we both appreciated their obvious enthusiasm; their belief in the star's potential as a recording artist, not just a gimmick; and, most of all, the fact that they seemed genuinely interested – virtually insistent – in involving Divine himself in such matters as choosing songs and helping to write lyrics.

We carefully allowed them to prepare a draft agreement – which would be signed as soon as legally possible – and, meanwhile, to start the search for a producer and a hit song. All three men were willing to take the risk of submerging themselves in Divi's career without receiving any formal signature from either him or myself. We both liked that. We were very pleased to start this new teamwork with a mutual respect, something we had not experienced with our earlier record deals.

Our Day in Court arrived. It was not an enjoyable experience. Bobby Orlando was livid and tried presenting Divi's legal representatives with financial statements at this last moment, but even those, way beyond their due date, were unacceptable in their (lack of) content. The judge declared that the agreement between 'O' Records and Divine had indeed been clearly breached and that we had made every reasonable effort to continue the relationship. He made his decision that a valid recording agreement no longer existed and that Divine was legally free to sign with whatever company he wished. In addition, the Court issued a warning to 'O' Records or any of its licencees against taking any steps to impede such new negotiations.

The matter of outstanding royalties was left to be settled separately and the Court issued certain instructions and guidelines on the pending lawsuit. Despite all our efforts – at considerable legal expense – over the years, Divine received no further payments from 'O' Records (or its subsidiaries) during his lifetime. Bobby Orlando continuously claimed that nothing was due to Divine as recoupable expenditure had exceeded Divine's contractual share of income.

On 18 April 1984, Harris Glenn Milstead signed an exclusive recording agreement in England with InTune Music Limited.

'I'm not saying all was a bed of roses – what is?' said Divine in response to media questions about the split with Orlando. 'But I thought I could progress more with someone else.' Divi always remained discreet about this break-up, which had caused him such a great amount of hurt, frustration and, he believed, loss of income.

And of his new signing: 'They seem to be able to see the future – visualise things,' he told the press. 'When I sat and talked with them they seemed to speak the same language as I did, I mean they understood what I was talking about and they more or less had the same ideas.

'I'm very lucky in that Proto Records is very eager to please. Barry Evangeli realises that the artiste has to like the song in order to properly get the song across to the public,' he continued. 'They'll give me the choice of material from whatever they have to work with. Then, it's discussed with the record company, and my management, and when all the parties agree, we go ahead and record.'

Divine was happy with the new arrangement and entered into it with his usual boyish enthusiasm when a new toy arrives to play with. He was totally co-operative and eager to be personal friends with his new recording colleagues. At first.

He was also having much more fun on the road, with Jay Bennett at his beck and call and the freedom to exploit once again the sexual possibilities of stardom.

We did a fun gig at a very straight rock venue in Essex, packed with girls and boys eager to be shocked. They roared at his vulgar humour, danced while he sang his hits (something Divine took a while to get used to, but now loved – getting very worried if they only stood still to listen, as in the old days) and – another recent introduction into his act – he brought a few fans onstage with him during his last song. There was never a shortage of exhibitionists in his audience, clamouring to bump and grind with the sweaty star, now jumping up and down in his five-inch heels with delight at the response to his own records. He would grab tits, grope crotches and fondle bums. The more he 'assaulted' his fans, the more they, and the audience, would scream with approval. Encores became difficult to perform as the fans never wanted to leave the stage once they were there beside their idol.

At this particular gig, the tape came to its conclusion, Divi had metaphorically Fucked Everybody Very Much several times and finally exited stage left to his dressing room, dragging a sexy young male with him. The newly found partner did not appear to be unwilling in this additional escapade into the unknown.

As usual, I forced my way through the crowd – still screaming for more – to Divi's dressing room and gave my usual 'secret' knock, letting him know it was me outside. I found his current assistant standing waiting too. 'Divi won't let me in yet,' he said with some surprise and bewilderment, knowing that it was difficult for his star to strip off the soaking wet, clinging costume by himself. I knocked again. Divi's voice shouted, 'Won't be a minute. Please wait.' At least he was polite, whatever he was up to. By this time the young lad's girlfriend had joined us at the door, also eager to know what her date was up to behind the barrier. In private with a drag queen.

Ten minutes passed, then the door opened and the youth rejoined his girlfriend. Business was conducted as usual with nothing being said about the delay until all autograph signings were completed and Divi and I were waiting for the car to arrive. We were alone in the dressing room. I looked at him inquisitively.

He grinned. 'Well,' he whispered, roguishly, 'when I groped him on stage I just couldn't believe it. I had to find out if it was all true. So when we got inside the dressing room, I just asked him to show me what colour underwear he was wearing.'

'Just like that?' I replied, amazed at his boldness. 'And what colour were they?'

'*Bright pink*!' he exclaimed with delight. 'And he just stood there with his leather pants around his ankles and his pink briefs bulging in my face.' Divine paused for theatrical effect. 'And then he talked on and on about his girlfriend and would I give her an autograph, while I took down his briefs and had a bit of fun!'

'And,' as if he'd forgotten the most important piece of news he wished to relate, 'it was all true. And even truer once I got going!'

Divine was living his fantasies. And why not? Nobody has to stay in his dressing room against their will, I told myself in an excuse for his behaviour. As we left the dressing room that night, the lad and his girl were waiting outside, arm in arm, she clutching to her chest the well-earned, signed photograph. They kissed Divine goodbye on the cheek.

'Get home safely,' Divi shouted over his shoulder to them both. He winked at me.

As usual, the next morning I went down to the hotel breakfast room before Divine. I passed his door. There was a tray outside with two half-eaten meals on it. And, delicately poised on top of a glass on the tray, as an amusing message to me, was a pair of men's briefs. *Bright pink*.

Divine had made another exciting discovery and one, I readily admit, that I never quite understood. Nor did he, but he was most willing to accept it. And use it.

He noticed that the lines waiting for autographs after the shows at the heterosexual venues he was now playing were as long as ever, although without so much of the over-the-top campery from the fans, which he quietly tolerated at the gay venues. Frequently, well-behaved couples would step in a little sheepishly for a signed photo, usually hand-in-hand to assist each other's timidness in facing this ogre head-on. Of course, as always, there would be the instant shock – and often, in these cases, relief – of seeing the gentle fat man sitting noiselessly in the corner.

Brief conversation would take place. The partners would leave, content with their souvenir. Twenty or thirty minutes later the male half of one of these such couples would return, mumbling some story about the girlfriend having to go home early, or drinking with some friends now. Could he possibly just ask for one more autograph for a friend? Divi and I became used to these speeches, they were always quite similar in content and delivery.

It was also a signal for anyone else to leave the room for a few minutes. We would make our excuses. Interestingly, Divi never seemed to feel a need to hide these new liaisons from me, presumably thinking that there was nothing wrong in inviting the guy back to the hotel as I knew he was straight! They would usually join us in the car journey back, attempting a somewhat boring butch conversation on the way. We would all try to be on our best behaviour, but sometimes the giggles would explode and I'm sure these guys became dreadfully embarrassed.

The signs would tell me that they had often stayed, if not the night then certainly for some hours. Divi was fascinated with this previously unthought of (or, at least, unapproachable) style of seduction. He never had to do the inviting. Was he bringing out the bisexuality in these visitors? Or were they just curious as to what was really behind this extremity of female sex symbolism on stage? Whatever, Divine was having a ball.

' "I think my fans in Europe are much more sophisticated. As a whole. Europeans are," remarked Divine. "Their culture is used to men dressed in women's clothing onstage, so it's not even thought about twice. It's just another actor playing another part . . . which in fact is all it *is*. Americans seem to have to label everything and have to pick. The minute you've got a woman's costume on, you're either a transvestite or a drag queen. Who knows?" ' (The *Advocate*, 1988)

13　Controversial . . . and Banned!

'In the end, I'm downright rotten,' said Divine about his role in the movie *Lust in the Dust*. 'But at least the character builds. In all my other films, I just used to barrel-ass on to the screen and didn't quit until the movie was through. That was the type of acting I specialised in . . . overacting.'

LA Weekly, 8–14 March 1985

ROTO RECORDS' OFFICE IN NORTH LONDON reminded me of Bobby Orlando's; tiny, cramped, untidy rooms full of boxes of promo records waiting to be mailed out. Each time I visited Barry Evangeli at his office, the same boxes seemed to be lying in the same corners. Before long, in addition to Barry and his staff of two, Pete Waterman, a young record producer, was based in the office, making it even more chaotic. Barry explained that Pete was temporarily using the space as his headquarters, while he worked on some ideas for Hazell Dean and others.

The Titchener brothers had cleverly promoted their new signing of Divine by announcing a search for suitable recording material for the controversial singer. They received hundreds of cassettes; some dreadful, some pornographic, most even worse. Nick and Ian were beginning to despair. 'Love Reaction' was moving off the British charts and Bobby Orlando's overseas licencees were now looking to InTune Music to keep the Divine product flowing. Then, along came 'You Think You're a Man', written for Divi by Geoff Deane, front man for the pop group, Modern Romance. Eager to get some reactions to the demo, Barry Evangeli played it to everyone who visited his office. Consequently, Pete Waterman heard nothing else for days. Needing to make some quick money while his other projects were still in the planning stages, Pete gladly accepted Barry's offer to produce Divine's next single. A few days later, Divine was in London's Marquee Studios, working as part of a team. And it was confusing to Divi how *many* people were actually part of this team – what did they all do? Barry, Nick and Ian watched every detail carefully as Pete Waterman brought in three young colleagues – Mike Stock, Matt Aitken and Pete Ware – to work with the star.

For the first time in a recording studio, Divine was indeed treated like a star. Everyone was patient and caring with him. They seemed to want him not only to be a creative part of this experience, but also actually to enjoy it. Divi was overjoyed and launched himself into the session with a previously untapped gusto. The vocals were recorded without problems – and Divi rushed off to Fortnum and Mason for tea, another task having been completed.

In 1946, when Gregory Peck and Jennifer Jones filmed the raunchy Western, *Duel in the Sun*, Peck joked to his co-star that the movie should be called *Lust in the Dust*. The quip became legendary in Hollywood circles and the nickname remained. Divi told me that Tab Hunter had been hawking around a spoof spaghetti Western filmscript, *Lust in the Dust*, to which he owned the production rights. Tab had found a business partner in 24-year-old Allan Glaser, a recent Twentieth Century-Fox intern, and they had formed Fox Run Productions in order to produce the movie themselves.

According to Divi, Tab had originally wanted to film it with Dolores Del Rio. Then there was some talk of a TV movie, co-starring Tab and Chita Rivera. Ever since *Polyester* and their instant friendship, Tab had had the business acumen to realise that the casting of Divine could be a real coup. 'If Des Moines was ready for Barbra Streisand as a man and Dustin Hoffman as a woman,' the producers noted, 'then they're ready for Divine.' And Tab had certainly noted the huge renewed attention from the media he had personally received when paired with a 300-pound man in drag.

Tab and Allan informed me over lunch of their plans to film in the autumn of '84. They wanted Divine. 'Getting investors,' Allan joked, 'is no problem. Most of them are so square they don't know what a transvestite is.' They proudly informed me that the movie would be budgeted at $1.5 million. I unhesitatingly requested a fee of $150,000 for Divi; I grandly thought my star was worth ten per cent of the budget. They clearly thought otherwise, swallowed hard and didn't finish their lunch.

Once again waiting for a new single to go through its initial club launch and enter the charts before the record company – this time Proto Records in England – required the services of the recording artist to promote it personally, Divi was back in Key West, with Lee and Jay. Our own relationship was becoming more and more strained by Divi's excessive spending and this distance between us. We were both hot-headed on the telephone; both of us nervous and tense through our effort to avoid getting into a row, we would frequently do just that. Divi and I could talk well, most of the time, face to face. Now our business was being conducted by long-distance telephone and it was far from satisfactory.

Divi had returned to the States with suitcases and parcels full of newly acquired clothes and Christmas decorations from England, delicate china and porcelain souvenirs from Holland, soft toys and dolls – to add to his growing collection – from Germany and crystal glassware from Scandinavia. All charged to his American Express card. What he couldn't carry with him was now arriving daily by freight (cash on delivery) at my home in New York. Divine never gave me warnings of these deliveries; my living room was full of boxes marked 'Fragile'. The situation was truly getting out of hand.

In the meantime the essential bills, such as the monthly travel agent's account (now regularly into five figures), lawyers' fees – still attempting to deal with 'O' Records – and the ever-increasing telephone bills, were not getting paid. And Divine would just slam the phone down if I even dared mention the word 'taxes'.

Jay Bennett started to call me from Key West, demanding, on his master's behalf, that I wire cash instantly to the island for their personal expenses. Then Divine's friend Stephen would call and inform me that he was visiting Divi for a week's holiday and would I please provide the air ticket on Divi's travel account and could he call round to see me this morning to pick up an envelope with $1,000 cash that his friend had asked him to bring? The travel account was for business purposes and therefore in my company's name, payment of the bills remaining my responsibility. Divi's personal bank account was empty. My star had even stopped calling me himself, for fear of yet another lecture.

There was a definite breakdown in communication.

Stephen stayed in New York. I charged my own ticket and arrived in Key West, unexpected. Jay cooked dinner and Divi smoked pot. By the end of the evening Divi had agreed with me that it was time for him to move back to New York. I had made it very clear that I thought our future relationship was at great risk through his current behaviour, reminding him that our own five-year contract was due for renewal in October of that year and, if things continued as they were, I would have to think very carefully about my decision to renew.

This carefully placed comment created panic in Divi. Suddenly it was as if the marijuana had lost all effect on him. Jay was hiding in his bedroom (although undoubtedly listening to every word behind his door), afraid to come near us because of our raised voices and very heated conversation. Divi and I rarely ever argued like this. Certainly, on reflection, this moment was as near as we ever came to breaking up our partnership.

We agreed that, as soon as he had the time, he would look for a home to rent in Upstate New York, not more than an hour's drive from Manhattan. This way he could combine the pleasures of a more relaxed life out of the city when not on tour, with easy access to myself and his other regular business commitments in town. He admitted to me that in any case he had been wanting to move away from Key West. The journeys home involved an aeroplane change in Miami and often a long wait before the uncomfortable, final thirty-minute flight in the tiny craft used on the Key West route. After the long, restless transatlantic journeys, he was finding this added inconvenience too much to cope with. And, he confided in me, things were not so wonderful any more with Lee. He felt it was time to live on his own again. With Beatrix, Klaus . . . and Jay, of course.

At four-thirty in the morning, when all had been settled and Divi had patiently listened to a longer-than-ever lecture about spending (which, of course, had absolutely no effect whatsoever on him beyond that evening), I phoned for a taxi to take me to Key West airport for the first plane out. I had no wish to stay longer on the island at this point. I wanted Divine to spend some time alone, thinking seriously about the purpose of my visit.

As I was about to leave, Divi reached into his familiar little brown suede bag, which he carried with him at all times, rummaged around in the bottom and pulled out a tattered, screwed-up document. He showed it to me as tears started running down his face. 'This is our contract we signed five years ago,' he choked. 'I've never been without it. Never. It's the most important thing in my life. I carry it with me everywhere and, when I'm feeling insecure or lonely on tour, I look at it and realise that I still have you there, *for me*. You're really all I have, you know.'

If the taxi hadn't arrived at that moment, I think I might have even got a hug out of the big bear.

My mission was accomplished. Divi was putting his priorities in order. We never talked about that meeting in Key West, but, two weeks later, on one of his visits to New York, he asked me if I would be willing to sign another five-year contract with him – our renewal – now, six months earlier than necessary. I did. Without hesitation.

'You Think You're a Man' was an instant hit; far greater than Divine's previous records. Our new team in England had done a tremendous marketing and promotion campaign. The clubs were begging for additional promo copies and the song was receiving regular radio play. Tour dates were put together overnight and the travelling players once again added to British Airways' profits for the year. This time, Divi took Jay Bennett with him and, tired of doing his own make-up, persuaded another friend, Jon Mathews, to accompany them. Jon was an experienced make-up artist, but, like Van before him, was unwilling to take on any additional task beyond this one-hour job each night.

' "You Think You're a Man" is electric "high energy" dance club rock, laying down an infectious beat, with an unforgettable vocal,' is how one of the music industry journals heralded the new single. 'If dance is your passion, make a point of finding this record.'

The record went straight to the top of *Record Mirror*'s influential Hi-NRG Disco Chart, where it stayed week after week. And then it started to cross over into the magazine's pop charts; the top 100 records in Britain. This is what we had been waiting for. 'Love Reaction' had crossed over the previous October, reaching number 65, but then vanished quickly. However, it had clearly opened the way for this next assault on the British. The day 'You Think You're a Man' first entered the pop charts, I was told the news by our record company as the magazine reached the shops, early in the morning. The Titcheners were already being besieged with requests for media interviews.

I tried to locate Divi. Eventually I tried Harrods, it being breakfast time. The kindly English lady in charge of the room answered the extension phone. 'Could you tell me if Divine is eating there at the moment?' I enquired.

'I'm sorry, dear, I don't know any young lady called Divine,' was her polite response. 'What does she look like?'

'I'm afraid you've misunderstood,' I continued. 'Divine is an American man, very fat, probably wearing dark glasses . . .'

'Oh, yes!' the lady interrupted me. 'You mean *Mr* Divine. Such a nice gentleman. I'll go and get him to the phone.'

Divine had found his respectability in, of all places, Harrods' breakfast room. *Mr* Divine, indeed!

'Hi, man, what's up?' he asked, guessing it could only be me who would interrupt his precious breakfast.

I told him the news. He shrieked down the phone with a scream that would have awakened any elderly Knightsbridge ladies still sleeping. I am told by his breakfast companions of that day that the good patrons of Harrods were treated to an a cappella version of 'You Think You're a Man' at full vocal throttle by our star, Mr Divine, as he returned to his table to announce his news.

Divi was ecstatic, overflowing with pride, excitement and joy – and, I'm sure, not a little bemusement – at this latest turning point in his career.

The record climbed to number 16. Divine's painted face and garish costumes were to be seen everywhere – on front pages of magazines and newspapers, on posters in shop windows, on greetings cards and badges sold on street corners. And beautifully photographed by Greg Gorman on his record sleeve, displayed, finally, with prominence in the record shops.

British television has one, long-running, all-important promotion show for new pop records: the BBC's *Top of the Pops*, transmitted weekly at prime-time viewing for the young potential record buyers. It is by far the most influential and result-oriented marketing tool in the British record industry. Once a record has reached the Top 30 in the pop charts, it is considered for exposure by the show's producers. But the BBC is notoriously conservative in its choice of prime-time viewing.

At this time, the TV station was being even more cautious, having recently banned the country's number 1 record – Frankie Goes To Hollywood's 'Relax' – from *Top of the Pops*. This censorship was reported in headlines throughout Britain, which, in turn, led to an unprecedented overnight increase in sales of the record and a retaining of the number 1 position for weeks to come. The BBC was aware that, by its actions, it had given FGTH more publicity than the band could ever have dreamed of, and had become involved in the kind of controversy it tried hard to avoid. Now, just a couple of weeks later, here was a 300-pound man, grotesquely dressed as a parody of a woman, six feet eight inches in his high heels, singing lyrics about thinking someone's a man, but being only a boy. And they could no longer ignore his song. They ran out of excuses to give to our very anxious and insistent promotion team. With the song at number 16, they had to invite Divine to appear on the show.

On 19 July 1984, Divine appeared on the BBC's *Top of the Pops*. Following the transmission, the TV station's switchboard was, supposedly, flooded with over a thousand calls, angrily complaining about 'the fat lady' their children had been exposed to that evening; 'it was disgusting, obscene'.

Once again, the scandal was spread over the front pages. 'I'm more shocked than all the people who phoned the BBC,' Divi was quoted everywhere. 'My performance was toned down and I kept to all the BBC's rules. God knows what would have happened if I'd done my real show.

'I'm surprised that so many people in Britain, which I consider my second home, have such closed minds,' he declared indignantly. 'I'm very hurt.'

The newspapers announced that the BBC had banned Divine from further TV exposure as he was just too offensive for their viewers. The BBC, trying to down-play this further controversy in which they had become involved, denied any official ban, but carefully avoided inviting Divine back to *Top of the Pops*, despite continuous pressure from Proto Records.

Sadly, though, I believe the British public smelled a rat with all this publicity and decided we had invented the complaints story ourselves in order to achieve the same increase in record sales as had happened for Frankie Goes To Hollywood. We hadn't. We were as confused by the furore as anyone. Divine had, truly, toned down his performance for television. But the record buyers were determined not to be manipulated by all this controversy and sales of 'You Think You're a Man' did not increase overnight. And then they decreased because we couldn't get further exposure on this most important outlet.

A final word on this incident. In September 1984, I was amused and delighted on seeing these two glaring, 'controversial' front-page headlines in *Weekly World News*, one of the cheap tabloid newspapers available at all American supermarket check-out counters: DRUNK DRIVER IS EXECUTED: HE WAS JAILED FOR FIRST OFFENSE – AND HANGED FOR THE SECOND! and BANNED! ROLY-POLY ROCK STAR SHOCKS THOUSANDS OF OUTRAGED TV VIEWERS.

As the previous year's working holiday in South Africa had seemed to be an acceptable compromise for Divine, I arranged a similar deal for us to visit Mexico, where, I was informed, 'Love Reaction' was on the disco charts. It was, to say the least, an extraordinary month of never quite knowing what would happen next.

Our host, owner of a small import record shop in Mexico City, seemed to have made no specific plans for Divine by the time of our arrival. Each day I would have a greasy breakfast with him in an outdoor café near to his shop and try as hard as I could to get some information. Would there be a show for Divine tonight? Where might it be? Could we possibly try arranging a sound check this time? If the situation hadn't been so bizarre, it would have been horrendous. But both Divi and I were determined to enjoy the holiday aspect of this trip, so we made every effort to stay in good humour, comply with our host's very-last-minute wishes and give the best we could.

We were in Mexico for one month. Divi's first performance was at the Caribbean Night Club, an intimate, sophisticated boite for the rich, not-so-young Mexicans. The patrons, elegantly dressed and sipping champagne at their individual tables, had no idea who the entertainer was that night. Divi jumped up and down, sang his songs, sweated and assaulted them verbally. He worked as hard as ever. The audience gave absolutely no reaction, neither during nor at the end of his performance, thereby putting our star through a performer's worst nightmare.

Our host congratulated Divi after the show – as if this past hour of hell for him had been perfectly normal – and insisted we joined the club's owner at his table. Very reluctantly, Divi changed clothes and joined me. The joint's owner, dressed in the finest of polyester and covered in gold jewellery, took pride in explaining to us that he was personally underwriting the cost of our visit to Mexico and that it had been agreed that in return he would get Divi's 'Mexican première performance' in his own club. Despite all the anomalies involved, Divine instantly fell out with our tour host, prophetically named Moises.

His last show in Mexico was, however, a never-to-be-forgotten event and in complete contrast to the first.

The constant radio promotion arranged by Moises during our visit had proved successful. 'Love Reaction' was number 1 and the Mexican kids were desperate to see Divine. A show was arranged at a partly completed, deserted skyscraper hotel in the middle of Mexico City. The entire ground floor – bare, save for its concrete foundation and glass window surroundings – would be the site. I did a long, complicated sound-check that day as the acoustics were appalling. Divi arrived at the venue, as agreed, at 11 p.m.

In this should-have-been hotel lobby stood at least 8,000 very young, dark-haired, extremely impatient kids. I learned that the show had been promoted on radio to commence at 8 p.m. and most had been waiting, in the claustrophobic, intense heat and under the most uncomfortable of conditions, for three hours already. I also learned that this was considered quite normal for Mexico.

By this time, the makeshift stage, from which I had carefully set the required sound levels that afternoon, had been totally destroyed by the restless audience. The dangerously over-crowded space was now under the control of uniformed police, threatening those in the front of the crowd with large wooden sticks, spiked at the end with vicious industrial nails. I was horrified.

Divi was now getting ready in his dressing room, some thirty feet above our audience, on what would have been the hotel's mezzanine floor overlooking the lobby. Obviously not wanting to give him any idea of the chaos below, I shouted, screamed and issued my ultimatums to anyone who seemed to be at all in charge. They immediately decided they spoke no English and returned my arm gestures with similar ones of their own. We were getting nowhere. I improvised, sensing this situation could be extremely dangerous. I decided that under no circumstances could Divi leave *without* performing. Mexico City's Chief of Police suddenly arrived and, through his interpreter, reinforced this decision in his own, most emphatic manner.

Within minutes, the technical crew and I transported all the rock concert sound equipment, hired for the night and carefully installed throughout the day, up to the mezzanine floor, together with the spotlights and whatever other essential equipment we could still get to through the mob.

My hands were bleeding from the rough equipment handling. My smart white suit for the evening's work was now covered in blood. My silk shirt had been torn down the front by an angry teenager. My hair was covered in spit, cigarette ends and the contents of crushed beer cans (that I suspected to be no longer beer, but the results of the boys not being able to find the toilets; if there were any). Not taking a moment to realise how I looked – or smelled – I rushed into Divi's dressing room to advise him that we were ready to start the show, only about 30 minutes later than he had been advised.

He took one look at me and exploded. He had no intention of going out into that crowd, if this is what they had already done to me! I hurriedly explained that I had now arranged for him to perform, dictator-like, from the mezzanine balcony, immediately outside the dressing room. The steps to this floor were guarded by police, the kids could not get near him. He was not persuaded. I told Divi about the Chief of Police. Divine put on his wig and heels.

His tape started and the pop star made the most theatrical of entrances, arms raised high above his head, as if he was the Pope blessing his flock. It took a few seconds for the audience, thirty feet below us, to realise he was now above them, performing on the precarious edge of the unfinished balcony. Those who had been waiting in the very front of the 'arena' were now placed directly *under* the overhanging balcony and could see nothing of their long-awaited idol. They pushed back, fiercely, violently. The crowd started to tumble like dominoes. My star continued to sing. Not being able to hear anything at all from the huge speakers directed down towards the audience, he just kept singing. Neither he, nor I, had any idea if he was singing the same song as was being played on the tape. (For once, it had been good news that they all sounded alike!) There was pandemonium downstairs and a sincere attempt at professionalism upstairs.

I dragged him from his 'stage' during the last song on the tape and used ten of the police to bundle him into a waiting car, engine running, before the tape finished and the kids could realise he'd departed. His assistant chased after him, grabbing heels, wig and tits as Divi — adrenalin now flowing — threw them on to the concrete steps, making it a hell of a lot easier to escape. I too improvised a secondary escape and — bruised, battered but higher on energy than I had ever been before — joined Divi an hour later in his hotel room.

He was sitting quietly on his bed alone, dressed in his dirty blue robe and smoking a joint, as if it had just been another night on the road. It was one of those special moments when I truly respected him. What a trooper. What a guy.

At four that morning, I was woken by a phone call from the owner of the hired sound equipment. He told me that the kids had indeed rioted when they realised Divi had gone without performing the obligatory encore, and had smashed all the plate glass windows surrounding the hotel's ground floor. The police, desperate to blame someone by now (so as not to have to take the blame themselves for allowing this fiasco to have taken place), had confiscated the sound equipment pending suitable reparation to the hotel owners. Moises, of course, was nowhere to be found. Would I come and sort things out for them?

'Fuck you very much!' I had great delight in screaming down the phone, before pulling the phone wires from the wall.

The next morning, regardless of whatever plans our Mexican host might still have for his visiting star, we were on the first plane back to the United States. The air stewardess, recognising Divine, helpfully translated a small item from Mexico City's morning newspaper. It was concerning the probable deportation of a large American pop star, due to his having caused a riot at his previous night's concert in the city.

We were never invited back to Mexico. But, once again, Divine had certainly left his own particular mark.

While in Mexico, I had received a call from Allan Glaser. The finance was in place for *Lust in the Dust* and they wanted to start filming within the next two to three months. They had hired Paul Bartel to direct. Could they now finalise Divine's deal? We eventually settled on a fee. However, at the last minute, I was advised that full capitalisation had not been achieved and the cashflow situation was precarious. Would Divine be willing to receive a considerably lower guaranteed initial fee, plus a deferred payment of the balance due from the movie's first profits? Reluctantly, Divi agreed, noting that it was still four times the fee he had received for *Polyester*. Screen Actors' Guild contracts were signed.

'I play a Mexican tart, Rosie Velez,' Divine told a journalist at the time. 'She sings in saloons. It's one of those "everyone's looking for the gold" films. I mean, my films are not exactly *The Sound of Music* and I'm no Julie Andrews, but I *am* looking for more of a mass appeal. I've had no offers yet, but I know people like Spielberg are interested.'

The original poster for *Lust in the Dust* proclaimed: 'He Rode The West . . . She Rode The Rest', which really just about sums it up. The film is set in the fictional town of Chile Verde, New Mexico, where a pair of deceitful sluts, played by Divine and Lainie Kazan, compete for the attention of Abel Wood (Tab Hunter) – the epitome of the straight-arrow hero of few words – and join the motley crew of crazed gun-slingers and ladies-of-even-easier-virtue living in the godforsaken outpost in trying to locate the gold said to be buried nearby. Of course, the map disclosing the secret is tattooed on the hindquarters of our two women of the world. Whoever gets them together and matches up the two halves, gets the gold. Simple, really. An honest-to-goodness sex farce.

Divi was pleased with the choice of Paul Bartel to direct, having seen *Eating Raoul*, his 1982 black comedy, and feeling certain that they would share a similar sense of humour and approach to the script. Indeed, Paul and Divi hit it off wonderfully from the first moment they met. It was also very exciting for him to be working on location – in Santa Fe, New Mexico – with such seasoned performers as Cesar Romero (when Divi told his mother that he was working with the veteran actor, 'she went crazy'), Geoffrey Lewis, Henry Silva, Nedra Volz and Lainie Kazan. 'No more amateurs to slow things down,' Divine was happy to note.

There was an even more exciting piece of news to come. 'I got the biggest charge,' Divine recalled, 'when I asked Tab who'd be doing the make-up. He said, "So-and-so is doing the rest of us, and George Masters is doing you." I said, "C'mon . . . George Masters? He did Marilyn Monroe, Rita Hayworth! He's even done Nancy Reagan." And Tab said, "Yeah, and now he's gonna do you." ' George Masters was indeed the acknowledged expert in his field. Divi was hugely flattered and more than a little overawed when, each morning at four, in preparation for the long day ahead, there would just be him and the Hollywood legend, working together before anyone else needed to join them.

The producers rented their star a charming bungalow in Santa Fe and Divi, Jay, Beatrix and Klaus settled in for the four weeks on location. It was, in the main, a time of happiness and satisfaction for the actor.

'I have my own trailer with my name written on it,' Divine told *People* at the time. 'I never had anything like that before. Every time I walk on to the set five people attack me from different directions – hair and make-up – and I think "What is going on?" When I was making films before, I would walk right across the room into the scenes and nobody would pay any attention to me. They've really spoiled me now.'

Off the set he created his temporary domestic life, with Jay preparing meals, his two beloved dogs providing adoration on demand and a friendly company of actors wandering in and out, gossiping, learning lines together and helping themselves to food. I received my nightly calls back in New York and, initially at least, my star seemed blissfully happy. I was also very proud of the comments being reported by the press, as other members of the film's company were interviewed. 'Divine is very serious and hardworking,' Paul Bartel said. 'He's just a natural. He takes direction, hits the marks and syncs to the playbacks. I think his personality is very accessible on the screen, regardless of gender identification.'

'Out of costume, he's nothing but a 300-pound beached whale,' Tab told the *New York Post*. 'But in costume, sparks come out of him. Whether you like Divine or not, he makes a statement. And he's got the comic timing of Lucille Ball.'

Lainie Kazan made a curious comment to *LA Weekly*. 'Divine is a combination of Little Eva and the Bethlehem Steel Company,' she said. 'I actually think of Divine as a woman now. I'm almost embarrassed to admit it, but I find her attractive. And I don't mind her being my sister at all!'

Divi took to Lainie at first and was eager to befriend her. 'We really do look like sisters,' Divine commented. 'Everyone was so worried at first, you know, how do we establish that Lainie and I are sisters without actually saying it? I said, "Listen, we both have big asses from the back and we both have killer hairdos, so don't worry about it. It'll happen." '

However, as filming continued, I became aware of two specific problems that were changing Divi's relaxed attitude. He had little patience with those late for work. He told me that Lainie often held up the entire filming process while she struggled with her costumes and make-up in preparation. Divi said that the actress complained bitterly about minor costume problems and used any excuse to cover for her lateness on the set. He just couldn't understand: if he could arrive on time – with far greater difficulties involved in these preparations – why couldn't she?

By the end of the month in Santa Fe, Divi was at breaking point with his co-star's behaviour. He liked her a lot socially, but this was work and for Divine social interaction was very much of secondary importance to what happens out on the set.

Far more serious, though, was the increasingly obvious feud between the director and Tab Hunter. This created both sadness and anger for Divine. He reported to me that Tab would constantly interfere on location as scenes were being set up by the director. As the film's producer, Tab believed he could influence every decision, but the cast – and most particularly Divine himself – were delighted with Bartel's direction and becoming more and more uneasy and short-tempered with their producer.

After many very public and disagreeable clashes between Paul and Tab, the director told Divine that he just wasn't willing to fight it out every single day and that he felt Tab had already destroyed beyond repair his own concept of the movie. Divi was greatly upset by all this, not the least because this dispute irretrievably altered his own respect and affection for Tab Hunter.

Divine received some great notices for his portrayal of a Mexican whore in *Lust in the Dust*. 'Just the sight of Divine gussied up in full dance-hall-girl drag riding a donkey that weighs less than she/he offers more laughs than a barrel full of teenage sex comedies,' said *People*. And *Variety* noted, 'In this, [Bartel] has been aided by an expert cast led by Divine. Picture is Divine's for the taking, and take it he does with a vibrant, inventive comic performance. Divine's naughty, suggestive reactions are often riotous, and his eyes prove constantly alive and expressive on camera.'

Moviegoer heralded the arrival of *Lust in the Dust*: 'In the tradition of such great screen couples as Spencer Tracy and Katharine Hepburn or Rock Hudson and Doris Day, transvestite actor Divine has decided to reunite with his/her *Polyester* co-star, Tab Hunter . . .', but the new 'William Powell/Myrna Loy' partnership – as Tab had labelled it after their first film together – was a short-lived one. Sadly, *Lust* flopped at the box office, although, like all of Divine's movies, it later became a popular video rental and is now considered by many to be a cult movie.

Divine blamed the film's failure on the differences of opinion between Paul Bartel and Tab Hunter. In any event, no more was ever heard of Divine's deferred fee from the movie's profits. Another lesson to be learned. However, two of Divi's warmest friendships and most rewarding professional relationships were to come as a result of making *Lust in the Dust*.

He first came across Greg Gorman when the photographer was hired by Fox Run to take advance publicity shots for the movie. There was an instant rapport between the two professionals that was quickly to develop into one of Divine's most treasured associations. The tall, handsome perfectionist was already established in Hollywood as a top star photographer, with such celebrities as Bette Midler, Robert Redford and Raquel Welch as regular clients. Divi adored and respected Greg and was thrilled when he discovered that there was a mutual admiration. Greg became Divine's personal photographer in 1984 and Divi resented having to do a session with anyone else once they had started to work together. Divine became one of the most photographed stars of his time, almost all of the most memorable and striking images of the star being shot by Greg Gorman, including the highly praised, award-winning record sleeves from 'You Think You're a Man' onwards.

Rob Saduski was provided by Fox Run as Divi's personal assistant on the set. During the month of filming, I heard many complimentary comments from Divi about Rob and was not at all surprised when he told me he had asked him to come on tour as his assistant. Rob was an absolute delight to work with; another true professional who, the minute he joined us as part of our team, made life much easier for Divine. He was to be by Divi's side, whenever he was working – on tour, in the studios or on stage – for the rest of the star's life. Even though he too was to suffer, at times considerably, from Divine's self-ishness and erratic moods on the road, Rob was never anything but totally loyal and devoted to his employer's welfare and professional image. There was a very strong bond of friendship between them. Both our lives changed for the better when Rob Saduski joined us in our worldwide adventures.

Back on the road, promoting 'You Think You're a Man' in England, Germany, Holland, Spain and throughout Scandinavia, Divi found a greater degree of satisfaction in his work, travelling with his new assistant. Divine even accepted the task of doing his own make-up again, while Rob prepared everything else. The association was going so well that it was no longer necessary for me to make frequent trips across the Atlantic. I would join them when there was a special event, such as a video shoot for the latest single or an important TV appearance, but I could now have a greater confidence in Divi's ability to be on the road without me.

Barry Evangeli informed me that the current hit single had been licensed to Liberation Records in Australia. The label was keen to bring Divine down under for a promotional tour, but Barry, aware of our needs by now, had warned them that Divine would require a fee and suggested they try to line up some disco shows. As Divi was unknown in Australia – none of his previous records, or his films, had yet been released there – the label decided it would be necessary to generate as much publicity as possible *prior* to his arrival on the continent, thereby creating a demand. Divi agreed to be fully co-operative with such publicity requirements.

The Melbourne-based *Tonight* television show requested a live-by-satellite interview, which was arranged on the roof of a building in Zurich, Switzerland, where Divi was currently appearing, one week before the scheduled trip to Australia. At the last minute, Divi's touring schedule had to be changed and, to meet the commitment of the TV interview – which could not be altered because of the necessity to confirm expensive satellite time – Divi was flown by private helicopter to Zurich and, despite a hectic, uncomfortable and inconvenient day's side-trip, arrived only ten minutes late. The TV station claimed this delay 'cost $15,000 and involved reorganising the entire northern hemisphere link-up'.

No one had warned either Divi or myself about the controversy that already existed prior to this interview. On promoting the 'exclusive satellite link-up', Channel Nine's chat-show star, Bert Newton, had invited two of his regular show guests – Derryn Hynch, a radio DJ/ interviewer, and Ian 'Molly' Meldrum, a TV pop show host – to comment. Hynch said Divine's films were 'pornographic' and Meldrum declared he would never show the star's pop video clip on his programme, *Countdown*. Newton himself joined the debate with, 'I find Divine grotesque and revolting and would not want to see his work.' The programme called for a ban on Divi's entering Australia. 'Australians shouldn't have to suffer failed foreigners trying to flog their acts here,' declared Hynch in righteous tones.

The brief interview commenced and Newton went on the attack, accusing Divi of being nothing but 'a gay porno star'. Divi, exhausted, unprepared and unaware of the furore, was visibly shocked. All he could do was immediately launch into his time-honoured defence of performing *that* scene in *that* film. He described his early films as 'avant-garde comedies, not pornographic at all'.

The interview was abruptly terminated as the satellite link closed down and Divi, livid and bewildered, was back in his helicopter, rushing to a waiting disco audience of Swiss fans.

In Australia, outraged TV viewers called to protest. John-Michael Howson, star of a rival TV talk show, came to Divi's defence. 'Divine is sleazy and tacky, but his films aren't pornographic,' he told the press. 'And as for Molly going on and being all punctured and bruised innocence, when on *Countdown* he promotes certain record stars who have the private lives of well-trained gutter rats . . . I get so bored with people who sit in moral judgement without knowing the facts. I'm sick and tired of all the rubbish and media hype which has been aired about Divine over the past week.'

The controversy made front-page headlines all over Australia. I guess the shit had finally hit the fan!

' "Do you feel your acting skills have grown?" I asked Divine. "Oh, sure, especially if you watch the very first films. I'm still not Sarah Bernhardt, but I'm up there with Helen Hayes. I think every actor grows with every project he's done. If you don't, it's time to quit and put it aside because you're not an actor. Yeah, I think I've gotten better. I am a comedian. A comic actor. My timing has gotten better." ' (The *Advocate*, 1988)

14 Divi Goes Legit

' "I'm less trashy than I used to be," Divine confessed. "Of course
I've never been really trashy in real life. But in my role as a comedian,
where I used to be utterly filthy, I am now more reserved. To tell the
truth, I've gotten interested in acting, which is a lot more than you
can say for many of today's movie stars. I guess I'm mellowing. I
mean there's enough vulgarity, enough trash on television. I've
always tried to work against the grain in my job as a comedian. But
now the grain is coarseness and foul language. Raunchiness is so
commonplace. It's everywhere, in movies and on TV, and so these
things don't have the shock value they once had." '

San Francisco Chronicle, 4 November 1981

ARRIVED IN AUSTRALIA ON 22 SEPTEMBER 1984. Divi and Rob arrived the
next day, in great humour after a fun overnight stop in Singapore.
It's fortunate that I had had time to cancel the planned airport press
conference (never a good idea, not knowing what state he would be
in on arrival), as Divi walked trouser-less through customs and immigration, wrapped in British Airways blankets. It seems he had spilled
some wine on his trousers during the flight. An air steward had then
burned a hole while trying to dry them in the microwave. How the
press would have loved that photo.

'Take one fat transvestite, a zealous radio commentator and a nervous teenybopper music show compere, mix in some vitriol and acidic
comments and simmer on a *Tonight* show for three days,' commented
Australia's *Sun*. 'If your subject isn't a well-done household name by
then, you've had it on the wrong heat. The irony of all this is that
Divine has become a sensation. In their efforts to sway public opinion,
Meldrum and Hynch have put Divine right out front.'

Because of the massive advance publicity, Divi was indeed very
much in demand. *Too* much. For the first time in his career, we were
obliged to cancel many of the appointments that our record company's
publicity department had arranged. They had literally filled each day,
from 10 a.m. to 6 p.m., with individual interviews, followed by his
show every night at nine in Sydney's Kinselas Night Club.

Divi magnificently hosted a packed press conference on his first day

— fencing off the obvious, controversial questions and promoting his talents and achievements to his heart's content — and then met as many individual members of the media as possible, given his full itinerary for the next three weeks. The Channel Nine publicity stunt — as many were now accusing it of having been — had also succeeded in filling a date book full of performance venues.

Kinselas was a 246-capacity cabaret venue and Divi was booked for a full week of performances. Admission ticket prices were high, so most of the younger fans who were now dancing to 'You Think You're a Man' were excluded. His first night audience was hostile; clearly waiting for this man who claimed he wasn't a porno star to show them exactly what he was.

'Talk dirty, Divine!' a man screamed from the neat rows of tables, only three minutes into the act. Others joined in. 'Yeh, forget the crap songs,' a woman added. 'Just talk dirty. We wanna hear some filth!'

Divi signalled for me to stop the tape. He was angrily stomping across the cabaret stage — no intimacy, *yet*, with this audience — and I could tell we were going to get a fabulous show. I had learned long ago that the angrier the *Man* when he stepped on stage, the more outrageous would be the *Female* Character. Divi *used* Divine a lot on stage to release his own pent-up frustrations. This impolite, offensive Australian audience had no idea what was to hit them now.

Divi launched into an attack of verbal diarrhoea. Even I, who thought he couldn't shock me any more, was open-mouthed. He abused this audience beyond anything they could ever have expected, instructing the electrician to bring up the house lights so that he could see their faces. The hecklers, of course, nearly vanished under their tables at this demand.

Every scatalogical remark I had ever heard him make — and many I had never heard before — came out in an avalanche of Anglo-Saxon words and references to individual audience members' bodily parts and functions. He even told the anecdote of *that* scene in *that* film, but with greater putrid detail than ever previously offered. And, in this book, I couldn't repeat the on-stage comments he made concerning the private lives of both Derryn Hynch and 'Molly' Meldrum. He was getting his own back to wild howls of laugher. This was his arena.

Divi was not going to be beaten. Nor abused by his audience. He gave them what they wanted. Trash. Filth. Obscenity. In bucket-loads. And, of course, they adored it. That first-night act in Australia continued for over one hour, with only seven songs on his tape. He received a standing ovation. The next day, all tickets were sold out for the week's run in Sydney.

Despite his sincere wish to clean up a heavily soiled image in this country, he was too much of a professional to disappoint his audiences. We talked at length the next morning over breakfast. He realised that, by giving them what they wanted, he would have put them in good humour to listen to his recordings. By the time they left Kinselas, they couldn't avoid being aware that he was a pop singer – or, at least, a disco diva – whatever else they might think he was. We set about writing a new script together. I can only hope those scribbled notes were not left on the breakfast table at the Sebel Town House Hotel for the lovely restaurant manageress to find.

Of course, we were not surprised that this act – given all the advance publicity and Divi's subsequent protestations – would not please the press. However, their barbed, vitriolic comments just attracted more of the curious to want to experience this unique entertainer for themselves. An example of Australian press reaction came from Leo Schofield, writing in the *Sydney Morning Herald*:

> And while I don't exactly think Divine should be run out of town, I'm at a loss to understand how such a vulgar, foul-mouthed, relentlessy unfunny and spectacularly untalented heterophobe performer can manage to attract an audience. . . . At the end of the show, Divine changes her frock. This is all the audience gets in the way of relief because it means the performer is off-stage for a blessed moment or two.

Some of Divi's Australian fans were making themselves even more easily available to him than the Europeans. Each day and night, there would be a few girls and boys waiting outside the hotel for his autograph. Or something more. Divi was grabbing a lot of 'ten-minute breaks' between press interviews, while a young female fan would wait patiently outside the hotel, without her young male companion. One late night, after a triumphant show at Kinselas, Ross knocked on Divi's bedroom door, requesting a signed photo. Ross stayed the night.

A week in Melbourne followed, Divi performing at a different venue – discos, rock clubs, university halls – for each of seven nights. Ross, about twenty, long blond hair and somewhat effeminate – and out of work – was now a fourth member of our party. Divi had an obvious crush on him and started to behave once again in the selfish, possessive way I recalled from the days on the road with Lee; Rob, however, had not experienced this before and was very hurt. Divi just ignored everyone else's needs and sensitivities while he had a boyfriend by his side. And this particular Australian loved it, clearly deciding he would take over as Divi's representative while in this new position of fame by association. He started to inform me of what 'Divi and I will be doing for the day', despite the business plans I had already confirmed.

Of course, Rob and I were having none of it. In spite of Divi's displays of jealousy, we gave Ross as hard a time back as he gave us. I refused to show even a false friendship for the sake of a cheap trick. I decided to make it open warfare; I had no time to spare in niceties as Ross's 'servicing' to Divi was affecting the star's commitments in Melbourne. It worked. Divi, once again, had to decide on his priorities. Ross was sent packing with a one-way air ticket back to Sydney, which, for a change, I had great pleasure in charging to our travel account.

The plush, modern hotel in Melbourne had one of those boards in the lobby, announcing the celebrities currently in residence. It was good publicity for the hotel – the tourists loved it – and most of the famous and would-be-famous were glad to have their egos boosted on arrival. The board currently displayed some twenty names, most of which meant nothing to us. At the very top of the list was 'Her Grace the Duchess of Hamilton', then, 'Divine'.

Divi's adoration of Britain's Royal Family had only brought about one, brief meeting to date – 'I met Princess Margaret when she opened an exhibition in Bath and she said that she knew all about me,' Divine told the press, adding naughtily: 'we had a long discussion about her sister!' Needless to say, he had still not had his tea with the Queen. But here, in this hotel, was a member of The Family (albiet very distant, and only by marriage) and *he* had the second billing. It took no time at all, through the hotel's very willing press agent, to arrange a meeting between them. We were told that Her Grace had read about Divi's scandalous arrival in Australia and longed to meet him.

The 39-year-old Duchess was in Australia to open the Heritage Festival at the State of Victoria's own town of Hamilton. The girl from Sussex had married Scotland's premier peer, the 15th in an illustrious line which extended right back to James IV of Scotland, and they now had four children. Her current trip to Australia was an effort to prove she could handle these official duties on her own when necessary. We were told she was delightful, but very nervous.

Divi and I were invited to drink sherry with Her Grace at six o'clock, prior to her official departure to Hamilton that evening at seven. Divi was over the moon and Rob spent the day preparing his spotlessly perfect outfit for the meeting: a three-piece Tommy Nutter white silk suit, white Maud Frizon lizard-skin shoes and all the essential accessories, including a discreet show of personalised Andrew Logan jewellery. Divi was perspiring with heat, nervousness and excitement as we knocked at the door of her hotel suite, at exactly 6 p.m. 'How should I behave?' he whispered to me. 'Am I supposed to bow, or something?'

Her Grace's travelling companion, Jeannie, opened the door and invited us in, apologising on the Duchess's behalf by explaining that she was taking a little longer to prepare than she had envisaged. We sipped sherry. Divine sweated profusely.

'Divine, is that you?' a gentle voice enquired from the other room in the suite. 'Oh, please come in. Don't stand on ceremony.'

Jeannie nodded her approval and we were shown into Her Grace's bedroom. The bathroom was at the far end and the door was open. Sally, Her Grace the Duchess of Hamilton, was sitting on the toilet seat, in her bra and tights, nervously trying to complete her make-up. Divi grinned and stopped sweating.

'Divine, my dear,' Sally said, without turning to greet us formally. 'I'm told you're something of an expert at this. You wouldn't be a darling, would you, and give me a hand? I'm all fingers and thumbs.' Within seconds, Divi had thrown his jacket on to the bed, rolled up his perfectly pressed, beautifully-tailored shirt sleeves and was sitting on the bathroom stool, gossiping away with Her Grace as he carefully applied her eye make-up. I was trying hard to suppress my laughter, but she caught me in her mirror.

'Oh, this must seem so strange to you, Mr Jay,' she offered. 'I do hope you didn't mind my talking to your star like that. I'm sure this is not quite the image you had expected.' Divi and I looked at each other and smiled. How many times had I made that comment to others about *him* in the past?

The task completed, Sally instructed Jeannie to go to the hotel manager's office and request her tiara from the safe. She then explained to us that the tiara is the gift she received – on loan, of course – from Her Majesty the Queen on her marriage to the Duke. She was entitled to wear one of the Crown Jewels. Divi's jaw dropped a mile. The sweat returned. While Her Grace struggled to get into her tartan ball gown for the occasion, he whispered to me, 'Bernard, I don't believe this is happening to me. I'm going to touch one of the Crown Jewels!'

Sally asked Divi questions about his career, and soon Jeannie returned. In her hand she carried a plastic Marks and Spencer carrier bag – I truly believe Divi had expected a red plush brocaded cushion carried proudly by a uniformed servant – from which she produced the beautiful tiara.

'Can you help me on with this, please, Divine?' Divi's hands trembled as he took hold of the tiara. Then – the moment of relief I had been waiting for – he just burst out laughing. Sally smiled and said, apologetically, 'Oh my, I've ruined another dream for you, dear Divine. I suppose you didn't expect that piece of elastic on the back to hold it in place.'

Divine fitted the tiara on Her Grace's head as if he were the Archbishop annointing the Monarch. He handled the elastic as if it were gold. This tender, loving moment remained one of the most treasured memories of Divine's life.

Elegantly dressed once again, Divi joined Her Grace as she made her formal departure for the evening. The Melbourne press were waiting in the hotel lobby. They were more than a little shocked to see *this* exquisitely dressed, beaming gentleman in white, escorting Her Grace to her car.

'Just a minute, please,' Sally requested of the photographers. She then led Divi by the hand to the celebrity display board and insisted the photographers take a picture of them together – her in full 'drag', him without – pointing to their names. The press adored it and the photo was everywhere the next day. Which only greatly increased the confusion in Australia as to exactly who – and what – this overweight person actually was. And what company he kept.

Divi triumphed again in Melbourne. He returned to Bert Newton's *Tonight* show, giving an interview, this time face-to-face with his host in the studio. Derryn Hynch had also been invited to meet Divine on the live show. The producers expected an all-out fight. What they got was a gentle, polite, perfectly attired professional actor quietly and calmly answering their questions. No matter how much they tried, neither Newton nor Hynch could ruffle Divine.

Then Divi asked Hynch what it was that so offended him. 'Had you ever taken the trouble to find out about my career before accusing me of being a porno star?' Divi enquired. 'Exactly what troubles you so much personally that you should get so heated up about me?' In for the kill. Hynch stormed off the studio floor and caught himself in the black curtains, trying to make a dramatic exit. He made a fool of himself.

Once again, Divi had won his day – by just being himself. The following week, Channel Nine announced it was axing the long-running four-nights-a-week TV show.

And the pop star Divine was currently number 8 in *Billboard*'s Hits Of The World Chart for Australia. Stevie Wonder's 'I Just Called To Say I Love You' was number 1, George Michael's 'Careless Whisper' was number 2; and Tina Turner, a singer Divi idolised, was falling behind him at number 14. Proof positive.

Then, the final charge for Divi in this adventure: an invitation to perform live on *Countdown*, 'Molly' Meldrum's show, on which he had declared with such venom only two weeks before, that he would never even show Divine's video clip. Somewhat conveniently, we thought, 'Molly' himself was in New York for the week, taping interviews, but a videotape of him was screened prior to Divi's performance, welcoming my star to his show. Such is the hypocritical world of showbusiness.

From Melbourne our record company sent us to Surfers Paradise, in the notoriously conservative State of Queensland. At the sound check in the 2,000-capacity Bombay Rock Club, I was informed by the venue's manager that 'four-letter obscenities are against the law in Queensland and, if Divine utters one word of filth or sexual innuendo from the stage tonight, he will be taken to jail'. In addition, as I had now accepted this instruction on the performer's behalf, I would be liable to the same penalty, I was informed.

I related the message to Divi. Very reluctantly, we agreed he would cut all the trash from his act that night and basically just sing the songs. We had no wish to go to jail, but he didn't want to disappoint the fans by not turning up for the show.

The rock hall was packed (which seemed to surprise the manager) and I started Divi's tape, sensing I should be in control of matters myself at this event. 'Native Love' was completed and the audience applauded. Divi stepped forward and instead of opening with his usual greeting – 'You want more? I can't hear you! You want more? Well, fuck you!' – he said, 'You want more? I can't hear you! You want more? Well, *tough*!'

It was all so inappropriate. Of course, the audience didn't laugh. They were waiting for the scandalous act they had been reading about for two weeks in their daily papers. Divi was clearly hating the show and I just played straight through the next four songs, without stopping the tape. I had no choice but to give him a break at this point as

Divi could not find enough energy to just keep singing one song after another for 40 minutes.

A pause. What would he do now, I wondered. The police were in uniformed evidence, standing – would you believe it? – at the side of the stage in full view of the audience. And then the unexpected happened. The timing was unbelievable.

'Show us your tits!' came the familiar order from a young male in the audience. 'Show us your tits!'

Divi could hold back no longer. After all, a good actor should always remain faithful to his script. 'Show us your willy, first,' came his stock response. I looked at the police. They didn't move. Divi, as always, repeated the instruction. The audience was starting to warm up, obviously loving this highly unorthodox interaction.

In all the years Divi had now used this method of putting down hecklers, the male object of his script had never taken up the star's suggestion. In Queensland, Australia, of all places, this boy, clearly indicating a very drugged state by his unsure movements, jumped on the stage and, before Divi could push him off – which he was about to do – the boy dropped his pants and completely obeyed the star's order.

The crowd cheered and roared their approval. The boy quickly jumped off the stage, vanishing into the audience. Divi looked at the police, who still hadn't moved from their vantage point. It was incredible. What he did next was, to me, at that moment, the most forgiveable and understandable piece of improvisation he ever attempted on stage.

Striding angrily to the very front of the platform, microphone in hand, he screamed: 'You can fucking get away with showing your dick in this godforsaken hole, but I'm not allowed to say "Fuck"! Well,' he continued even more aggressively. 'Fuck you! Fuck you! Fuck you very much!'

That did it. The police moved in and 'assisted' Divi off the stage. I raced round to the dressing room, where our names and addresses were duly taken down, passport numbers noted (we always carried them with us in case of such an incident) and formal warnings given. We were not charged, but were advised to leave Queensland as quickly as possible.

The first commuter plane from Queensland to New South Wales the next morning had never seen three more willing passengers.

The publicity from this visit to Paradise created two more sold-out concerts in Sydney before we left Australia. The record was selling everywhere and Divi had earned excellent fees from the tour. We had all achieved our objects. On our departure at the airport, Liberation Records presented Divi with an XXL T-shirt, reading 'TUFF YOU VERY MUCH!' He loved it.

Divi, Rob and I returned to England to tour once again and made a one-day side-trip to Munich, where Pete Waterman and his team were completing some studio work together. They had written a song for Divine—a kind of cocky response to the complaints from viewers after the *Top of the Pops* fiasco—titled 'I'm So Beautiful' and were eager to record it. So Divi joined Stock, Aitken, Waterman and Barry Evangeli to make a second single for Proto Records.

Divi had longed to get rid of his bothersome, trouble-causing playback tapes—the tape decks provided were forever breaking down—and use a live band on his tours. There were obvious problems to be solved (apart from the one of additional expense) because the disco tracks were not recorded by live musicians, the sounds having been created from synthesisers and other electronic equipment. Pete Ware took on the task of bringing together three other musicians—he would play keyboards himself—and became Musical Director for the band, Divine Intervention. It proved necessary to use the tapes to augment the live musicians, so we stil had the problem Divi had wanted to leave behind, but we also appointed an experienced road manager who, along with driving the minibus and handling the cash, would be able to maintain the equipment to a more reliable standard.

Our booking agents had no trouble obtaining the higher fees I demanded—to cover the increased expenditure—as Divi was riding high on a wave of success from 'You Think You're a Man' and was now the most popular and sought-after-dance-music-venue attraction in Britain. In addition, I was told, many venues—such as the university campuses, for which Divi was now in demand—were delighted that a live band was accompanying the star as their customers felt cheated by playback acts.

So now we were a team of eight on the road and Divi was thoroughly enjoying this new role as Front Man. There were even times—much to my and Rob's astonishment—when Divi would be the life of the party on the long daytime journeys, regaling his musicians with outrageously camp anecdotes. They loved it all and became fond of their star, treating him, initially, with something approaching reverence.

Divi gave a concert (with our band, we could now call it this) at Warwick University, where young female students screamed and yelled at the front of the stage, a few of them tearing off T-shirts and underwear and throwing the items at the star. It was quite bizarre: how far we had travelled since that legendary body-part signing in Atlanta. The girls would also storm the dressing rooms and beg Divine for photos and other souvenirs. Often, we would find them waiting outside our hotels, but, much to the frustration and bewilderment of the boys in the band, the girls would *only* be interested in Divine. The phenomenon of the female rock 'n' roll groupie is a difficult one to fathom, made even more so by their lust for this unusual looking man in drag.

'Alan Rudolph called my office in New York and said he wanted to meet me,' Divine proudly recalled of the way he was cast in Rudolph's film *Trouble in Mind*. 'So we met and he gave me a script and said, "Here, I've written this part for you. And I want you to do it; and, if you want to do it, it's yours." And I said, "Wait a minute. I don't have to read for this? I don't have to do anything?" He said, "Well, no, a star of your calibre doesn't have to read. I wrote it for you and you're my first choice. If you don't want to do it then I'll find someone else. But I would love for you to do it."

'Of course, my manager was sitting there,' Divi continued. 'I would have done the movie for nothing, but you can't say that because he would have had a heart attack. So I had to pretend like I was cool and didn't really want to do it. "Well, we'll call you," I said, thinking *sign the fucking contract!* But it worked out find. We called the next day and they were quite thrilled.'

And that *was* – allowing for a slight dramatisation on Divi's part – how it happened. The film's producers, Carolyn Pfeiffer and David Blocker, just called one day and said they were bringing Alan Rudolph to meet me. When they explained what it was about – that the role was a male one – I just suggested Divine be at the first meeting too. It wasn't necessary to go into complicated business negotiations. To be honest, if it had been necessary, I *would* have let Divi do it for nothing. It was such a wonderful opportunity for him. And just at the time he needed it. He was ready to prove to his public what he had believed for so long – that the dress wasn't an essential prop in order to hire Divine.

Rudolph's original description of the character Hilly Blue was 'a pasty mess of hermaphrodite evil with clear and cold eyes like melted snow and pale and doughy skin. The voice is a raspy falsetto.' 'It's a case of the right actor playing the right role,' said the writer/director of the casting of Divine.

Rudolph's *Choose Me* was one of the most acclaimed films of 1984.

As a director, he was already known for taking liberties with himself as a screenwriter, creating a collaborative atmosphere with name actors whose regard for him was such that they accepted comparatively low salaries to work with him. Keith Carradine and Genevieve Bujold were two such actors. Kris Kristofferson and Lori Singer were already joining them to star in *Trouble in Mind*. Another of Divine's dreams came true when he saw the movie's poster, announcing 'Divine as Hilly Blue' under these names.

If this wasn't legitimacy, then what was? And Divine yearned for it so badly. *Trouble in Mind* was a godsend.

Kris Kristofferson played Hawk, an ex-con and ex-cop vying with Keith Carradine, as Coop, for the affections of Lori Singer, who played Georgia, an innocent waitress working in the café run by Genevieve Bujold's worldly-wise Wanda. Divine was Hilly Blue, the gangster kingpin of Alan Rudolph's fictitious Rain City.

Location filming, scheduled for March 1985, was in Seattle. Divi would be required for thirteen days only. 'While Divine doesn't occupy as much screen time as the other characters,' Rudolph explained, 'Hilly Blue's presence and power pervades the exaggerated world the film has created.'

The filmscript was not easy to read. Alan Rudolph gives free rein to his stream-of-consciousness imagery – to the association of characters, situations and settings that flow with their own inner logic. As the director/writer himself claims to 'never know what my films are about until they're done, and only then when someone else tells me', it was no wonder that the script of *Trouble in Mind* was beyond Divi's comprehension. I tried to summarise the plot for him, but he still understood very little of what was intended. In the event, it only seemed necessary for Divi to get a grasp on his own character, so we concentrated on his lines.

For the record, which might surprise many, Divi – at least during the time I worked with him – *never* read a script in full. Even with John Waters's movies, John would discuss the role with him, I would talk about the basic story-line, and then Jay Bennett, or another, would help him learn the lines of a specific scene the night prior to it being shot. Divi admitted to me that he never really knew exactly what was going on in any scene he filmed. His was a natural ability to create a character and he was willing – or lazy enough? – to rely on that ability. With the help of his directors, it worked for him. But it quite shocked me; what a risk he was taking.

The first time we watched a screening of *Polyester* together, he laughed out loud throughout. He told me after that it was only now that he understood what Francine Fishpaw was going through, as he'd never read the script. I'm sure he never managed to understand *Trouble in Mind*.

As filming had already been in progress for a few weeks before Divi arrived, he was more nervous than ever as he realised this cast would all be buddies by now and he felt very much the outsider. Would they take him seriously?

He told journalists, 'With some of the stars I'm working with now, I say to myself, "I can't work with them. I can't do a scene with Kris Kristofferson. He's a famous movie star." And Alan Rudolph said, "So are you." I replied, "It's just not the same thing to me." Kris was very nice. Could not have been sweeter. He came over and said, "You're one of the guys," and tapped me on the back. It was great. But sometimes I feel like Baby Huey. That huge duck with the little parents. They're all these normal people on the set, and then they bring me out.'

However, once again, I took great pride in receiving regular reports from the film's production office of Divi's absolute professionalism and how the director and cast had all 'fallen in love with him'. Indeed, during the two weeks in Seattle, Divine had no problems to speak of, except for not understanding what the film was all about.

Divi amused me with another anecdote about his efforts to get to know his cast. 'Genevieve Bujold and I were in the make-up room and she said to me, "What is this shit? This Divine shit?" She offered to take me to a Neil Diamond concert, she offered me a ride in a limousine. I said, "Darling, it'll take more than a ride in a limousine to get me to a Neil Diamond concert!" And later that night she turned up on the set and she said, "You were right, it wasn't worth the ride." '

Early on in filming, Kristofferson badly damaged his hand and had to stay in hospital for a few days. This put the entire schedule back and the producers decided, as they were contractually entitled to do, that they would need Divi for a week beyond the original completion date of 26 March. Divi's very unusual two-edged career – both edges now running parallel to each other – once again created a problem. I had confirmed a well-paid engagement in Hong Kong for 30/31st March for him to open a new nightclub as the star attraction.

The producers of *Trouble in Mind* were most obliging and re-scheduled so that Divi could fulfil his obligation in Hong Kong and then immediately return to location filming in Seattle. I picked up Divi

and Rob Saduski from the set, where they had been working throughout the day. We travelled overnight to Hong Kong and were taken to
our hotel suites. On arrival, Divi literally cried with joy on finding a
huge bouquet of flowers in his suite, wishing him luck in Hong Kong,
'from Kris, Keith, Lori, Genevieve and all in Rain City'.

While Divi tried to sleep off the jet-lag and – goodness knows how he
managed it – somewhat reluctantly bring his mind back to the Female
Character, I visited the Canton, the elegant new nightclub next door to
our hotel and being readied for its grand opening the next evening. A
huge poster outside proclaimed:

CANTON WELCOMES DIVINE
The Most Beautiful Woman In The World
starring in
The Year's Most Eagerly Awaited Event

They had omitted the essential word 'Almost' after his description. I
knew Divi was not famous in Hong Kong; surely the guests at this most
chic of openings – flying in from all over Asia, I was assured – would be
expecting Miss World to entertain them, from the wording on the poster. Would they have any idea that this description was a joke?

The following morning, severely affected by jet-lag, Divi met the
Hong Kong media. They were indeed bemused, but they loved him and
gave him the depth to explain, in his inimitable way, what his act was
all about. His photo and quotes were all over the papers later that day. I
stopped worrying about a potential 'trades description act' lawsuit. As
usual, the press had described *everything* in detail.

The Canton was designed for about 150 night revellers. The opening
night attracted over 500, all it seemed holding invitations. There was
chaos in the street outside and there were police on horseback attempting to control the elegant, but impatient crowd. There was no way I
could sneak Divi, fully prepared in costume and make-up, through the
hotel's front door and into the side entrance of the nightclub, as I had
planned earlier in the day.

The hotel manager told us of an old, unused tunnel connecting the
two buildings. A few moments later, the hotel manager, Rob Saduski
and I were walking through the sewers of Hong Kong, six inches deep
in filthy water and, I was convinced, surrounded by rats, with six
Chinese waiters carrying Divi horizontally above their heads to avoid
his getting wet – or bitten!

Yet again, under the most difficult of circumstances, Divi was fantastic, holding his well-over-capacity audience spellbound. I don't think many of them understood what the act was about, but, by the time Divi appeared on stage, weary yet dry, they were drunk enough to just let themselves go and laugh. And they howled at him. Mostly when he was singing.

The next morning we were back on a plane to Seattle. On our arrival, a limo provided by the film company took Divi straight to *Trouble in Mind*'s location. He went to his dressing room, changed into his movie costume – a Tommy Nutter-designed tuxedo – and started acting. When he completed his spectacular death scene – blown to pieces by a flying bullet – filming came to a brief halt while the cast and crew applauded. Kristofferson walked over to him and publicly announced, 'You know, Divine, I wasn't at all sure about you when we first met, but, by heavens, you really are one of the guys.'

This had to be the most satisfying moment in Divine's career and one of which he, justifiably, boasted to all who would listen. That brief, unrehearsed speech from the multi-talented star was the biggest compliment Divine could be paid. What he had waited all his life to hear.

The critics were confused by Rudolph's off-centre *film noir*. The reviews were mixed. But, once again, Divine received a set of personal notices, some of which he could be justly proud. 'There are ample flourishes and moments . . . but the only one who manages to hold up the film's heavy philosophical weight is Divine, in his first all-male role,' stated the *Hollywood Reporter*. 'Playing a Sydney Greenstreet-twisted villain, Divine's world-weary asides . . . are marvelously counterpointal to the film's ennui noir decor.' The *New York Daily News* noted: '. . . the real surprise is the female impersonator Divine. He turns Hilly Blue into a deliciously campy, roly-poly bad guy.'

But, as Divine knew better than anyone, you can't win 'em all. 'Among several terrible performances,' commented the *New York Times*, 'Divine stands out – he gives camp a bad name.'

However, in January 1986, Divi was thrilled to read in the *Los Angeles Times*, 'Looking back over the last 12 months for noteworthy movie items is like browsing the table for bargains during the last hour of a yard sale. . . . Still, the year had its moments. There was the fabulous Divine, playing both a winsome prairie hooker (*Lust in the Dust*) and an evil gang lord (*Trouble in Mind*).'

Within a month of completing his latest film, we were all back in

Europe for essential promotion of his new single, 'I'm So Beautiful'. For Divi, this meant the usual, endless days of interviews, TV appearances and club gigs, interrupted only (when he was in London) by breakfast at Harrods and tea at Fortnum and Mason.

Peter Stringfellow's Hippodrome Club had become the most successful disco in London; a sort of English Studio 54 of the eighties. Monday night was 'Gay Night' and Divi had already proved, several times, to be a hugely successful draw, packing the venue to well over capacity. Peter was generous with the fees he paid to Divine and he appreciated that we would always go out of our way to make the Hippodrome appearances more theatrical, more of a special event.

With our new band on stage, augmented for this occasion by eight male bodybuilders – whom Divi ceremoniously stripped from Stars and Stripes boxer shorts to Union Jack bikini briefs – and a brilliant display of fireworks, lasers and lighting effects, he did two shows for the American Independence Day Celebrations, one on the Monday 'Gay Night', the other on the following Thursday.

'I'm here representing Freedom, Liberty, Family Values and the fucking American Way of Life,' Divine roared, rising on the hydraulic stage from the basement level of the club, draped from head to toe in the American flag. Both Peter Stringfellow and I were delighted to see he had attracted as large a crowd – and as great an ovation – on both nights, despite the gender orientation of the audience.

On the Thurdsay night, I had invited my best friend's sons to see Divi. I knew they had never before seen a live concert by a pop performer and, knowing I managed Divine, they had been longing to meet him. Detective Constable Alan Goss, whom I had known since 1971, had given me permission to bring his fifteen-year-old boys to the show and, being concerned for their welfare – they have always looked upon me as their godfather – I stood them within the security boundaries of the stage. Matthew and Luke were overjoyed and Divi treated them kindly, making them feel very special. Being identical twins – and very fashionable at the time with their long blond hair and slightly dandyish mode of dressing – they attracted a great deal of attention from the audience while they were watching the show.

Back in Divi's dressing room – where he held the usual post-Hippodrome reception for friends, celebrities and hangers-on – the boys were entranced with the glamour of stardom. They decided there and then that they too wanted to be pop stars. They asked me if I would manage them. I advised them, thinking of their father's probable reaction to this conversation, to finish school and then we would talk about it. I wasn't aware, at the time, of any musical talent they might possess, but it wasn't difficult to realise that their stunning looks could help take them a long way.

Divi had his photo taken with them that night so they could have a permanent souvenir of their special evening. Three years later, they became the best-selling pop duo Bros, for a while the two most photographed faces in Britain. Divi would have been very proud of them. And, I'm sure, have taken more than a little credit.

'Divine is in danger of becoming the finest character actor since Alec Guinness, or a stale cartoon on the order of Viva, Candy Darling and Tiny Tim.' (*Washington Post*, 26 Feburary 1988)

15 Bored, Depressed and Lonely

' "I guess I love the attention, I love traveling. I love the people I've been able to meet that I wouldn't have been able to meet under other circumstances," Divine said. "Just that my whole life is completely different and I love living it. There are times when you think 'Why? Why do I bother? Jump off the roof?' But they are very brief, because I am very busy and I love what I am doing, so that's why I'm driven to this. I like to make people laugh." '

The Hamptons, 13 August 1981

IN THE FALL OF '85, Divi moved home. He rented a charming cottage on an estate by the Hudson River, about a hundred miles north of Manhattan. It was perfect for his needs at the time; he could behave like the Country Squire, inviting his friends to stay for weekends, cooking barbecues out on the patio, visiting the local antique shops and sitting late at night smoking pot and dozing off by the private swimming pool, to which he had access. Everything he owned was moved back up north again and lovingly placed around the house.

The ever-growing collection of soft toys – including teddy bears from all over the world – was beautifully displayed in an attic room. Expensively framed posters of his shows and films covered the living-room walls, while a montage of career photos was carefully positioned in his bedroom. Very quickly, it became Divine's Home and he was content there, together with his houseboy, Jay Bennett (now on a weekly salary and with a contract he had drawn up, detailing exactly what he would – and mostly wouldn't – agree to do), the two now large and heavy bulldogs, and, to my surprise, Lee. I liked Lee and always felt he was a good friend to Divi, but I was confused, having been told the relationship was now over. Divi assured me that Lee was living with him only in the capacity of *companion*, as he too had become tired of the never-ending party life in Key West.

With the cost of moving and all the charges Divi had made at local stores to enable him immediately to turn the rented cottage into his home – the locals being only too willing to give their new celebrity instant credit – the cashflow problems were becoming impossible to handle once again. He was still totally dependent on the income from the club tours and, as before, I could not manage to bring his net income from these gigs much higher than 40 per cent of the gross. He was demanding more and more luxury on the road, now staying at top hotels and flying in travelling companions whenever he felt bored. I was very reluctant to argue with him about such excesses as I knew how tough and tiring these tours were for him. My attitude was that if the additional luxuries enabled him to have some enjoyment, then he deserved them. However, this meant that the net receipts back in America were, in proportion, less and less. And his personal expenditures when at home were increasing at an alarming rate.

Meanwhile, InTune Music had produced another compilation album of Divi's hits. *The Story So Far* featured not only the two singles recorded in London, but also some of the Orlando tracks, which, the Titcheners informed me, they had licensed from 'O' Records through the Company of Two Pieters in Holland.

The album brought the following comments from Ted Mico, writing for Britain's *Melody Maker*:

> Who would have thought this year's disco queen would weigh in at 1/7th of a ton, and discover a means of making pounds out of pounds. . . . The growling Divine has no difficulty grappling with the feverish synth chords of 'I'm So Beautiful', wrestling with its unrepentant Boystown cliché, before beating them both into submission by the first chorus. . . . It's ironic that a drag queen can produce almost 23 minutes of dance without a drag, with music that is less emasculated than most of his prissy contemporaries.

We were waiting patiently for detailed financial statements from In-Tune Music Ltd. On signing the recording agreement in April 1984, Divi had been paid an advance against royalties of $10,000. The company had taken up its option to renew for a further year, paying their client a further advance of $15,000. Knowing that there were already production costs for two singles and two accompanying videos to be recouped from Divi's share, we were not yet expecting to see huge cheques arrive in the mail from InTune. But, after our previous experiences, we were watching carefully for valid paperwork. It was slow in arriving, which made us nervous. The Titchener brothers were very concerned to deliver everything to us as contractually obliged, but they explained their own frustrations in trying to obtain all the relevant figures.

Other matters were beginning to greatly concern both Divi and me about our relationship with InTune and Barry Evangeli. 'You Think You're a Man' and 'I'm So Beautiful' had been extremely successful recordings, achieving high chart placings and, we presumed, good sales in the territories in which they had been released. Our producing team—by this time known as Stock-Aitken-Waterman (Pete Ware had been dropped)—were themselves achieving even greater success with the band Dead or Alive and other artists, including Hazell Dean. We had been informed that InTune had argued with Pete Waterman over the expenditures involved in producing the two Divine singles and Waterman had subsequently declined any further approaches to work with us. We knew that Divi's success in making dance-music singles was very much to do with the current popularity of the record's producers. In Bobby Orlando and Stock-Aitken-Waterman he had two such popular and in-vogue producers.

In 1985, Divi made three more singles under his agreement with InTune—remakes of pop classics 'Walk Like a Man' and 'Twistin' the Night Away' and one written for him, 'Hard Magic'—all produced in the studios by Barry Evangeli, Nick Titchener or Pete Ware, none of whom were name producers who would attract attention to the releases. Although the three singles became popular club tracks and appeared in all the gay- and disco-oriented charts, they were not achieving anything like the cross-over success Divi had recently become used to.

Certainly, Divi was rarely out of the British press at the time. Proto released a picture disc of 'Walk Like a Man', shaped like a pair of men's briefs and 'showing huge Divine squeezed into a dress and clutching on to a scantily-clad young man,' according to the *Daily Mirror*. Some record stores refused to stock this version of the single 'where teenagers might see it'.

'I don't think today's youth is so prudish that they'd be upset by my little joke,' Divi responded. 'Underpants is not a dirty word. I never wear them. They're too confining for a personality as large as mine.'

Although Australia had certainly now been added to Divi's increasing worldwide fame, we were very worried that other previously successful territories—such as Benelux and Scandinavia—were hardly being serviced at all. Imports from Britain were arriving overnight and therefore the clubs were playing his records and the demand, though decreasing, was still there for club gigs in Europe. Because of the dispute we had with 'O' Records, we were unwilling to continue the relationship with the Company of Two Pieters. We found, to our shock, we no longer had licencees in these territories. At least the Bellaphon label had welcomed Divine for West Germany, but they were slow in promotion and complained of too many imports arriving from Britain prior to their own domestic releases.

Worst—and most frustrating—of all was that Evangeli appeared to have no credible contacts in North America and there was no sign whatsoever of a distribution deal being signed. Divi had now had nine singles—all successful in some territories and in varying degrees—but *none* of them had yet been distributed in his home country, the United States of America.

The imports from Britain—and the promos from 'O' Records—had made club hits throughout the country of all nine singles, enabling Divi to remain the star most in demand for personal appearances. America was even discovering the European videos Divine had been making to assist in the promotion of his singles. 'U-68 has just begun playing three of the divine one's most recent rock videos,' *New York Daily News* reported. 'Stations in Europe have been playing these clips for a while now, but U-68 is the first outlet on this side of the Atlantic to risk life and limb. Included are brilliantly appalling visualisations of the "singer's" European hits, "I'm So Beautiful", "Hard Magic" and the one number Divine was truly born to sing—"Walk Like a Man".'

But, everywhere we went together, we received complaint after complaint about not being able to buy the records in the stores. It was incredible to us. Here was the most visible of all disco recording artists— receiving more public exposure through his movie roles and general media coverage than any other in the history of this field—and there was no American deal. I begged Evangeli to come to the States and visit labels with me. I was convinced that, together, we could establish a distribution contract. Record labels knew that the artist's management did not hold the rights to sign licensing agreements and, although I was making some good contacts myself, they were not willing to open up formal discussions without the licensor—the copyright holder—at the desk. Consequently, with Orlando's distribution network problems, Divi's records have never been officially distributed in his own country—where he was most famous.

Meanwhile, Divi's parents had been invited to spend a few days with him when he was living in Key West. 'We had a wonderful time,' Frances told me. 'I took him and Jay Bennett shopping, then made him a pan of lasagne. We played his recordings and he seemed to enjoy having us around.'

He was also now making regular visits to the family home in Margate, the frequent return engagements at Fort Lauderdale's Copa proving useful in facilitating such reunions. I was welcomed with open arms each time I arrived with him (which he encouraged, as he was delighted to let me do all the talking for him, my advising his parents with a carefully censored outline of the latest career developments); both Frances and Harris were generous and warm to me. I loved to see the obvious delight they took in having their son back with them. I truly enjoyed these visits, but stopped accompanying Divi once he had the courage, and sometimes the temerity, to invite other friends to join him. I was no longer necessary and his friends were often clearly uncomfortable with my presence.

But there was also another reason why I stopped socialising with the Milsteads. I was becoming an unwilling conspirator in his efforts to convince his parents of his monetary success. I was forbidden by Divine to even hint about the cash problems he had. Just like his friends in England, his parents understandably believed that Divine was getting rich.

When you speak to those who have no practical experience of the entertainment industry, boasting of your current movies from which you received rave reviews, your nine worldwide hit singles for which you have been awarded Gold Records, your Country Home with its own swimming pool . . . when you arrive in a floor-length black mink coat and wear a large diamond in your ear . . . those listening are entitled to believe that you're rich. Divi wanted his parents to believe this – it was an important part of his needing their forgiveness and their pride in what he had achieved.

He started to send them expensive gifts and surprise them with long phone calls from all over Europe. 'I found that when I travel,' Divi told *Number One*, 'if I don't bring a few presents home, they're not as glad to see you for some reason!' He talked to his parents of sending them on a holiday cruise – first class of course – to join him in England. He promised his mother the fur coat she had longed for all her life. They were only too willing to believe him. But I was very uncomfortable with this deception. Divi's return to his parents' welcoming arms was one of falsehoods, of deceit. Although understanding the reasons behind it, I did not want to be his accomplice. And it was already beginning to cause me very embarrassing problems.

During one of his visits home, Frances had allowed her son to use her credit card at the local Sears department store. He had told her that he needed to pick up a few inexpensive items for his country home and that these particular items could not be found easily in upstate New York. She proudly accompanied Divine, the film star, dressed in his trademark dark glasses and Maud Frizon pumps, and enjoyed the shopping expedition with him. Divi thanked his mother for her kindness in purchasing these few household items, but conveniently forgot to return her credit card.

The next day, while the happy family relaxed in the back garden, enjoying the Florida sun, an excess of mother's home cooking and re-established relationships, Divine announced he would take an hour or so away to visit a local friend. Frances happily handed her son her car keys. Divi, it appeared, managed to stay awake behind the wheel long enough to reach Sears once again. As usual, the credit card was burning the proverbial hole in his pocket.

About two months later, I received an irate phone call from Mrs Milstead. She had just received the latest statement on her Sears account and discovered charges in excess of $1,000 (for her – living on a carefully planned retirement budget – a lot of money), which she had immediately questioned and been informed that the store was in pos-session of the signature of Harris Glenn Milstead for these purchases.

'How could Glenn do this to me,' she screamed down the phone. 'He has all that money himself and Harris and I are having to be so careful with our few funds. I just don't understand it.' I longed to explain to her, sensing that in the long run it would be better if they faced up to the truth; that her son continuously lived well beyond his means and that, on my desk at the time, was a bulging file of bills he had recently incur-red and could not afford to pay. But, of course, I remained loyal to my client and managed to temporarily calm Frances by assuring her that I would speak with Divine instantly. Before she rang off, she made me promise that I would send her a cheque that same day from her son's bank account to meet the debt. She obviously thought that was a simple task.

Why didn't she call Divine directly? I wondered. Was it that such a conversation would bring back too many painful memories; that she would prefer to indulge herself in the film star fantasy he had carefully planted? I called him and reported my conversation with his mother.

'That motherfucker owes it to me,' he bellowed. 'Why the fuck is the bitch bothering you? If she has a problem, tell her to call me.' I was shocked. That kind of outburst had no validation. I lost a great deal of respect for Divine over this very brief phone call.

Of course, I took on the task of paying Sears directly – over a period of time – from Divi's earnings. This enabled both mother and son to avoid any further conversation about the incident. It would seem that for Frances, even these many years later, it was best left that Glenn could still do no wrong.

Divi was eager to spend some time in Los Angeles, visiting friends and, if Greg Gorman could spare the time, getting some new photos taken. Pati Mayfield, my good friend and neighbour, started to relieve me of the time-consuming and frustrating task of working as Divi's booking agent. She was already experienced in the rock 'n' roll business from some years back, so it took her no time at all to become an expert at organising Divine's gigs – and the essential cashflow. Pati was a wonderful colleague to work with. She made instant friendships with the club owners across the States and, consequently, firm enemies of the other, mostly shady and unreliable booking agents that had dabbled with offers to Divine over the years. Pati soon became my personal assistant and Divi's full-time booking agent for his North American club gigs. With her efforts, tour dates were in abundance.

Two were arranged to earn some cash on the West Coast. The first was in a venue in east Los Angeles. Divi's 'dressing room' was behind a precariously balanced screen at the back of a tiny stage placed in a far corner of the vast dance floor. The club was packed with over 2,000 young Latino and Hispanic kids, high on the music and their drugs. The owners had insisted on paying me Divine's $3,500 fee as it came in at the pay booth. I carried to our cramped space a plastic bag stuffed full of crumpled one-dollar and five-dollar notes, which had taken me over half an hour to count and therefore delayed the start to the show. Divi was impatient, ready to get out on the stage and get it over with. The disco speakers were blaring in our ears and we couldn't attempt any conversation. I decided it was best to leave the bag behind the screen, where no one could go during the show and I could keep an eye on it from out front, rather than take the time now to fold the bills neatly and attempt the unlikely task of fitting them all into the money belt around my waist.

I positioned myself by the side of the stage, sensing there might be problems with this unruly crowd. Divi's tape, operated by Rob Saduski at the other side of the building, played its familiar announcement:

'Ladies and gentlemen – please welcome – the One – the Only – *Divine!*'

Those at the front of the cavernous hall watched Divi and screamed the lyrics of the familiar opening song. Those at the back danced to the music, oblivious of the sweating star jumping up and down on the makeshift stage. He was on his third song as I became aware that those who had been crowding the stage were suddenly leaving to go to the back of the room.

At that moment, true chaos broke out. A fight between three youths had developed at the back of the hall during Divi's act. Knives had been produced. The police were summoned and, as the venue had a reputation for violent outbreaks (of course, no one had warned us), they were there within minutes. A policewoman had rushed into the fight and had been stabbed. Now it seemed the entire Los Angeles Police Department had arrived on the scene. There was sheer pandemonium as kids tried to escape from the building, arrests were made, handcuffs attached, helicopters blazed their spotlights through the windows and sirens were blaring outside. An ambulance arrived to take the policewoman away.

Throughout this drama – which all took place within the space of a few moments – Divi was totally unaware, singing away to his tapes, spotlight shining in his eyes and music blasting his ears.

He couldn't hear me shout at him, so I rushed up on stage and grabbed his arm. He didn't understand what I was doing and pushed me away with some considerable force. Rob was trying to find his own way through to us and had left the tape running. As long as Divi could hear his music being played, he was determined to entertain, to earn his $3,500. I had no choice but to rush back on stage and pull his wig from his head, something I would never have dreamed of doing under anything but that kind of circumstance. I knew well that, in his mind, there was nothing worse than losing his wig in front of an audience. But this *did* seem to be a time for drastic action. He reacted as if I was insane and pushed me behind the screen, where I fell to the floor, still clutching his wig, my star towering above me, his sweat falling in gallons on my face.

Before he could crush me with his heels, I screamed out what was going on. As I did this, the police raced on to the stage and behind our screen. Divi, now acting from basic instincts, grabbed the black plastic bag full of loose notes and started trying to stuff it down the front of his dress. As far as he was concerned, he had been prepared to do his entire show and there was no way these fuckers were going to get any refund, whatever the reason the show had been cut short.

The police sergeant's face was a never-to-be-forgotten picture. I was still struggling to get up off the floor. Divi, wigless and make-up pouring down his face, was trying to hide a bag full of money—dollar bills were already falling out of the bottom of his miniskirt. Rob reached us just in time, and the police sergeant arranged an escort out of the building, much to his colleagues' amusement at the sight of this very unusual looking parade from backstage.

We were stranded in the middle of violent east Los Angeles, our car and driver nowhere to be seen. Police helicopters were still flying above us and road blocks were already in place. And Divi was still in full drag, clutching the precious plastic bag to his soaked tits. Our kindly police sergeant realised our dilemma and arranged a motor-cycle-escorted drive back to the hotel. As far as I knew, Divi's tape was still playing inside that particular war zone!

Our other gig on the West Coast was at the Palace in Hollywood—a sort of hybrid of London's Hippodrome and New York's Ritz. Although a disco, it featured live performances by many well-known rock bands. It was unusual for a disco star to do anything there beyond what is termed a PA: to arrive unannounced and sing the one particular song—to playback—that the singer's record company was currently pushing. Five minutes, in and out. And, of course, no fee. But Pati had negotiated a large fee for Divine and he, knowing this venue would be packed with the rich and famous of Hollywood, wanted to give the very best of shows. At Divi's expense, we flew in from England his road manager, Tim Sweeney, and musical director, Pete Ware. We engaged three other first-class musicians in Los Angeles, together with the usual disco dancers and back-up singers, and rehearsed for three days. Judging from the audience's reactions throughout his 50-minute set, we were content to have put yet another successful show—in an important venue—behind us.

However, two days later, the *Los Angeles Times* reported:

As a disco singer Divine falls a little short—and when Divine falls, you hear it . . . pop music's answer to football's Refrigerator revealed a voice that made Wendy O Williams sound like Julie Andrews and a frame that made, say, Simon Le Bon look like Twiggy. . . . The evening still could have been fun on the deranged, freakshow level that Divine knows so well, but the frightwigged chanteuse was content to play the coarse, raunchy red-hot mama, a nightmarish Mae West catering to the crowd's eagerness to whoop it up.

European touring itineraries were now being arranged at a feverish pace as Divi's singles crossed boundaries and turned up in unexpected places. It had become essential for me to travel with him again as his road managers couldn't cope with the tensions created by the star's moods and selfishness. He had grown bored with his band – realising that musicians who could often be drunk on stage were actually less reliable (and much more expensive) than faulty tape decks – and took far too much advantage of staff, demanding more and more spending money and, in one case, sulking and becoming incommunicative when he finally had to face up to the fact that a particular road manager was not to be seduced.

Divi had grown tired and depressed with touring Holland and Germany; the endless car journeys, the tiny, uncomfortable village hotels with only single beds, no room service and no elevators. Whenever he was back in these countries – frequently, as John Seine continued to provide us and his agency with an income – I would receive his demands to cancel the tour and let him come home. He was sad, lonely, bored and restless. Nothing Rob nor I could do would help. I would have private phone conversations with Rob and he would tell me that things couldn't get much worse. At one point, Divi had stopped talking to him at all and would take no interest in preparing for his shows. He had also – I would hear from angry agents and record companies – refused to give any more interviews or television appearances.

But the itineraries were confirmed and Divi could not afford to cancel and damage his reputation to that extent. Pati and I worked on an immediate change of plan; a travel schedule that, although frantic, we thought might interest our star with its differing locations.

On 17 June, Divi, Rob and I arrived in Finland, where he was to perform six gigs in six towns on six nights, including two Midsummer Eve Festivals, where the country's teenagers gathered – in huge camp sites buried in the deep forests – to undergo a kind of sexual initiation. Pop groups were flown in from all over the world as the finale to these weekends of pubescent discovery.

The end of the six-day tour left us in the middle of the country, far from an international airport. Divi refused to make the five-hour car journey back to Helsinki, so our promoters quickly arranged for us to take a commuter plane from a nearby private airfield. The plane would be rerouted in order to pick up its celebrity passengers.

We left the pretty, but uncomfortable Finnish hotel very early in the morning and drove to the airfield. No breakfast was available at this hour. Divi was in a foul temper, having not slept at all in the hotel's narrow, hard wooden bed. We were scheduled to meet the plane at seven; we arrived at the airfield at the not unreasonable time of 6.20 a.m. Divi screamed abuse at Rob at the top of his voice, blaming him for 'all this waste of time when I could have been trying to sleep' and suggesting that Rob had no interest in Divi's welfare. Rob backed away, aware that Divi was not going to stop now. There were two staff in the tin-hut reception area, clearly very embarrassed by this uncouth display of bullying.

I walked out, thinking that Divi might calm down if he didn't have me as an audience, and began to walk along the narrow, unfinished road leading from the hut, realising that I had become as bored with my colleague's selfish behaviour as he had with his own work. I decided I would leave them as quickly as possible and return to New York. I didn't need to suffer his insensitivity any more; I wasn't being paid to be his road manager. Suddenly I was aware of four voices bellowing at me. I turned and saw the tiny plane about to land, only a few yards away from me now. I had been walking down the middle of the runway. I ran for my life.

Divi was so amused by this that his mood changed abruptly. Rob relaxed in this, probably only-too-brief, moment of insanity. And I wondered what I would have to do next to keep my star amused.

We flew, via Helsinki and London's Heathrow, to Tel Aviv. 'Native Love' was number 6 in the Israeli charts and Divi had been invited to give three shows in the city's only rock club. On his opening night the sound system was so inadequate that it broke down twice in mid-song and Divi stormed into his dressing room and tore down all the drapes and wall hangings in his fury. After this disaster, there was a reception in a gay disco. Divi was introduced to a cute young Israeli, who then spent the night with him.

The next morning our Israeli promoter joined us to translate the morning newspaper's account of the previous night's show. The paper, of course, was written in Hebrew. There was a large photo of Divi in the middle of the page. Our colleague laughed, explaining that there really wasn't a specific Hebrew translation available of the name Divine – as the word would only be used in religious reference – so a literal translation of the headline accompanying the photo could be read as 'God Comes To Israel For the First Time'. Divi grinned, finding that quite acceptable.

When the others had departed, Divi and I started to chat. I tried approaching him about his recent, intolerable moods. I knew he really adored Rob – and very much appreciated how important was his help – so I thought I should warn him that his assistant was seriously thinking of packing his bags.

'I can't take this life any more, Bernard,' Divi opened the conversation. 'There's just no point. I work and work and work, dragging this ugly body around the world. And at the end of it all there's no money and no lover to go back home to.' I decided to listen and say nothing. 'It's not your fault,' he continued. 'I know you do your best for me and sometimes I must be the worst kind of pig to be around, but we just don't seem to be getting anywhere, do we? Sometimes, Bernard, I think you expect too much from all this. You're so determined, but it *isn't* going to happen. They'll never accept me the way we both want.

'I *hate* what I'm doing now. There's no fun left in these shows. It's the same old thing night after night. Let's face it –' he stared directly at me – 'there's been no offers of movies since *Trouble in Mind*. I'm going to spend the rest of my life putting on the fucking dress and jumping up and down to stupid songs, making a fool of myself.'

In my own mood at that time, it was difficult to know how to reply to him. I wanted to reassure him, once again – as I had done so many times in the past – but something in my mind told me he just might be right in what he was saying. I knew his recording career was rushing downhill and the demand for personal appearances was decreasing. I tried getting back on to the only subject I felt certain he might warm to.

'Divi, when we get back to the States, you must let me go to Los Angeles and just stay there as long as it takes for me to find a talent agent to represent you. I don't have the contacts to find you movie roles and I'm never at my office any more because you want me on the road. Of course you've had no offers since the movie,' I tried to explain. 'They're not going to just jump up from their desks and say "Hey, let's drop John Candy. Forget about Rod Steiger. What we need is Divine!" We've got to find someone to *tell* them that's what they need. There *must* be someone out there interested enough in you by now.'

He listened attentively and agreed that that was what I should do. We chatted further about film ideas and I thought his mood had calmed.

'The boy last night.' Divi suddenly switched subject. 'The one from the disco. He's fabulous. Great sex. Can you call him – he gave me his home number – and ask if he wants to travel with me and come back to America? I'm sure he'd love to do that. And that would make me happy.' A pause, and then the voice of the spoilt child once again. '*Please*, Bernard. You do want me to be happy, don't you?'

'Divi, you're being unbelievably childish, living in a dreamworld,' I retorted in a temper. 'First, the kid's nineteen. Second, you don't even know him. And third – do you remember?' I asked, recalling our conversation with the youth the previous night. 'He's now in the army!'

I accurately report my star's response: 'Bullshit. *You* can get him out of the army. Use your influence. I'm a star here. Call someone.'

I stormed out of his room, slamming the door as he screamed that he'd commit suicide and jump off his balcony – nobody cared a damn about him.

For the next 36 hours Rob and I neither saw nor heard anything of Divine. He wouldn't answer his phone or come to the door. He had bolted the door from inside, so my spare key was no use. Room service told me they had had no calls to deliver food to his room. He ignored scheduled press interviews and I fumbled with excuses to our promoter.

Every few hours I strolled nonchalantly to the outside of the hotel, below his balcony. There was no huge dent in the concrete from a fat body landing there.

From Israel we travelled to Paris for a show at a new disco. The airline lost all my luggage, so my mood didn't improve. However, in an effort, I believe, to try to make amends with Rob, Divi suggested we celebrate Rob's fifth anniversary of abstension from alcohol. Rob was a serious and devoted member of AA, reading his self-dependency book each and every day. Divi suggested we had dinner at the restaurant on the first floor of the Eiffel Tower.

I called the restaurant ahead and arranged VIP treatment, saying we would arrive at seven and had to depart by nine in order for Divine to prepare for his show. Our star went out shopping and returned late, causing our arrival at the Tower to be delayed by an hour. This gourmet restaurant was not to be rushed; in our one hour there all we were served was a bottle of champagne that Divi ordered – and a mineral water for Rob. Not exactly the best kind of celebration for a recovering alcoholic. But Rob appreciated the gesture and the Paris show went wonderfully – star and personal assistant working side by side in harmony. For a change.

The following day, 29 June – only twelve days since we had arrived in Finland – Divi was due to be the star attraction of London's Gay Pride celebrations. We had, to date, avoided letting Divine be a figurehead at any predominantly political gay event, although he received many such invitations. He and I both had the same firm principles about 'coming out' in public. On starting to work together in 1978, we had discussed this problem and made the decision; Divi neither had to announce the fact that he's gay, nor deny it. The public may presume whatever they wish – and, we realised, they most probably would – but he did not feel the need to stand up as a representative of any particular community.

Until recently, he had chosen to be quite ambiguous about his preferences when asked. 'Love doesn't come from your pants,' he told England's *New Musical Express.* 'I've been in love with men and with women. There is one special woman who I have known for a long time. Some day I'd like to marry her.' The journalist then wryly commented, 'The idea of Divine and his bride charging up the aisle in matching wedding dresses springs to mind pretty obviously, but the way Divine is toning down the camp and dressiness, you can bet the occasion will be more along the lines of Elton and Renate.'

Although he was always loyal to and appreciative of his gay audience, he was also very well aware that it wasn't every one of them who approved. 'I am trying to say to people, "Learn to laugh at yourself",' he said. 'Gay or straight, it helps if you can look at yourself for what you are and either accept it or do something about it.' For those gays who believed he demolished their public relations efforts, he added, 'I cannot believe anyone can be so prissy and humourless. I am sure they are closet numbers who go home from the office, slip off their three-piece suits, and cook dinner wearing a silk slip and high heels.'

When he finally decided to stop avoiding the issue and answer the probing journalists directly, his astute comment was more amusing than revealing. 'Don't tell me about minority groups,' he told them. 'I am a gay actor trying to make his living wearing a dress. Now that really *is* a minority group.'

Our good friends at Heaven in London had approached Divi about being this year's guest performer on Gay Pride Day. Divi and I agreed that he owed it to the club that started it all for him in Europe. And this particular community who had always supported him so loyally and enthusiastically. However, we were still insistent that his participation – without fee of course – be as an entertainer and not interpreted as a political statement. He would make no speeches from the stage.

Heaven's man in charge came up with the novel idea of Divi performing two songs, standing on the roof of a hired pleasure boat as it sailed slowly along the Thames and passed the Jubilee Gardens, where the celebrations would be taking place.

It was a huge success. The sight of Divine, in a body-hugging silver-blue gown, precariously balanced in heels on the sloping roof of the small craft, gently rocking on the tide of the Thames, while the makeshift speakers screamed 'You Think You're a Man', was definitely one for sore eyes. As he performed, gyrating to the beat in his usual outrageous manner, another pleasure boat – this one full of innocent tourists – passed by. I noticed their tour guide busy trying to explain this extraordinary additional London attraction of a huge bum, swaying and rocking on top of a boat, to music that they couldn't hear in their position on the Thames.

It had been a hectic trip, full of dramas, intolerances, successes and some fun. But the close experience once again with Divine told me without doubt that I must make it possible, sooner rather than later, for him to earn his living from a more secure base and in a lifestyle more suited to a lonely, frustrated, overweight actor.

I had to find him a Hollywood agent. It was time – at long last, after seven years of handling *everything* ourselves – to start building our team. Or, I seriously feared, we might lose the team leader.

'"I was completely losing touch with reality and I didn't care," Divine admitted. "I was unbearable and difficult to work with, all the things I hate in other people, to the point I was suicidal. I didn't care if I lived or died. I really hated my life. And everything about it."' (*Washington Post*, 26 February 1988)

16 Bi-talented and Bi-coastal

'The third song to come our way is a version of Divine's new single, "Little Baby". During the instrumental portions of this, as in previous instrumental moments, Divine struts from side to side of the small stage waving at us his tongue and his breasts, the latter of a shape and consistency that suggests shrink-wrapped auto parts rather than, well, breasts. It is somehow reassuring to catch him from time to time laughing to himself at the sheer folly of it all. . . . When "Little Baby" – which I earnestly hope will be a hit and bring the ample American back to *Top of the Pops* – is over, Divine leaves us, trailing obscenities in his wake.'

John Peel, the *Observer*, 25 January 1987

BY 1986 DIVI HAD APPEARED on every major American television talk show, with the exception of the two most influential: the venerable *Merv Griffin Show* and the powerful *Tonight Show With Johnny Carson*. My frequent efforts to have Divine invited as Johnny Carson's guest fell on deaf ears, until the comedienne Joan Rivers took over every now and again as Guest Host. The producers invited Divi on to the show with Ms Rivers, but only if he wore drag, which, they told us, she was insistent upon. Not only had we made the decision some years back not to accept such invitations, but the thought of the Female Character Divine trying to chat professionally with the forceful, loud-mouthed Joan Rivers – herself often described as a parody of a drag queen – was horrific. Nothing could be gained from such an experience.

Divi himself knew the value of TV talk-show exposure. 'I've been on David Letterman's show a couple of times and Tom Snyder and the morning chat shows,' he said. 'It's been great for me – the best thing that could happen. I'm one of those people who always say that television killed the movies. Now, people just sit at home and get stoned. I still believe that – I love to go to the movies, to go out – but my television appearances let me reach an enormous audience who would never see me otherwise.'

On 13 February 1986 Divine taped *The Merv Griffin Show*. They showed a clip from *Trouble in Mind* and then brought the star – in his sartorial best—to the famous sofa, as first guest on the show. The interview was excellent, referring constantly to Divi's recent triumph as a character actor. Merv Griffin seemed to have a genuine respect for my star. Divine was surprised and delighted to receive the compliment of being invited to stay on the sofa for the rest of the show, chatting with the famous host and his other celebrity guests. Divi beamed when Merv shook his hand after the taping and personally invited him to return to his show whenever he was in Los Angeles in the future.

Dining in Hollywood later that night, Divi was once again in total contrast to the offensive, sulking, lazy bully we had suffered only a few weeks before in Europe. Here was an elegant, handsome, successful character actor enjoying his steady movement up the ladder of fame. 'That's making it,' he declared, 'when Merv Griffin invites you to be a regular guest.' He was content for the moment. Three weeks later, Merv Griffin announced his immediate retirement from hosting television chat shows, after thirty years in the business.

Greg Gorman had watched the TV show's broadcast the following week and was impressed. He too saw the terrific potential for such a character actor—out of his skirts—in the movie industry. He also knew of our intense frustration at not being able to find a talent agent bold enough—and important enough—to field Divine in this medium. And also into that of network television: why couldn't this actor take on specially written guest star roles in Love Boat, Dynasty, Hotel or Dallas? Greg discreetly arranged a meeting between myself and a friend of his, Belle Zwerdling of Progressive Artists Agency in Hollywood.

I liked Belle from the moment I met her, over lunch at Le Dome on Sunset Boulevard, and it took only minutes for me to be certain she was the answer to our problem. Belle was a fan of Divine's and spoke of the many possibilities open to him once the industry could be persuaded to take him seriously. It was agreed that she would speak with her partner and get back to me. If they were interested in signing Divine as their client, the next step would be, of course, to meet the actor himself. I assured Belle of my star's kindness, sincerity, ambition and professionalism. 'You couldn't want a more adorable guy on your books,' was my parting, somewhat tongue-in-cheek, comment.

Divi met Belle and her partner soon after, again over the inevitable Los Angeles lunch. I managed to kick him under the table enough times to give them the impression that he was staying awake and interested in chatting with them. As excited as he was about this development, his attitude before lunch had still remained, 'Why don't they just fucking sign me and get on with it? Do I have to play *girlfriends* with them as well?'

Whenever Divi felt he was required to make small talk for business purposes, he referred to it as 'playing girlfriends'. He was convinced that those inviting him were expecting the Character Divine to entertain them, not the Man. 'The other night I had dinner with a friend I hadn't seen in a while,' he told the writer Hal Rubenstein, 'and he told me his room-mate warned him not to eat with me because "God knows what *she* will do, probably stand up on the table and moon and vomit all over people". C'mon, fellas, give me a break.' He just couldn't understand why there were some who felt they could not properly represent him until they started to know him. To Divine, representation was just a job of work to be done.

Progressive Artists Agency signed a two-year exclusive representation contract with Divine for cinema and TV roles. It was agreed that they would not involve themselves with his music career. True to fashion, just as he had done when signing the management contract with me in the seventies he departed from the meeting to go shopping and start spending the money that – he had no doubt – would instantly roll his way now he had a Hollywood agent.

Leo Ford was gay America's current wet dream. The six-foot, twenty-year-old blond was on exhibit everywhere: in gay movie theatres, on best-selling videos and in show-all magazine photo spreads. He was a highly marketable commodity as the most popular young stud in gay – and some bisexual – porno movies. His escort services were advertised in magazines at $400 an hour and he had recently been touring the gay bars of America with his stage act, the climax of which could only be described as exactly that.

Divi had met Leo briefly at a wild afternoon of partying some months before at the Marlin Beach Hotel in Fort Lauderdale. I remembered introducing them to each other when a mutual friend told me that Leo was 'dying to meet his screen idol'. I didn't know at the time that they had exchanged phone numbers. Now I was receiving reports that Leo was constantly to be seen with Divi when he visited Los Angeles, without me, and Rob had started to call – in some astonishment – to advise me that the infamous Leo Ford was flying in to some of the disco gigs Divi was currently doing across the States.

What was I to make of this? Heaven forbid that Divi was actually running up an escort services bill of $400 an hour; by now he would have been bankrupt. My informants advised me that they were sharing one hotel room. I was finding it difficult to believe that this was Divi's latest adventure in *true love*. Whatever was behind it, I was very nervous. I could understand that Divi would be greatly flattered by attention from such a sex symbol, but I couldn't help wondering what was in it for Leo? Of course, the gay community loved the pairing and I soon began to receive press cuttings from America's gay news magazines, showing photos with accompanying headlines, such as 'The Queen of Trash and The Prince of Porn together again'. This association was becoming a gay *scandale*. And why hadn't Divine told me anything about Leo?

Just as Divi was beginning to be taken seriously by the American public at large; just as the word 'transvestite' and its gay association was not included in every sentence written or spoken about him – Merv Griffin didn't use it once – my star was taking a huge risk. This kind of publicity could create a backlash he could not afford.

I confronted Divine and he took great offence at my disapproval, assuring me that Leo was a friend and admirer and accusing me of, once again, wanting to ruin a close relationship. I forbade him to have Leo accompany him at gigs, and to be seen in public with him. I told Divi that, if it was so important for him, he could continue the 'friendship' behind closed doors. After I'd given my star a lecture on the importance of public relations, he stormed out and sulked for two days.

Leo was flown into New York to present his notorious performance at a gay disco. Divi urged me to accompany him to the show and talk to Leo, promising me that I would then have no further worries. By this time, it was absolutely clear to me that Divi had developed another of his crushes. Leo Ford had become his priority in life. I watched the evening's star attraction go through his paces – the extremity (forgive the pun) of which really did make Divine look like Julie Andrews – and met young Leo after in his dressing room. I admit I was totally charmed. He was gentle, intelligent and quite clearly in awe of Divine's fame and talent. He behaved impeccably and took me aside to sympathise with my own worries about their public exposure together.

'I keep telling Divi I shouldn't join him on these gigs he's doing,' Leo insisted, 'but he will send these air tickets to me and I can't stand him being so lonely when he phones me.' At least I now knew the extent of expenditure involved in this new amour. Air tickets were within reason; and I was content now that no huge escort bills would be presented. I came to the conclusion that Leo had a genuine fondness, respect and admiration for Divine and was enjoying what, to him, was an association with a *legitimate* star! But my star was infatuated. And they *were* sleeping together – something that would have made thousands of fans around the world very jealous indeed. Of either of them. Under pressure from both Leo and myself, Divi agreed to go underground with his latest friendship.

Belle Zwerdling advised Divine that it might be best if he moved to the West Coast, where he would be available at a moment's notice to attend a reading or a casting meeting. Belle was quite concerned about her activities on her new client's behalf being a waste of time if he were not instantly on call. 'In Hollywood, you have to be readily available,' Belle told Divi, 'or they'll just offer the part to someone else who is.' Divine needed no persuading. Living in Los Angeles meant living next to – or perhaps even with? – Leo Ford.

We fought bitterly over the decision. I had no intention of moving my home and business to Los Angeles without first having good reason to do so. To date, Belle had produced no firm offers, nor even a meeting with a producer or casting agent. Until such time as Divi had regular employment on the West Coast, it just didn't make sense. There was no star in the world more used to jumping on an aeroplane when necessary; Divi was already racking up many more miles each year than any airline steward. If Belle needed him – and would give us twenty-four hours' notice, which I thought not to be an unreasonable request – I was prepared to guarantee his attendance. Unless, of course, he was in Europe earning his living, which, like it or not, had to remain his priority due to his extremely precarious financial situation. Belle was happy to accept my compromise. Divine was not.

Leaving Jay, Lee and the bulldogs in upstate New York, Divi left for LA, where with the very limited cash available to him – his American Express card having been revoked for non-payment of monthly bills – he was only able to rent a very modest, unfurnished one-bedroom apartment in an unfashionable area of Hollywood. Leo Ford provided a mattress and one chair. Totally against my wishes, Divi was now a resident of both New York and Los Angeles. Bi-coastal as well as bi-talented.

Two months later, Divi returned to his dogs and whatever little security he had in his life. He had learned a few lessons meanwhile. Belle had not managed to arrange even one relevant meeting for him while he was in Los Angeles and so he had received no star treatment.

Leo quickly became bored with his companion's laziness and lack of celebrity status while he was out of work and returned to live with his long-term lover, whose existence Divine had denied to himself throughout this period. And Divi's phone didn't ring – no one wants to know you when you're down and out. In New York, Divine was far from down and out. We welcomed him back.

He gladly accepted another European club tour, needing to feel in demand and to be the star attraction once more. But in Holland he was no longer packing the clubs – he hadn't had a hit record there for ages – nor was he recognised in the streets. It was a shattering blow for him and he resented the Dutch, conveniently forgetting how they had been responsible for his earning his living over the past few years. He travelled to Iceland, which he hated with a vengeance – 'The most boring country and the most boring people,' he unwisely told an English journalist – and then made a return visit to Israel.

It was at this time that his impatience and intolerance of his current lifestyle peaked. His tempers were more violent and unpredictable than ever. 'I just want to finish it all, Bernard,' he sobbed to me. 'My life is a disaster. I'm going to commit suicide. There's nothing left to live for any more. I've gone as far as I can. I've no more dreams left.'

Remembering that this was the exact hotel, in Tel Aviv, in which he had last talked of suicide, I tried to reason with him that his despondency and desperation were due to loneliness and a hatred of touring, not lack of career success. This time, though, I didn't go downstairs to check the dents in the sidewalk below his balcony. I stayed by his side almost twenty-four hours a day. I was very concerned about his state of mind, but uncertain quite what to do.

That night in Tel Aviv, after a spectacularly successful show in the packed 5,000-capacity Cinerama Disco – and even that didn't improve his mood – I lay awake, sensing that Divi should not be left alone. At about 3 a.m. my phone rang and I recognised his steady, heavy breathing at the other end. He said nothing but I heard sobs. He put the phone down. I used my spare key to enter his room without knocking and climbed on to his bed by his side. Tears were cascading down his face. He seemed so vulnerable. He grabbed my hand and I put my arm around his shoulders, hugging him to me like a child. We said nothing. He just cried and cried for what seemed like hours. He eventually fell asleep and I stayed the night, not wishing to move and risk waking him. It was the only time I spent the night in Divine's hotel room. Just like every other intimate gesture between us, we never spoke together of it.

On returning to London, we were to receive confirmation of our worst fears. I had been demanding financial statements from InTune Music and the Titcheners had promised them, prepared up-to-date, on our arrival that day at the Holiday Inn in Marble Arch. There was no envelope waiting for me at the hotel's front desk, so I immediately called the record company's offices. Nick and Ian Titchener both came to the phone. I listened, shaking with anger, as the story unfolded.

Barry Evangeli had been assuring them that his company's accountants were busy preparing the statements, which were to be presented to InTune Music prior to Divine. Ian Titchener had called Proto's accountants that morning to complain that they had still not received them. He was informed that Barry Evangeli had left the country overnight for Cyprus, that Proto Records was seriously in debt and that the accountants had been instructed to commence a process of liquidation of the company.

The reputable firm of accountants had no up-to-date figures to provide on sales of Divine's records, nor of the considerable advances we had been told Evangeli had been receiving, on behalf of InTune Music Ltd, for new territories such as Japan. Proto Records had no assets worth listing and no liquid funds to distribute.

Lawyers advised us that there was no point in making a case against InTune Music Ltd as they were looking, in turn, to Proto Records for payment. Should we wish to pursue an action against Barry Evangeli personally, we would have to appoint legal representatives in Cyprus. Our lawyers advised us against committing ourselves to such a huge expense with very little likelihood of an eventual settlement.

No record royalties. A few small advances over the years. But virtually no money ever came to Divine from all those record sales, all over the world. We had had *watertight* contracts. We had eventually hired lawyers. Was it my fault as his manager? Over the years of touring we became friendly with most of the dance music recording stars on the performing circuit. I would talk with them about the problems we were having in obtaining royalties on record sales. Almost without exception, they would report to me an identical story. I am not aware of any one disco singer, however successful and who did not eventually manage to cross over into long-term pop stardom, who achieved any sort of wealth from that period of music history. Most are now having to earn regular salaries from work outside the music industry in order to support themselves. Or still try to obtain the odd club gig or two, singing their long-past, oft-forgotten hits.

There *are* many who became rich from disco. But, it would seem, not the performers. The risks involved in signing with ephemeral, undercapitalised record labels, together with the necessity to continuously provide the public with new product—whether you had been paid for the old, or not—were just too great.

Hazell Dean's management was fortunate in obtaining her original studio master tapes—and all rights to them—in the process of Proto's liquidation. But although such tapes of Divine's were the copyright of InTune Music Ltd and not Proto Records, the Titcheners were informed that no tapes of Divine's recordings had been located since Evangeli's departure.

About a year later, a re-issue of several of Divine's 12-inch singles, either recorded by or licensed to InTune Music Ltd, mysteriously appeared in the shops under the Receiver Records Limited label. We received a modest advance against royalties.

On 8 December 1986, in a final, somewhat desperate effort to keep his recording career moving, Divi signed a new agreement with the loyal Titchener brothers, this time under the guise of the illogically named company, Don't Panic Productions. Two further singles were released.

'Little Baby' was written and produced for Divine by Bruce Woolley, who had achieved recent success with songs penned for Grace Jones, including 'Slave to the Rhythm'. 'Now I'm looking for a whole new sound,' Divi told the press almost apologetically. 'The high-energy thing was fun but it seems to have gone its way. I'm making a new record with Bruce Woolley and we're hoping to make it danceable.'

USA's *Dance Music Report* was enthusiastic about the result of this new partnership. 'Divine's new record is quite a satisfaction,' it noted of 'Little Baby'. 'This time using a less Euro-beat feel and more of an underground rhythm section Divine belts it out smoothly. The cut is less rough than usual and has a hummable melody line and a more serious dance appeal than one might expect. This is a departure from past hits that could break Divine bigger than before.' Sadly, *DMR*'s prediction was not accurate. 'Little Baby' vanished without trace almost overnight.

Divi's final experience in recording was a clear sign of a career sinking. Almost everyone and his brother had a hand in writing, producing, editing and mixing 'Hey, You!'. England's *Music Week* said, 'Divine waddles back after an absence of over a year, as if you noticed, with maybe his catchiest high enery dance track to date, and one sure to make a sizeable impression [sic] on the dance charts.' It appeared briefly at Number 49 on the Hi-NRG Top 50 Chart.

Clearly, Divine's recording career–at least as a disco singer–was at an end. But, with Belle Zwerdling networking on the West Coast on Divi's behalf, and some recent worthwhile contacts of my own on the East Coast, we continued to be optimistic of the future with the more important side of his career–acting.

Divine guest-starred on syndicated television in an episode of George A. Romero's popular series, 'Tales from the Darkside', playing the leading male role in *Seymourlama*. Although this was only viewed by a limited audience compared with the exposure of a networked evening sitcom or mini-series (which he longed for), it was very much a step in the right direction: Television–A Male Role–Top Billing.

With this additional tape–and achievement by Divi–under her arm, we waited for Belle to call him West. But she reported to me she was having a much more difficult time than she had originally envisaged and that the only possibility on the horizon was a guest cameo role on Fox TV's *Married . . . with Children*. Despite all his excellent credits and media reviews, the plain fact was that studio bosses were scared of the name Divine. They *still,* she assured us, associated it with dog shit. But Belle was determined to break through. The agency willingly took up its option on the second year of representation, confirming to Divine that they saw him as a long-term challenge, but one they were proud of accepting.

On one of our many phone conversations from coast to coast, Belle seriously suggested that we contemplate using the name Glenn Milstead for male roles and Divine for females ones. She felt it would be easier to 'open doors without having them quickly shut in my face again' if the name Divine was not mentioned. I found this suggestion quite ludicrous and unacceptable. Divi had spent over twenty years trying to make Divine famous. It was ridiculous to think of giving all that up now and trying to sell his services under a name which meant zero to the public.

On my reporting this conversation to Divi, he reminded me of a journalist's comment he had loved, from the *Los Angeles Herald Examiner* some years before:

Forget about divine guidance. Scratch also divine light, divine being, Dan Devine, Andy Devine, divine intervention, unutterably divine and simply divine. Divine, ladies and gentlemen (and others) is a guy who used to be called Glenn who grew up in a suburb of Baltimore, Md., to become a very famous movie star.

Divine it was to be. Glenn remained in Baltimore.

And Divi moved back to Manhattan, now bored with the time taken to commute between New York City and upstate New York. Phillip and Ed had found a country house, from which they were operating their successful new business. Divi returned to East 58th Street, the difficult landlord and the inefficient plumbing. With Jay, Beatrix and Klaus, of course.

I tried to find new sources with which to revive Divi's sagging recording career. Even Bobby Orlando contacted me, suggesting Divine return to his fold. Divi and I became very excited about meetings we had with Steve Bronski and Larry Steinbachek, of Bronski Beat fame, who were eager to write and produce for him. They did write a single for him to record, 'Cha-Cha Heels', but, sadly, he didn't find the time to go into the studio with the guys before March 1988.

Meanwhile, Divi was restless and, of course, short of cash. In a rather sad effort to broaden his earning potential, he accepted an agent's offer to attend an audition for a commercial voice-over, reading the role of a *lemon*. Dressed as elegantly as he now could, Divi waited his turn, surrounded by old-time vaudeville comics who now made their living from this unsung department of our industry. They didn't know Divine; he didn't know of them. It was pathetic for a pop star, a film celebrity, to be *this* desperate. Following the audition, we went for an expensive meal in a chic Manhattan restaurant – where he received a standing ovation on entering – and never heard another word from the voice-over agent.

It was now six years since he had worked with John Waters. As before *Polyester*, Divi and John continued to meet infrequently, on a friendly basis – Christmases, visits to Baltimore, the odd TV interview together. For a while there was talk of Divine starring in a sequel to *Pink Flamingos*, tentatively titled *Flamingos Forever*. In an interview with the *LA Weekly*, Divi said, 'I love John. I've known him since I was sixteen years old and I think he's brilliant. I would do his movies if we had to film them out in the cold up in Alaska, as long as he'd let me sit in a fur coat or something. He wants me for his next film, a sequel to *Pink Flamingos*, and, whenever he's ready, I'm ready. How could I ever say no to the person who gave me my start?' he continued. And then, I thought, a rather unfortunately worded declaration: 'You don't go shitting on the people who've given you breaks.'

But say *no* he did. I read the script of *Flamingos Forever*, in which, among other atrocities, Divi was required to float off to Heaven on a giant turd. I related the storyline to him and he was adamant. What was, in the early seventies, a mind-blowing exercise in Poor Taste was now, we both believed, sheer Bad Taste. Divi felt the public would never accept such an infantile effort in shock tactics some fifteen years later and by people fast approaching middle age. He declined John's approaches. Fortunately, the subject was taken no further as John himself put aside the project on Edith Massey's sudden death.

Other than this episode, there was no firm news of a potential John Waters project for Divi. Until I received a call from a Stanley Buchthal, asking to meet me to discuss Divine's contract to star in a movie for which he had become an investor and co-producer: John Waters's *Hairspray*.

' "They say I'm selling out," Divine complained. "I don't really call it selling out. Same person. Still do the material I want to do. What did Frankie sing? I did it my way. I stuck to my guns. Give people what they want and they laugh and have a good time. That's one of the best things you can do for anyone." ' (*Chicago Sun-Times*, 28 February 1988)

17 A Household Name

' "At the *Hairspray* première," Divine proudly told me, "Maryland's governor declared it 'John Waters Day' and the Mayor of Baltimore hugged me, telling me how much he liked all my films, especially *Pink Flamingos*. That's the kind of politician *I* like, and that's how I hope a lot of people will start feeling about me." '

TGIF, 26 February 1988

JOHN WATERS HAD BEEN PITCHING HIS IDEA of *Hairspray* to mainstream studio executives for some time, knowing he needed to make as near to a conventional Hollywood movie as he was able. But, just as Divine had been throughout his career, John was plagued by *Pink Flamingos*. 'The main guy watches it in his private screening room with his wife,' John declared, 'and I'm dead.'

It would seem that John had also come around to believing that it was time to leave the flamingos – and the supporting trash – well behind. 'I don't have the anger I had at twenty,' he said. 'If I did, I'd be bitter. There's no such thing as a fun, angry forty-one-year-old. They're usually jerks. I hate bitter people. I've done the other stuff. If you can get a wider group of people to see it, that's the challenge. It's much more delightful than to make a movie for the same little group of people.'

Eventually, Stanley Buchthal met John and agreed to develop a deal, selling it to New Line Cinema. New Line, in turn, hired Baltimorean Rachel Talalay to work as line producer on the movie. Rachel had got her own start in the movie world seven years earlier as a production assistant on *Polyester*.

The movie's plot grew from a short essay in Waters's book *Crackpot*, about Baltimore's fabled *The Buddy Deane Show*, a teen dance TV show which ran from 1957 to 1964. Waters himself had even danced on the show as a teenager.

In *Hairspray*, the time is 1962 and all the glamour-crazed teens of Baltimore are fighting to get on the *Corny Collins Show*. Chubby teenager Tracy Turnblad achieves her own social standing when she becomes the show's star, battling for the title of Miss Auto Show 1963 against the 'peaches-and-sour-cream' rich girl, Amber Von Tussle. The girls' mothers, Edna Turnblad and Velma Von Tussle, join in the struggle, while Tracy discovers the wrongs of segregation by befriending a group of black outcasts from her own school. Tracy and her friend Penny lead a campaign to help integrate the *Corny Collins Show* and, of course, all ends happily ever after for our heroine.

Once again, the director had started to round up some of his Dreamlanders, including Van Smith, Pat Moran and Mink Stole. The *Washington Post* noted that 'the director's penchant for using the same group of players is reminiscent of Woody Allens', prompting the amusing response from Divi, 'I'm the Mia Farrow, I guess.'

In addition, John was determined to bring together one of the most eccentric casts seen in a movie for many years, to include performers such as Sonny Bono, Pia Zadora, Jerry Stiller, Ric Ocasek, Ruth Brown and Debbie Harry—all unkindly described by the *Baltimore Sun* as 'a selection of used-up former celebrities whose failed careers are part of the joke'.

Early chats that had taken place with John about this script had Divine cast as Tracy Turnblad, but, on attempting to raise his $3 million capitalisation, he soon realised that a commercially viable PG-rated movie—for that was what he was after—could not feature a 41-year-old man dressed as a girl and having heavy petting scenes on screen with sixteen-year-old wholesome American boys. Buchthal gave me an up-to-date filmscript and said that John had re-written the role of Tracy's mother, Edna, with Divine in mind.

At that first meeting with the co-producer, I was also told that both he and John Waters were very keen indeed to get Divine's commitment to *Hairspray*, but that New Line Cinema was opposed to the casting, convinced that the combination of John Waters and Divine once again would only bring back the to-be-avoided-at-all-costs comparisons with the early movies.

While appreciating Stan Buchthal's honesty, both Divi and I were quite shocked. Divi knew that New Line Cinema had made much money over the years from his performances in the 'celluloid attrocities' they now rented out successfully around the world. This news of their current disloyal attitude made Divi even more determined to get what *he* wanted from doing this movie, before just agreeing to it for John's sake. Interestingly, in an interview with *Melody Maker* in July 1988, after Divine's death, John himself admitted, 'But I do know one thing. They'll never say it to my face, but a lot of studio execs will be relieved that the next time I have a project, they won't have to deal with the Divine issue. Even after all these years, he *scared* them.'

I read *Hairspray* and adored it. I read it again and the same thought bugged me as had done on the first reading. There was a fascinating, well-rounded cameo character role of Arvin Hodgepile, the bigot who runs the TV studio that airs Corny Collins' show. Divi, too lazy as ever to read the entire script, agreed that playing the mother's role made a lot more sense for his career; he had already had his own, personal doubts about accepting the teenage role of Tracy, should it have been offered. I described Arvin Hodgepile to him and he fell about with laughter. He adored the idea of playing both roles, knowing that the dual exposure in one movie might finally prove his talents as a character actor to the powers-that-be.

I was very relieved that, this time, Belle Zwerdling was doing the negotiating on Divine's behalf. Daily reports now came of her conversations with Stanley Buchthal. It appeared that he loved the idea of Divi playing the two roles but John Waters was dead set against it – 'Divine is my leading lady,' was the message given to Belle, 'and that's what he must be in *Hairspray*' – and New Line still didn't even want Divi in the movie at all. Belle and I decided to stand firm. First of all, John and New Line had to sort out their differences. I could only presume John pulled rank as Belle was soon relaying that it was time to discuss Divi's fee and other contractual details. I thought there was little point in doing that until we had sorted out John's problem with the cameo role, as Divi would certainly want a higher fee for playing both roles.

Eventually, after very much deliberation – and once again at the last minute – negotiations were completed and the contract signed. Divine was to play both Edna Turnblad and Arvin Hodgepile – we just held on and on until whoever still didn't agree gave in – and his fees and profit percentages were confirmed. Regarding billing, Divi and I felt that his name should be above the title only with Ricki Lake's, who, although unknown, was now cast in the other leading role of Tracy. On the understanding that no one would receive any special billing on posters, we finally agreed to the producers' wish of equal billing, in alphabetical order, with five other members of the cast. However, Divi was quite offended, on finally seeing the movie's poster, that both Ric Ocasek and Pia Zadora, with one-scene joke cameo roles, had indeed been awarded 'special appearances by' billing.

Divi checked into the hotel of his choice in Baltimore and, with his usual enthusiasm and energy for filming, threw himself into the excitement of making a new movie. However, all was not well. After the first day, Divi called me in New York and complained bitterly. While other guest stars, such as Debbie Harry, had individual trailers in which to change and rest, Divine had been consigned to the warehouse-like general male dressing room. He was horrified, having to prepare himself to become the frumpy, obese, lower-middle-class mom, while all the young, inexperienced kids hired for the dance sequences stared and giggled at him. I complained, through Belle, to Buchthal. Pat Moran told Divine she couldn't understand what all the fuss was about; after all, he was a member of the original Dreamlanders. The second day's filming didn't provide Divine with his trailer. He was livid. Urgent ultimatums were issued. Divi was taken to his personal trailer on the third day and, from then on, treated like a star, but things were never quite the same between him and the Dreamlanders after that incident. There was much evidence of jealousy and resentment at his star treatment. Inevitable, perhaps? But sad, too. Surely they could have seen that Divi had well-earned his professional star status over the years?

But at least Divi could now show some enthusiasm at the endless media interviews he did while filming, telling the *Washington Post*, 'It has better lighting, better sound people, individual trailers for the stars. Just like a real movie!'

The rest of the time filming in Baltimore went well and was fun for Divine. Belle, Stanley Buchthal and even John Waters himself would call me to pay Divine the most wonderful compliments, both for his professional behaviour on the set and for his portrayals of both roles, as seen from the rushes. Indeed, on reading the media stories as they started to appear during the production process, I noted that John was enjoying taking great credit for his casting of Divine as Arvin Hodgepile. Divi adored all the young actors and dancers and spent hours spinning wonderful yarns with them about his years on the road as a pop star. They sat at his feet in awe and watched, incredulously, as he performed all the 'sixties dances for them.

On his nightly calls to me in New York, Divi had only one ongoing concern, reminding me of our conversations when he was filming *Polyester*. Once again he was having trouble working with his director. Both Paul Bartel and Alan Rudolph had given Divine a great deal of direction, careful guidelines as to what they wanted on screen from the characters the actor was portraying. Although not used to this kind of detailed discussion, he had benefited from it, feeling that the work was much more satisfying once he could be certain he was providing the results the director desired. In addition, he had felt appreciated for his acting abilities. Back with John Waters, it seemed to be a matter of Divi discovering who *he* wanted Edna Turnblad to be and then just getting on with it. He longed for more specific direction, but that was not John's way of working. At least, not with Divine.

Filming completed, Divi deserved a holiday and once again he chose the island of Ibiza, renting a beautiful villa with its own swimming pool, high in the central hills. We had stayed there in previous years and the delightful couple who owned the home—and looked after the guests during the summer—welcomed him fondly. Cash to spend had been taken care of by the five days in Malta and guests arrived and departed at regular intervals through the month, celebrating their friend's new-found freedom from the restrictions of marijuana. Andrew Logan and his sister Janet, Michael Davis, Robyn Beeche and her friend Michael Duffy, Jon Turner and my friends Alan and Margaret Goss came from London; Greg Gorman joined them all for a few days from California. It was a time of sheer joy, with our star behaving with an eccentricity of spirit and a love of life that surprised and delighted everyone. He was the most perfect and charming of hosts, preparing meals, mixing drinks at the pool and constantly clowning from his bedroom balcony. Although we had decided to politely decline an invitation for him to appear at the island's famous Ku Club this time— I didn't want him to even have to think about becoming the Female Character during this holiday—our party of revellers would attend nightly and, as before, receive VIP treatment. Divi relaxed and awaited the release of his new movie with patience and zeal, feeling certain once again that life in the future was going to bring everything he had always dreamed of.

Premières of *Hairspray* were scheduled for February 1988, so Divi agreed to go back on the road in England to keep the cash flowing until he could busy himself with being a film star. 'Little Baby' and 'Hey, You!', although not hit records, created enough interest on the club and campus circuit to enable Albert Samuel, our long-time booking agent in London, to put together a reasonable tour. Divi and Rob joined Tim Sweeney, the tour manager, again, while I flew in from the States only for specific events, including the most outrageous and triumphant of all his disco appearances.

Peter Stringfellow had invited Divi to return to the Hippodrome, but I knew we needed an extraordinary idea to top everything we had done there before with such success. I decided I wanted Divine to make his entrance riding – and singing – on an elephant. The club's enterprising technical director tracked down Bully, the Baby Elephant, and after all the advance publicity heralding the event, the venue was almost closed for licensing contraventions. It appeared that the Hippodrome was not licensed as a circus! After hectic, final-moment negotiations with at least ten different government and city agencies, Bully was brought to the underground dressing room, supervised by his trainer, representatives from the RSPCA and bewildered civil servants. He arrived at about 9 p.m., before the club opened.

By the time we arrived, Bully had been listening to the loud disco music playing above him for three hours. I immediately paid a visit to our co-star for the night, who was on his four feet, excitedly dancing – in step – to the rhythm of the beat. Even when Divi's extraordinary weight was carefully placed upon him, he continued dancing. As the hydraulic stage rose and the solidly packed audience became aware of exactly what we were doing, the applause became almost deafening. Divi started to sing, the trainer could only *just* manage to hold on to his charge as the baby elephant disco-danced his way across the stage, and we gently – and precariously – led Bully and his very unusual passenger through the thousands surrounding the dance floor to the side exit, where Divi disembarked and Bully was taken home.

When Divine returned to the stage to complete his opening song, he received the greatest ovation he had ever experienced in all his more-than-1,800 shows around the world. Amazing, we thought, how simple things can thrill spectators: we noted that the pairing of Divine with a baby elephant was one to repeat in the future.

The day after his triumph at the Hippodrome, Divi took my arm as we were walking in the West End of London. Energised on stardom and fame, he took the courage to bring up a subject that had been forbidden by me some months back. Two years previously he had passed Asprey's, one of London's most famous and high-priced stores, and viewed a large brown, crocodile-skin hold-all in the window. He fell in love. Determined to become its proud owner, he placed a $500 deposit in cash and informed the salesman that he would return forthwith to pay the balance and claim the coveted item. During the years that had passed, he had never managed to hold on to enough cash to settle the account and the patient deputy manager of Asprey's had pleaded with me several times for my client to visit him again. This particular purchase, priced in the region of £2,500, had become a *cause célèbre* with me. It seemed to represent the epitome of his over-spending, his indulgence in unnecessary luxuries, his sheer extravagance. I had no intention of letting him complete this folly until he was rich.

Divi used all his persuasive charms that morning, clinging on to my arm and listing my virtues and attributes *ad nauseam*. Of course, he got round me. But not without a little blackmail of my own, forcing him to accept a return engagement to Iceland the following month, from which he could earn the fees to complete this purchase. I 'loaned' the cash that morning to Divine on the condition that the Iceland fees would replace the amount from our British bank account, which was supposed to be used purely for professional cashflow purposes when in England. He ran all the way to Asprey's, like a child. The precious bag was smuggled through customs into the United States and was rarely ever allowed out of its protective cover, lest its surface should be damaged in transit. Consequently, very few of his friends ever actually saw the much-boasted-of possession.

Somewhat reluctantly, Rob had accepted another offer of work, as Divine was not guaranteeing full-time employment to him and he was never certain when he would next be paid. Rob was temporarily working with Madonna, so Divine took a boyfriend with him to Iceland. They returned without the awaited balance from his fees. On my challenging him, he responded, 'Ah, but there were other things I needed to pay for as well as the bag, Bernard, so I had the right to take the cash from Iceland as the only reason I said I'd do the gig in the first place is because I needed the money to pay for my purchases.' I stared in disbelief. 'Well, I don't know why you're angry,' he continued. 'I haven't run up any new debts by going to Iceland, have I?' Nothing ever changed.

Divine had been totally irresponsible about money since the day he was born. Not only his, but others' too. As far as he was concerned, if there was money around, it was to be spent. As quickly as possible. By him. I even tried appointing business managers in Los Angeles towards the end of 1987, as I thought it would take the burden of his accounts and cashflow problems from me and we could concentrate on career moves in the future, avoiding the many arguments that were always caused by his over-spending. But it only made matters worse as he immediately played one of us off against the other, thereby now having two different sources from whom he could 'steal' his own money.

The crocodile bag, the Tommy Nutter suits, the growing collection of rare china and pottery, the expensively framed posters and photographs all needed a more suitable home, Divi decided suddenly one morning in New York. So he went apartment hunting and found a 24th-floor penthouse in a modern building on the Upper West Side, with spectacular views of Manhattan and the Hudson River. Of course, his good friend Stephen assisted him in his search and encouraged Divi to commit himself to this overnight three-fold increase in rent. Divine signed the lease, before I was informed, and the rental agency called me for the advance payments required. He was so fond of creating these little surprises for me.

However, despite the untimely expense of moving, it was a pleasure to see his renewed enthusiasm for his daily life as he moved into his chic penthouse. Before long, it was a true reflection of his own, contradictory personality. One corner of the vast living room would be African in theme, with the zebra-skin rugs and elephants' feet carefully displayed on the floor, surrounded by wicker baskets, wicker chairs and voodoo dolls. Another corner would be like a floor display at Harrods, with a beautifully upholstered, overstuffed giant sofa, scatter cushions covered in the best of silk, a Persian carpet on the floor and valuable antique china delicately placed on the black-and-red Japanese motif side tables.

The entrance hall would resemble a tropical jungle, with daily replacements of exotic fresh flowers, charged to a newly opened credit account with Pati Mayfield's friends, who just happened to be florists. Two of his closer friends, Bob and Judith Pringle, would visit regularly and accompany Divi to the jacuzzi in the building's private health club. Jay Bennett, of course, was plucked from his involuntary retirement and given the spare bedroom, in return for a minimum of household duties.

Divi adored entertaining in his new home, and finally being able to show off his bizarre purchases from his travels. Only I understood how he had sweated and toiled along dark motorways and in huge discos with long-forgotten names and faces to earn these prizes. I too, on visiting him, had to smile and enjoy his new domestic bliss.

But I had to return to my office and face the ever-fattening pile of his monthly bills, credit debts, tax demands and sundry invoices. And the daily florists' accounts.

Paul Bartel invited Divine to play a three-minute cameo role in *Out of the Dark*, a low-budget spoof murder mystery he and a colleague were producing in Los Angeles. Divi was thrilled to accept, once again overjoyed to see his colleagues recognising his character-acting potential, without tits and frocks. The role of the caustic, hard-bitten

LA detective was great fun for him. It involved two days of filming in north Hollywood and, for Divi, it was one big party. If ever there was an actor who was at his happiest on movie sets, it was he.

Paul Bartel had brought together many of the team from *Lust in the Dust*, including its assistant director, Michael Schroeder, now in the director's seat. Paul himself was playing another cameo role, along with James Katz (*Lust*'s Executive Producer), Tab Hunter and Lainie Kazan. Rob Saduski took over preparations for the character's look and, when our star emerged from his dressing room in a trilby hat, grey moustache and second-hand, baggy suit, none of his friends recognised him.

By the time *Out of the Dark* was released, Divi was dead and the producers, Paul Bartel and Zane Levitt, paid their bit-part actor the great compliment of dedicating their film to him. 'Divine cannot be replaced,' Levitt told *Frontiers*. 'There may be another Tom Cruise, and I'm sure they're working on it somewhere, but there's never going to be another Divine.' Unfortunately, the movie attracted little attention beyond being misleadingly promoted by local cinemas as 'Divine's Last Film'.

Meanwhile, New Line Cinema was gearing up for a huge promotional campaign to accompany the release of *Hairspray*. And there was no one connected with the film in more demand than Divine. The publicists reported to me that they were having no difficulty in lining up interviews and soon confirmed this statement by handing Divi an amazing schedule of press, radio and television appointments. For the first time, Divi entered into his marketing duties with relish. He was no longer afraid of falling asleep while someone was talking to him. He was bubbling with energy and excitement, eager to spread the word of his fame. He talked brightly and coherently and charmed the journalists and photographers. Every article that was printed was full of praise for Divine The Man. It was as much a revelation to him as it was to any of us. Although still plagued with the transvestite label, he was keen to explain that he was also playing a male role in *Hairspray* – and had just completed another cameo male role in Los Angeles. The phrase 'character actor' was never off his lips. He hammered it home in every interview he gave, determined to see it in print, even if the old labels still accompanied it.

In the past he had never bothered to read his press interviews, bored with the same old references to dog shit and drag queens. But now Divi would be at his local news-stand early every morning, the first to buy whatever magazine or newspaper was featuring him that day. And immensely proud when he would see his face on a front cover, displayed all along the Upper West Side. 'Things people told me would never happen are happening,' Divi said. 'I'm clawing my way to the top as a man, no less.'

The *Los Angeles Times* requested a photo session at a sophisticated Manhattan restaurant, where Divi patiently pretended to sip cups of tea all afternoon. *Time* printed his photo. *People* did yet another feature on the actor. Hollywood's *Celebrity Bulletin*, privately circulated to advise members of the media who's in and out of town, featured Divine as 'Celebrity Of The Day'.

And his personal zenith: *Interview* magazine called to announce that his would be the cover photo, illustrated by his friend Richard Bernstein, on their February issue. Popular New York writer Hal Rubenstein was assigned to interview Divi for the magazine's six-page feature. The conversation between them took an entire day and, Hal told me, Divi never even looked tired once. Another full day was spent in the photographer's studio, taking glamour shots of the actor, both in his disco outfits and in Tommy Nutter's stylish suits.

If one could take the liberty of guessing what was the happiest day in Divine's life, I would offer as a suggestion the day the February 1988 issue of Andy Warhol's *Interview* hit the stands. Divi walked up and down Broadway, just staring at the fabulous colour portrait beaming over all Manhattan. 'I was on the cover of *Interview* magazine this month,' he told the *Washington Post*. 'Nothing made me happier. I waited for fifteen years. I knew Andy. I'd call him once a week and say, "I want the cover."' To Divine, this feature was the best and most important tribute he could be paid.

The first public screening of *Hairspray* was at the Miami Film Festival.

'One day Glenn called and said, "Mom, you have to go shopping for a new dress because I'm taking you to the Miami Film Festival to see *Hairspray*",' Frances Milstead proudly recalled. 'I got so excited to think Glenn was finally asking me to go with him to a theatre. I was so excited that I started to call and tell everyone I knew, to tell them the happy news. They were all so happy for me.'

New Line Cinema sent a limo to pick up Mrs Milstead from her suburban home outside Fort Lauderdale. Divine, perfectly attired in his tuxedo and experiencing, at that moment, almost everything his heart desired, was there to accompany his mother. 'Glenn was holding my hand in the limousine to Miami,' Frances told me. 'I felt he was nervous and so I asked him. He said very little, so I laughed and said, "Never fear, Mommy is near." He cracked up.'

Divi also recalled the day with fondness. 'My father's in a wheelchair but my mother came to the Miami Film Festival the other night,' he said. 'I told her to stand up. I was on stage. She was weeping. They're both very proud now and very happy. She's like Shirley Temple's mother all of a sudden.'

Divine brought his mother to the grandly orchestrated première of his movie in Baltimore. He rented her a fur coat for the night, saying he had bought it for her as a gift, but that it had to be returned the next day for some alterations. Yet again, he was determined to impress; to allow his parents to believe he was independently rich. I wondered, that splendid evening, how he intended explaining to her the long delay there would need to be before she would ever receive that coat again as her own.

Divi spent the glamorous evening with me at one side and his mother at the other. Hundreds of flashbulbs captured the touching image of the grinning, handsome star and the oh-so-proud, beaming mother. Frances Milstead had finally started her 'second life'. From now on she knew she would be experiencing all the wonderful adventures – through her son's fame – that she had been sadly denied due to her devoted husband's disabilitating illness. She gave interviews to England's Jonathan Ross, for a Channel 4 documentary he was preparing about John Waters and Divine, and to journalists searching for their 'human angle'. They were not disappointed.

'I'm still close to my son, and see him when he performs in South Florida,' she told them. 'The only thing that bothers me about his career is he never told us he was a drag queen. We had to read about it. Apparently, he's very good at it. But I'm not ashamed of my son. I love him.' Some details were offered through rose-coloured glasses, to say the least: 'While growing up, my son was not unlike other boys. I never had any problems with him at all,' Frances assured her attentive interviewers. 'He was good-looking, very affectionate, and he did well at school. It makes me depressed to see him as heavy as he is now. Every mother wants a doctor or a lawyer. But this is the world today. You have to accept it. I figure we might as well accept him. As long as he's making a living . . .'

We lunched with Frances at the Baltimore hotel the next day and Divi started planning the 50th wedding anniversary celebrations he wanted to give for his parents in the same hotel later that year. No expense would be spared by their son. Nothing was too much trouble. Frances cried with joy.

The furthest thing from her mind that afternoon was that it would be the last time she was to see her baby Glenn.

Hairspray received upbeat media notices and became an instant success in theatres from New York to Los Angeles. Divine's dual performances were praised almost unanimously – and mainly posthumously.

'John Waters may never win an Academy Award,' said Mike Davidson, writing in *Manhattan GX*, 'which is a shame, because he deserves one, if only for bringing Divine to a mass audience. . . . With one look of motherly love, Divine gives more subtext than any close-up since Garbo! Divine was not always as accomplished an actor as he is in *Hairspray*. But the spark was always there. If the true test of a star is that when he is on screen it is impossible to look at anyone else, then Divine was truly a star.'

Divi and I took the train back to New York. As soon as we arrived, Belle called from Los Angeles, congratulating the star on his rave reviews. And giving him the great news: the role in *Married . . . with Children* had been confirmed that morning. He was to fly in for the taping in less than three weeks' time.

Divine couldn't have been happier. His was becoming a Household Name.

'Besides being a wonderful performer, Divine was one of the few truly radical and essential artists of this century. If there had been no Divine, someone exactly like him would have to have come into existence in order for American culture to continue its march forward. He was an audacious symbol of man's quest for liberty and freedom.' (Paul Thornquist, Jersey City, the *New York Post* letters, March 1988)

Postscript

First the paramedics arrived to confirm his death. Then I waited for the Los Angeles Police Department and the Coroner's Office to take the body away. It took six hours in all. Rob Saduski returned from the TV studio, devastated. Greg Gorman and Belle Zwerdling arrived. I busied myself in my usual efficient fashion, trying to avoid facing up to the reality of the situation. There was much to do.

There would have to be an autopsy, I was told. 'After all, this is Los Angeles and a star has died mysteriously.' Hollywood was conscience-smitten at the time over adverse media coverage of the coroner's office and its public relations image.

I called Mr and Mrs Milstead in Florida. They asked me to handle everything as Harris was too ill to fly to the West Coast and Frances didn't want to leave him alone. Then I called New Line Cinema – I wanted them to deal with the media and make the formal announcement. Within half an hour of my discovering Divine's body, photographers were waiting outside the hotel.

The third phone call I made was to our doctor in New York. The paramedics needed to know for their report if Divi had been taking drugs or if there was a known illness that might have caused the sudden death. Divi had visited Barry Goozner for a general check-up just four days prior to his trip to Los Angeles. Once again, Barry had given him a clean bill of health, apart from another warning about his weight – now 375 pounds. Barry was shocked, stunned; he had become fond of Divine as a friend as well as a patient. He gave the paramedic the necessary information. But I don't think Dr Goozner was totally surprised at the news.

The press started to call. 'How long had Divine known he had Aids?' was one question coldly thrown at me. 'Did he meet a stranger the night before? Were there any signs of a struggle?' was another. How cruel they were. Until the coroner's formal announcement, they seemed prepared to suggest anything. I don't know how the story was started, but most papers reported that he choked to death in his sleep.

It took two days for the Los Angeles Coroner's Department to pronounce the official cause of death: hypertrophic cardiomyopathy with cardiomegaly. An enlarged heart. The coroner told me that Divi most probably would have died quietly and painlessly.

New Line Cinema informed me that John Waters had called a press conference in Baltimore. He announced that there would be a public funeral in Divi's home town. Nobody discussed any of this with me, who still had charge of the star.

Divi's body was placed into the coroner's bag and six of us carried it down the steps from his suite. I asked the hotel manager if he would politely request the sunbathers to return to their rooms while the body was carried through the pool courtyard to the front entrance. We fought with some photographers as they tried to take shots of his body being thrown into the van. It was ghoulish.

Later, I turned on the TV to watch the news. Sure enough, Divi was the local headlines and – would you believe it? – the voice, speaking over the still photo of Divi in his favourite suit and bow-tie, announced, 'Today, the famous *character actor*, Divine, died in his sleep in Los Angeles.' No mention of the word transvestite. I screamed back at the TV set. 'Don't tell *me* that, you bastards! I've been trying to tell that to *you* for the past ten years!' So that's what it takes for the media to finally pay attention.

Outside my hotel suite there were journalists camped out in sleeping bags, waiting for me to speak with them. My star really had become famous. How he would have loved all this.

Three days later I put Divi on his final plane trip, back to Baltimore. His parents had arranged two days of viewing prior to the funeral. On my arrival Frances and I hugged each other and cried together for a brief moment. Then I handed her Divi's diamond stud, that she had instructed me to remove from his ear and deliver to her.

The only detail of the Baltimore funeral arrangements that I became involved with was a request to his parents that people be asked to send flowers, not money to a charity. Divi so adored flowers that I felt he had the right to be buried surrounded by them. They arrived by the vanload; wonderful marks of respect and affection from friends, unknown fans, long-forgotten relatives, work colleagues and even some celebrities who had admired him but hardly known him.

Elton John's tribute almost filled the room. Whoopi Goldberg, whom Divi had recently enjoyed meeting, sent white flowers with white balloons, and the message 'See what happens when you get good reviews!'

John Waters spoke movingly at the funeral, making much reference to Divi's early life. I was not asked to add my own tribute, this was clearly a Dreamlanders funeral. But Divi had long ago resigned his membership.

Divine was buried at Prospect Hill Cemetery in Towson, Maryland, next to the grave of his adored grandmother. His parents paid him the greatest tribute of all, by inscribing the name Divine along with Harris Glenn Milstead on his stone.

The morning after the funeral I visited Mr and Mrs Milstead in their hotel suite before they returned to Florida. There were many arrangements to be made with Divine's belongings. I had urged my colleague many times over the years to prepare a will. He would not hear of it, insisting that it would be a premonition of his death. His parents were his next of kin and therefore inherited what was his. Once again, they asked me to handle everything for them.

I would have given almost anything not to have had to go through with the next particular conversation, but I had no choice as they were already requesting details of the royalties due to him from his films and records. I informed them that, not only did Divine have no money at all, nor did he own his own home, but that he was very heavily in debt.

Despite Divi's accountants having verified all the information I have provided to Mr and Mrs Milstead, I don't think they have ever come to terms with the facts. The difference between the reality and the carefully planted fantasy of his financial situation has been difficult for them to handle. Consequently, their reluctance to accept this reality has caused me much hurt and grief since his death; and, ultimately, the loss of my friendship with his parents.

To coincide with the release of *Hairspray*, the Titchener brothers had planned another compilation album, to be titled *Maid in England* (pun intended). On each of Divi's record sleeves, he had made a personal dedication – to friends, relatives or work colleagues. With the pressure of the *Hairspray* openings, I had forgotten to discuss the dedication for the new album and wasn't aware that Divi had already prepared it himself for the printers in London. Two weeks after his death, Nick and Ian sent me the first copy, which included his chosen dedication: 'This one's for Bernard (who was made in England). Here's to the next ten years and lots more albums. Love Divi.'

Even the music journalists had a new-found respect for my star following his death. Forever labelled the Queen of High Energy, it was fascinating to note the word change in writer Chris Halstead's final comment on *Maid in England*. 'This album was supposed to relaunch Divine's career, but has instead become a monument to the *Monarch* of Hi-NRG.'

A final gesture. Before his body was flown back to Baltimore, the kind people at Callanan Mortuary in Hollywood allowed me a private moment with him. The day before, I had chosen the clothes in which he was to be buried: a black Tommy Nutter suit, black polo-neck shirt – and a small, favourite item of Andrew Logan's jewellery. He was now laid out, dressed and embalmed in his coffin, hands carefully placed on his stomach.

I thanked him for all the fun, cursed him for all the bad times and kissed him on the cheek. Then I carefully placed into the inside pocket of his jacket, a photo of him playing with Beatrix and Klaus. Together with the torn, tattered, much-abused copy of our original contract together. The one he always carried with him. For his reassurance that I was there, for him.